FOOT SOLDIERS FOR DEMOCRACY

FOOT SOLDIERS FOR DEMOCRACY

THE MEN, WOMEN, AND CHILDREN
OF THE BIRMINGHAM
CIVIL RIGHTS MOVEMENT

• • •

EDITED BY
HORACE HUNTLEY AND
JOHN W. MCKERLEY

INTRODUCTIONS BY
ROBIN D. G. KELLEY AND
ROSE FREEMAN MASSEY

UNIVERSITY OF ILLINOIS PRESS
Urbana and Chicago

© 2009 by the Birmingham Civil Rights Institute
All rights reserved
Manufactured in the United States of America
1 2 3 4 5 C P 5 4 3 2 1
∞ This book is printed on acid-free paper.

Library of Congress Cataloging-in-Publication Data
Foot soldiers for democracy : the men, women, and children of the Birmingham
civil rights movement / edited by Horace Huntley and John W. McKerley ; introductions
by Robin D.G. Kelley and Rose Freeman Massey.
p. cm.
Includes bibliographical references and index.
"Second volume of oral histories produced by the Birmingham Civil Rights Institute
Oral History Project (BCRI OHP)"—Pref.
ISBN 978-0-252-03478-7 (cloth : alk. paper)
ISBN 978-0-252-07668-8 (pbk. : alk. paper)
1. African Americans—Civil rights—Alabama—Birmingham—History—20th century.
2. Civil rights movements—Alabama—Birmingham—History—20th century.
3. Civil rights workers—Alabama—Birmingham—Biography. 4. Birmingham (Ala.)—
Race relations—History—20th century. I. Huntley, Horace, 1942- II. McKerley, John W.
F334.B69N438   2009
323.1196′0730761781—dc22
2009026687

CONTENTS

PREFACE

This book is the second volume of oral histories produced by the Birmingham Civil Rights Institute Oral History Project (BCRI OHP). Since 1994, the BCRI OHP has collected more than four hundred interviews with movement participants from across the social spectrum. The first volume of oral histories culled from the project's collection, *Black Workers' Struggle for Equality in Birmingham,* focused on the ways in which the city's black union members fought to transform their labor organizations into vehicles for racial justice as well as working-class empowerment. While drawing on many of the same themes as its predecessor—especially the central role that black workers played in shaping the city's civil rights history—this book also casts a wider net. Rather than focusing on a single subsection within the larger movement, it examines black community activism across lines of class, gender, and generation. As a whole, the interviews in this volume seek to capture the solidarity, the fragmentation, the love, the anguish, the agony, the ecstasy, the courage, and the cowardice of the people of Birmingham in their defense and defiance of civil and human rights during the twentieth century. They remind us of the long history of racial oppression in the city, state, and nation, but they also express the hope inherent in the ability of ordinary people to organize in defense of their common humanity.

The introduction to this volume is in two parts. In the first section, "Foot Soldiers for Democracy," historian Robin D. G. Kelley continues his tradition of writing about "race rebels" by using the BCRI OHP interviews to give a new perspective on the Birmingham movement and the vital role played by the numerous men, women, and children who have remained nameless and faceless in most movement accounts. As he demonstrates, the Birmingham movement included "a broad range of activists whose personal histories and experiences illuminate the movement's rich diversity and complexity." The second part, "Look for Them in the Whirlwind," is written by a Mississippi student activist, Rose Freeman Massey, whose firsthand knowledge places her in a unique position to comment on the meaning of young folks' participation in the movement. She offers an analysis from the perspective of one who has experienced encounters similar to those of the student interviewees. Massey argues that understanding the civil rights movement in Birmingham requires hearing and understanding the perspectives of young people in general and students in particular.

As both Kelley and Massey suggest, the dramatic battle of "Birmingham '63" had its roots in long-standing traditions of black resistance and mutual aid. Black men and women had first come to the city during the late nineteenth century in search of employment and freedom from the oppression of the countryside. Many black men found jobs doing the dirty and dangerous work for companies such as Tennessee Coal and Iron and its successor, U.S. Steel. Black women often cooked and cleaned for white employers in Birmingham and its surrounding communities. Many interviewees recalled that they or their parents had found work "over the mountain," referring to the affluent white suburbs south of Red Mountain. Still other black men and women built the foundations of the city's black middle class, turning education, skill, and good fortune into positions as ministers, teachers, business owners, and medical and legal professionals. While often divided by class, color, culture, and neighborhood, these black Alabamians turned to the resources and ingenuity of their communities to negotiate the culture of white supremacy around them. Faced with constant threats to their dignity and safety, they formed mutual aid societies, social clubs, unions, sports teams, choirs, and numerous other groups of coworkers, churchgoers, classmates, neighbors, and friends.

The movement that confronted white supremacy in Birmingham during the 1950s and 1960s drew on these traditions but did not spring forth from them fully formed. Instead, as these interviews reveal, the movement was shaped and nurtured by a relatively small group of committed activists, the people James McPherson called the "faithful few." Led by Fred Shuttlesworth, a brave and charismatic minister, these activists formed the core of the Alabama Christian Movement for Human Rights (ACMHR), a local organization created in 1956 in the wake of Alabama attorney general (and soon-to-be governor) John Patterson's injunction against the National Association for the Advancement of Colored People. Dedicated to the overthrow of white supremacy through nonviolent direct action, the ACMHR first took on the lack of African American police officers but soon expanded its campaign to confront segregated bus seating, schools, parks, water fountains, and lunch counters. The example set by Shuttlesworth and other activists inspired more men and women to become involved in the movement, but the ACMHR and its members continued to struggle against the fear and apathy of many of the city's black residents. Activists also faced resistance from conservative black leaders, who chafed at Shuttlesworth's threat to their position as community spokesmen and feared that the movement's confrontational tactics would only invite more violence from whites. Even from within the ACMHR, members struggled with the organization's commitment to nonviolence in the face of white fists, bombs, and guns.

Indeed, the threat of white violence was so real that the movement's internal challenges paled by comparison. ACMHR activists and their allies forever faced the specter of intimidation and even death. Employers threatened to fire workers who participated in the movement, and bombers and arsonists destroyed the churches and homes of activists. While on their way to mass meetings, activists were frequently stopped for minor traffic violations, encounters that were accompanied by threats of bodily harm. Police officers photographed activists and auto tag numbers, and informants attended meetings and tape-recorded the proceedings. After meetings had begun, they were frequently disrupted by firefighters announcing that the overflow crowds constituted a safety hazard and by callers claiming that explosives had been planted inside buildings. As the movement gained in strength, the intensity of the violence increased as well. On May 14, 1961, a hostile white mob assaulted the Freedom Riders as they arrived in Birmingham. Two years later, archconservative Eugene T. "Bull" Connor, the city's longtime commissioner of public safety, directed police and firefighters as they used dogs and high-powered hoses to attack activists, many of them children. On September 15, 1963, four little girls were murdered by a Klansman's bomb at the Sixteenth Street Baptist Church, and whites gunned down at least two other black youths.

The movement survived these acts of violence and intimidation in large part because of its ability to mobilize the city's young people. As both actors and symbols, young people catapulted the movement before the eyes of the world through their central role in the massive demonstrations of April 1963, the Children's Campaign in May, and the tragic bombing in September. From Japan to Germany, Canada to Egypt, the brutality of Birmingham's firefighters and policemen was broadcast by television and printed in magazines and newspapers. The Southern Christian Leadership Conference, an umbrella organization that coordinated nonviolent protests across the South, provided essential direction and support, but the demonstrations were made possible only by connections forged between young people in their daily lives. As Washington Booker III recalled, "I heard people say that the leadership didn't want to use the children and that it was some of the field-workers' idea. But as soon as the idea got around among the kids, it was over. We liked it, and we moved on it."

Looking back on the movement, interviewees saw both successes and failures. On the one hand, they took pride in the political and economic opportunities that followed the collapse of legal segregation in Birmingham. Many of the interviewees had taken advantage of these opportunities to pursue higher education, gain better jobs, and advance their children's education and living standards. Some had been instrumental in registering black residents to vote and in reshaping the city's political life through the election of Birmingham's first black mayor, Richard Arrington. On the other hand, many interviewees also expressed a sense of regret at the movement's decline and suggested that the time had come for a new generation of activists to mobilize the traditions of resistance and mutual aid in the service of the broader community. Looking forward to the revival of the mass meetings and the freedom music they inspired, Carlton Reese observed, "We've come a long way, but yet we still have a long way to go."

EDITORIAL METHOD

All of the interviews that appear in this volume have been transcribed, cataloged, and indexed and are available in hard copy in their entirety. The original interviews were structured to gather information on place of origin; parents; siblings; education; work; and experiences related to birth, childhood, migration, and race.[1] In this volume, the interviews are presented chronologically by age of the interviewee to highlight the ways in which individual motivations and forms of community activism changed over time. A headnote introduces each interviewee, summarizing his or her background information and explaining how each individual's experience relates to the Birmingham story. While we have removed some unnecessary or confusing language, we have tried to retain the original flavor of the interviews by keeping the interviewee's words whenever possible. For example, many interviewees used the honorary title of doctor to describe respected people whether or not they possessed an earned doctorate. Since this usage captures an important relationship and nowhere obscures the meaning of the interviews, we have retained it throughout. All words or letters added by the editors have been placed in brackets, and portions of the interviews have been rearranged for purposes of clarity and continuity. We have used two methods for supplying additional information within the interviews. For short identifications, we have inserted material within brackets; longer identifications and references requiring more detailed discussion have been supplied in endnotes. To aid readers interested in only selected interviews, we have repeated notes when necessary. All changes have been guided by our goal of making the interviews accessible to the largest possible audience, and we encourage anyone interested in the unaltered texts to consult the recordings and transcriptions maintained by the Birmingham Civil Rights Institute.

NOTES

1. For a more detailed commentary on how individuals were identified for the BCRI OHP, see Horace Huntley and David Montgomery, eds., *Black Workers' Struggle for Equality in Birmingham* (Urbana: University of Illinois Press, 2004), vii.

ACKNOWLEDGMENTS

This project would have been impossible without the able assistance of many who gave unselfishly of their time and talents. They include Yvonne Agee, Tanyika Blevins, Beth Campbell, Eleanor Caver, Michelle Craig, Liz Draper, Kimberly Falkner, Desiree Fisher, Tiwania Glover, Bette Hanson, Lola Hendricks, James Jones, Dr. Ricky Lee of Miles College, Nakeshia Jackson Leverette, Kecia Lightner, Corrie May, Binnie Myles, Braden Phillips-Welborn, Ahmad Ward, Eric Watson, Carrie Weeks, and Laura Williams. Odessa Woolfolk, president emerita of the Birmingham Civil Rights Institute Board of Directors; Wayne Coleman, archivist; and Braden Phillips-Welborn greatly assisted in reading and rereading interviews. Laura Anderson, assistant archivist, assisted in the development of the biographies and proofreading. We give a special thanks to the staff at the Central Branch of the Birmingham Public Library, especially those of the Archives Department and the Department of Southern History and Literature. Laurie Matheson, Jennifer Reichlin, and Breanne Ertmer of the University of Illinois Press have been consummate professionals in guiding us through the publication process. Our editor, Ellen D. Goldlust-Gingrich, has been superb. We thank the anonymous reviewers for their helpful suggestions. Paul Ortiz's forthright analysis and suggestions helped us to rethink our organization and emphasis. Angela Fisher-Hall was instrumental in acquiring permission to utilize the various photographs. Dr. Lawrence Pijeaux, executive director, and the Birmingham Civil Rights Institute's Board of Directors assisted financially and offered encouragement throughout the process. Thanks also go to the *Birmingham News* for allowing us to use the newspaper's photo archives.

INTRODUCTION

FOOT SOLDIERS FOR DEMOCRACY
ROBIN D. G. KELLEY

We've all seen those images: hundreds of black men and women, some very young, facing down trained attack dogs, high-powered fire hoses, tear gas, and billy clubs at the hands of Eugene "Bull" Connor's finest. Scenes of black people kneeling in prayer, dragged and beaten by police, teenagers pushed across the ground by fire hoses capable of taking bark off trees, and children packed into paddy wagons on their way to the city jail have become the iconic images of the civil rights movement. And like it or not, such images projected Birmingham, Alabama, to the rest of the world as a city of hate, the heart and soul of Dixie-style racism.[1] But more than anything, the film footage and stills from Birmingham's spring 1963 demonstrations moved many distant observers from a position of indifference to one of indignation.[2]

Those pictures still haunt us today, reappearing in virtually every visual document of modern America, every celluloid treatise on race. Yet the hundreds who put their bodies on the line for the cause of democracy—as well as the invisible ones who raised bail money, offered training in nonviolent tactics, cared for the injured, made signs and sandwiches for the movement—are never named. There are no captions identifying the dozens of young people lying in the streets assaulted by hose-wielding firemen. Sure, we recognize the bigwigs—Dr. Martin Luther King Jr., Rev. Ralph Abernathy, Rev. Fred Shuttlesworth—and more serious history buffs know the names of other visible actors such as A. D. King, A. G. Gaston, James Bevel, and Diane Nash. But who were the foot soldiers who stood up to such vicious violence? Who were the folks who made this movement, whose courage forced the city to negotiate and the federal government to intervene? Who were those unnamed idealists who, in deeds rather than words, helped author King's renowned "Letter from Birmingham Jail"?

Thanks to the untiring work of Horace Huntley and the Birmingham Civil Rights Institute Oral History Project (BCRI OHP), we can now begin to bring these anonymous faces into relief, fill in the names, and tell their stories. This remarkable book introduces us to a broad range of activists whose personal histories and experiences illuminate the movement's rich diversity and complexity. As you will discover, the foot soldiers for democracy came from all walks of life; they included barbers such as James Armstrong, domestic workers such as Emma Young, educators such as Johnnie Summerville and Carlton Reese, and entrepreneurs such as Eva Lou Russell. We meet movement "security guards" such as Joe Hendricks, an aircraft worker with a ninth-grade education; Henry M. Goodgame, an ironworker who went on to earn a law degree; Korean War veteran and steelworker James Summerville; and the college-educated James Roberson. These men and women demonstrated when they could, spent time in jail, and often stayed up all night to protect their neighborhoods, their churches, and the homes of movement leaders from the wave of bombings and violent attacks that turned Birmingham into a war zone. We hear stories like those of National Association for the Advancement of Colored People (NAACP) activist LaVerne Revis Martin, who discovered a bomb planted at the Bethel Baptist Church, and Paul Littlejohn, a future bus driver who was arrested for his activities in the bus boycott movement.

In Birmingham, African Americans stood at the eye of the storm. The city, we must remember, was considered the linchpin of the segregationist system; a victory there was mandatory if the movement was to succeed anywhere else. Long before the 1963 demonstrations, local activists regarded Birmingham as the civil rights crucible. In 1956, the year the state of Alabama outlawed the NAACP, Shuttlesworth founded the Alabama Christian Movement for Human Rights (ACMHR), which launched challenges against segregation in public facilities and the color bar denying African Americans city jobs as clerks, bus drivers, and police officers. The movement certainly experienced its fits and starts, but by the early 1960s, all eyes were on Birmingham, and the Southern Christian Leadership Conference (SCLC) prepared to send its heavies to face Bull Connor. For King, Birmingham represented the backbone of segregation. "We believed," he wrote, "that while a campaign in Birmingham would surely be the toughest fight of our civil-rights careers, it could, if successful, break the back of segregation all over the nation. This city has been the country's chief symbol of racial intolerance. A victory there might well set forces in motion to change the entire course of the drive for freedom and justice."[3]

While SCLC certainly brought greater international attention to the Birmingham struggle, local people—particularly the schoolchildren who insisted on participating in the civil disobedience campaign—and their willingness to organize and fight back made all the difference. The costs were heavy; hundreds of young protesters were jailed, beaten, and hosed down. For nearly all of these kids, their first experience as activists turned out to be a horrifying and unforgettable ordeal, but as the oral histories in this book show, the violence and repression often only steeled their efforts. The televised coverage of police attacking and arresting unarmed children, often while they were praying and singing, made the world aware of the horrors of segregation and the moral authority of southern black folk. After May 1963, the Kennedy administration could no longer look the other way, especially if it wanted to maintain its authority as the self-proclaimed leader of the "free" world. Pressure brought by these foot soldiers ultimately moved the federal government, which in turn compelled Birmingham's city fathers to negotiate a settlement.[4] The movement won its demands for desegregated public facilities and lunch counters, a commitment from various business establishments to hire and promote African Americans, and the release (on bail at least) of the demonstrators. Of course, the settlement represented only a partial victory, and racist violence continued to plague Birmingham. In the most deadly and dramatic expression of these unresolved tensions, a brutal bombing at the Sixteenth Street Baptist Church on September 15, 1963, cut short the young lives of Addie Mae Collins, Denise McNair, Carole Robertson, and Cynthia Wesley and left an indelible mark on the nation's conscience.[5]

The oral histories included here not only enrich the archives of the black freedom movement but also force us to revise the history of civil rights struggles in Birmingham and throughout the South. They give us an even greater sense of the price grassroots activists paid for their participation. We may recall that four girls paid the ultimate price when they were murdered by white supremacists on a quiet Sunday morning, but we are less likely to know the story of sixteen-year-old Johnny Robinson, whom the police gunned down just hours after the church bombing, or of Virgil Ware, shot and killed later that day by a white teenager who had recently attended a Klan rally.[6] The stories in this volume also tell us about the walking wounded, like LaVerne Revis Martin's daughter, whose forehead is permanently scarred from glass fragments caused by a white supremacist's bomb. Martin also tells us how she and a colleague were forced to take a lie detector test after she discovered an undetonated bomb near the Bethel Baptist Church and police accused the two of having planted the device. Martin's story resonates with other memories included here of the day-to-day police harassment activists endured. The oral histories also paint a vivid portrait of what it was like to be arrested, to ride squashed like sardines in a paddy wagon, to survive in a Birmingham jail—in other words, what policing was like when there were no cameras around. Yet stories of arrest and incarceration were not always tragic tales of misery. On the contrary, many of the younger people interviewed speak of the exhilaration of being in jail with other kids, some of whom took pride in the fact that they were making history, while others took pleasure in clowning around with their friends.

Less dramatic and more pervasive were the episodes of economic terrorism—activists facing the threat of being fired or losing their jobs as a consequence of their involvement. Reese, for example, tells of his inability to secure a teaching job in Birmingham because of his activities. After two years teaching in Mississippi, he eventually returned to Alabama, but he found a job in Shelby County, just outside of Birmingham. The situation for activist educators was especially complicated since they had to negotiate ways to retain their jobs while encouraging students to walk out of school to join demonstrations. The testimonies in this book include a few anecdotes about teachers and principals telling students that walking out was a violation of the school code while pointing them toward the doorway.

Because young people were fundamental to Birmingham's 1963 civil rights campaign, these oral histories also teach us a great deal about the social ramifications of mobilizing children and teenagers for change. What was it like to be a twelve- or fourteen-year-old kid on the front lines fighting for freedom? What motivated these kids to risk so much? Moreover, what was it like for parents to send their kids on marches or watch them go to jail? How did they try to explain segregation or the movement to their children? How did these young activists bring home the movement to their parents and grandparents? In some cases, the interviews reveal that despite their status as movement heroes, many of these children were also adolescents engaged in typical adolescent behavior. Willie Casey confesses that his initial involvement in the movement was motivated largely by the desire to get out of taking an exam. But participation transformed him. Soon after the demonstrations, Casey and his family moved to Cincinnati, Ohio, where his activism landed him in jail again, this time charged with inciting a riot.

The oral histories also reveal rich insights into gender differences in the movement or at least in how the movement is remembered. A few male interviewees make passing remarks about women's nonparticipation, chalking it up to "fear." Yet the overwhelming participation of women in the movement as well as the stories women tell paint a dramatically different picture. Emma

Young, then a middle-aged domestic worker whose testimony is filled with astute commentary on various civil rights leaders, recalls that her husband was too afraid to join the movement. Jimmie Lucille Hooks, an ACMHR activist who prepared children for civil disobedience, also belies the idea of women being afraid when she describes herself as "just not afraid of nothing." When her children were arrested, she marched into the Juvenile Court and made such a fuss that she got custody of them without posting bail. Furthermore, her motivation for fighting criminal justice officials speaks to a very important concern for women that has been largely ignored in the literature on the civil rights movement: the fear of rape in jail. Finally, the testimony contained here is filled with stories of black women's militancy, not just during the heyday of the movement but among previous generations of women. As Emma Young remembers, her mother left Camden, Alabama, sometime during the 1910s because she wanted to go "someplace where she could do better and not let white folk take all she had labored for."[7]

The spirit of resistance always embodied a unique combination of fear, courage, and hope. No matter how many photographs or hours of videotape we watch of the events in Birmingham or anyplace where black people are struggling for freedom, images can never capture the complexity of this spirit of resistance. Sometimes only words, expressions of feelings rather than descriptions of events, can capture the intangible elements of the black freedom movement. These beautiful stories reveal that the activists' most emotionally wrenching experiences were not necessarily being spat on or arrested but having to attend a funeral for four little girls murdered for no reason other than the color of their skin. Sometimes it is not the tear gas or the pain of the billy clubs that generate tears, but the songs—those timeless songs about which Professor Reese talks. And more often than not, the tearing down of physical racial barriers paled in comparison to the feeling of seizing the dignity and power that segregation sought to deny black people. Jimmie Lucille Hooks's explanation for joining the movement captures the fundamental importance of this struggle for dignity and power. Bill collectors and other powerful white people felt they had the right to "just open [my] door and walk in." "You never were 'Mrs.' or 'Miss,'" she adds, "you were always by your first name, boy or girl. . . . When they were talking about the civil rights movement, I was ready, too much ready to get involved. To this day I don't regret it one bit."

Indeed, judging from the oral histories, it is hard to imagine any of these foot soldiers regretting their participation in the movement, no matter what the cost. One might even argue that the movement was transformative, instilling them with a sense of possibility as well as a lifelong commitment to community service. Their stories of life after the movement are almost as inspiring as their movement tales. Nearly all of the activists included here have remained active in their churches, on boards, and in neighborhood organizations, and a few returned to school, earned advanced degrees in law and education, and committed their lives to community institutions. For example, the remarkable Eva Lou Russell, owner and operator of the Fraternal Café, turned to her lifelong interest in poetry and emerged in her autumn years as the Rapping Grandmother, publishing and performing verse about black pride, love, and history.

Many foot soldiers have stories yet to be told; many unsung heroes have songs yet to be heard. Without these people, there would have been no movement. They are history makers who rarely, if ever, receive credit for their deeds and vision. Nor do they seek credit, which is perhaps fitting for people willing to lay their bodies on the line for others. Joe Hendricks eloquently sums up their viewpoint when he insists that he deserves no credit for his contribution to the movement: all that "glory [goes] to God."

LOOK FOR THEM IN THE WHIRLWIND
ROSE FREEMAN MASSEY

I grew up and came of age working in the civil rights movement in my hometown, Greenwood, Mississippi, and other little towns all over the state. The memories of all the people, places, and events are as vivid as if they occurred yesterday. As I have moved on personally and professionally over the years, I sometimes find myself stunned, struck, and awed by the vivified images of more than forty years ago. Until recently, I attributed my propensity to revisit this period in my life to my appreciation and understanding of history. Now I know it is more than just an appreciation for the past. After reading these interviews with the children of 1960s Birmingham, I realize that the dialectical relationship between oppression and opposition continues and that we must not forget; if we do, it can happen again. The oral tradition is alive and well. There is no one better to tell the story than the survivors, the eyewitnesses. To bear witness is powerful.

For many of us, the turbulent 1960s are receding into history, gone, lost in the oblivion of contemporary life. This is not the case for the survivors, those who lived, struggled, and breathed faith, hope, fear, triumph, and loss more than forty years ago in Birmingham. A whole generation of African American men and women will never forget what they felt, saw, and heard—too much, too soon. The interviews of the BCRI OHP reveal young people's courageous efforts in the face of America's culture of racism, violence, and discontent. Memory often compresses the past, leaving victims of oppression with a blurred, distorted, mixed portrait of themselves that has been created by the oppressor. But these interviews offer the children of 1960s Birmingham the opportunity to reclaim their humanity and thus themselves. They tell their stories with clarity, intensity, coherence, and a vibrant mysterious eloquence, conveying the excitement and spirit of their generation.

From churches to drinking fountains, movie houses, parks, public restrooms, and schools, segregation dictated the pace of life in the Old South. Custom, law, black disfranchisement and ultimately the threat of violence buttressed the region's racial caste system. Violations of custom or law could provoke swift retribution. Birmingham was no different. In the early 1960s, it was America's most racist, segregated, and repressive city. Birmingham's African American adults worked in white-owned mills, mines, and kitchens. They had obligations and responsibilities and were thus vulnerable. If they marched, voted, or sat down at a lunch counter, they could lose their jobs or their homes. Practical reasons, therefore, led the city's children to become a force in combating white terrorism. They came from communities and hamlets such as Pratt City, Bessemer, Blount Crossing, Fairfield, Woodlawn, Irondale, and Birmingham proper. Some were just babies who attended elementary schools such as Hudson, Riley, Sandusky, or Henry C. Bryant. There were older kids who attended junior high and high schools such as Dunbar, Irondale, Fairfield Industrial, Ullman, Parker, Hayes, and Wenonah. There were some college students from Miles and Daniel Payne Colleges. Circumstance chose them to crowd the stage of history, and their accounts offer an accurate representation of the complexity of the times and help to illustrate how the city has come to be what it is today.

These interviews are fresh, pure, and raw, which is the beauty of oral history. They focus on antiblack racism and economic exploitation, two of America's longest-lasting problems. Annetta Streeter Gary remembers the dehumanizing experience of having to go to the back of the bus. When she went to jail, she was separated there, too, by color. She and her peers struggled with the agony of being socialized in two different worlds, one white and one black. All of the children grew up with stories of the Ku Klux Klan and police brutality, and all too often such tales were soon repeated in firsthand experience. Washington Booker states that he and his friends had daily run-ins with the police: "We knew them to be torturers and murderers." James Ware's thirteen-year-old brother, Virgil, was shot to death on the day of the bombing of the Sixteenth Street Baptist Church. Such events must have life-altering effects on the psyche of a young child. How long does it take for a psychological wound to heal? How do you purge the horror from your spirit? I don't know that you can ever do that.

In Birmingham during the 1960s, history chose the children to stand in the eye of the storm. They rose and responded to the occasion. From their number came untold stories of courage, acts both large and small. They bore the brunt of the high-pressure water hoses and faced the crazed frenzy of raw bigotry and police dogs. These young people who were bound together by a common thread helped to create the most significant social movement in all of American history.

But what in fact was the thread that bound together these children? What gave them and other young people of this period the courage to stand and face Bull Connors all over the South? Some observers and participants have suggested that the music imparted courage. Most of the interviews reference the freedom songs and how they affirmed the solidarity of black people. The lyrics of songs such as "Ain't Gonna Let Nobody Turn Me Around" and "We Will Never Turn Back" were and still are awesome. These songs gave me a feeling of power and an assurance that God was with us because we were right. Another prevailing theme is the human spirit's incredible ability to buoy itself on faith. The spirit and faith of "We Shall Overcome" is almost surreal. You had to be grounded in faith.

Participants recall that people wore faces of fear but also of determination, dedication, and faith. They firmly believed that things were going to change. Some of the interviews suggest the mystique of how things just seemed to happen, and there are constant references to how everyday people simply appeared to be moving with the spirit of the time. Some of the participants believe that events had been predestined. Others remember being gripped by fear, but it was not a paralyzing fear, just a realization of what they faced. In its wake, they felt themselves driven forward by some unknown force. For most of the interviewees, forty years of hindsight have made the situation seem a little surreal.

The Birmingham stories also speak to the power and purpose of the mass meetings held in black churches. Since its beginnings, the black church has been one of the most viable and stable institutions in the black community.[8] The black church—often the one institution that whites did not control—has served as a place of worship, a school, and a meeting place and thus became the logical place to hold mass meetings. The mass meetings put fire in your bones. They were very exciting, exhilarating, and moving.

First came songs of struggle, inspiration, and strength, followed by prayer, speeches, and testimonials from the local people. Out of the mass meetings came a sense that God was on your side and no police dogs or jail could turn you around. It didn't matter how dangerous it was or how petrified you were. You just stepped out on faith. The power of the mass meeting was incredible; it was definitely a galvanizing force. It let the people know they could do anything. According to Malcolm Hooks, the "mass meetings had a very profound effect on me as well as some of the rest of my brothers and sisters." He goes on to suggest that the mass meetings produced a complete metamorphosis, akin to a spiritual awakening: "It was almost as if you were caught up. . . . [I]t's very strange trying to explain it, because that's exactly what it was. You were caught up in a feeling. You were being directed, and we were moving almost as if we were being led to do it." Carolyn McKinstry says, "I personally felt very, very inspired and motivated when I listened to the speeches at the church. I wanted to be part of that. It just felt exciting, it felt good, it felt right, and I wanted to be part of it." Shirley Smith Miller attended mass meetings with her mother and felt that the prayer and singing made her feel as if she could beat all odds. Carl Grace recalls, "Dr. [Martin Luther] King would speak, [and] it was like I could sense an anointing, . . . and that anointing would touch me." The mass meetings gave the people the courage to stand up and face the police and the dogs and do whatever had to be done.

These children embraced the tenacious spirit of Marcus Garvey's words: "Look for me in the whirlwind or the storm, look for me all around you, for, with God's grace, I shall come and bring with me countless millions of black slaves who have died in America and the West Indies and the millions in Africa to aid you in the fight for Liberty, Freedom and Life."[9] Young people grasped the thunderbolt, heard the awful roar of the ocean's many waters, and engaged the enemy. These interviews constitute a vibrant history that must be read to approach the truth of what happened in Birmingham and all over the South.

NOTES

1. Numerous studies have detailed the role of race in the development of Birmingham and its surrounding communities. They include Robert J. Norrell, "Caste in Steel: Jim Crow Careers in Birmingham, Alabama," *Journal of American History* 73, 3 (December 1986): 669–94; Robin D. G. Kelley, *Hammer and Hoe: Alabama Communists during the Great Depression* (Chapel Hill: University of North Carolina Press, 1990); Henry M. McKiven Jr., *Iron and Steel: Class, Race,*

and Community in Birmingham, Alabama, 1875–1920 (Chapel Hill: University of North Carolina Press, 1995); Robin D. G. Kelley, *Race Rebels: Culture, Politics, and the Black Working Class* (New York: Free Press, 1996); Glenn T. Eskew, *But for Birmingham: The Local and National Movements in the Civil Rights Struggle* (Chapel Hill: University of North Carolina Press, 1997); Daniel Letwin, *The Challenge of Interracial Unionism: Alabama Coal Miners, 1878–1921* (Chapel Hill: University of North Carolina Press, 1998); Brian Kelly, *Race, Class, and Power in the Alabama Coalfields, 1908–21* (Urbana: University of Illinois Press, 2001); Diane McWhorter, *Carry Me Home: Birmingham, Alabama: The Climactic Battle of the Civil Rights Revolution* (New York: Simon and Schuster, 2001); Horace Huntley and David Montgomery, eds., *Black Workers' Struggle for Equality in Birmingham* (Urbana: University of Illinois Press, 2004).

2. On the impact of the images generated by the 1963 mass protests in Birmingham, see Howell Raines, *My Soul Is Rested: The Story of the Civil Rights Movement in the Deep South* (New York: Viking Penguin, 1983), 139–41; Taylor Branch, *Parting the Waters: America in the King Years 1954–63* (New York: Simon and Schuster, 1988), 760–61, 786, 804, 806; Eskew, *But for Birmingham*, 1–7, 227, 267, 272–73, 304–6; McWhorter, *Carry Me Home*, 370–76. For examples of Charles Moore's photographs of the Birmingham demonstrations, see also Michael S. Durham, *Powerful Days: The Civil Rights Photography of Charles Moore* (Tuscaloosa: University of Alabama Press, 1991), 90–119.

3. King quoted in Andrew Young, *An Easy Burden: The Civil Rights Movement and the Transformation of America* (New York: HarperCollins, 1996), 185.

4. For detailed examinations of the 1963 Birmingham demonstrations and their influence on local, national, and international policymakers, see Branch, *Parting the Waters*, 756–801, 807–9; Eskew, *But for Birmingham*, 3–17, 259–331.

5. On the ambiguous legacy of desegregation for Birmingham's African Americans, especially the young and poor, see Kelley, *Race Rebels*, 87–100; Eskew, *But for Birmingham*, 299–340; Judith Stein, *Running Steel, Running America: Race, Economic Policy, and the Decline of Liberalism* (Chapel Hill: University of North Carolina Press, 1998), 59–66.

6. On Robinson's death in the context of increasing police brutality in Birmingham during the mid-1960s, see Kelley, *Race Rebels*, 90–93.

7. Scholars of African American and women's history have increasingly demonstrated the central role that black women played in various reform movements as well as the ways in which prevailing ideas about race, class, and gender shaped women's responses to Jim Crow. These studies include Nancy A. Hewitt and Suzanne Lebsock, eds., *Visible Women: New Essays on American Activism* (Urbana: University of Illinois Press, 1993), esp. the essays by Darlene Clark Hine and Deborah Gray White; Jacqueline Jones, *Labor of Love, Labor of Sorrow: Black*

Women, Work, and the Family, from Slavery to the Present (New York: Vintage, 1995); Glenda Elizabeth Gilmore, *Gender and Jim Crow: Women and the Politics of White Supremacy in North Carolina, 1896–1920* (Chapel Hill: University of North Carolina Press, 1996); Tera W. Hunter, *To 'Joy My Freedom: Southern Black Women's Lives and Labors after the Civil War* (Cambridge: Harvard University Press, 1997); Belinda Robnett, *How Long? How Long? African-American Women in the Struggle for Civil Rights* (Oxford: Oxford University Press, 1997); Leslie A. Schwalm, *A Hard Fight for We: Women's Transition from Slavery to Freedom in South Carolina* (Urbana: University of Illinois Press, 1997); Chana Kai Lee, *For Freedom's Sake: The Life of Fannie Lou Hamer* (Urbana: University of Illinois Press, 1999); Elsa Barkley Brown, "Negotiating and Transforming the Public Sphere: African American Political Life in the Transition from Slavery to Freedom," in *Jumpin' Jim Crow: Southern Politics from Civil War to Civil Rights,* ed. Jane Dailey, Glenda Elizabeth Gilmore, and Bryant Simon (Princeton: Princeton University Press, 2000), 28–66.

8. Historians and other scholars have begun to see black religion and church organization as contributing to both accommodation and resistance to white supremacy. For varied perspectives on the role of religion and the black church in the African American freedom struggle, see E. Franklin Frazier, *The Negro Church in America* (New York: Schocken, 1974); Joseph R. Washington Jr., *Black Religion: The Negro and Christianity in the United States* (Boston: Beacon, 1964); Gayraud S. Wilmore, *Black Religion and Black Radicalism: An Examination of the Black Experience in Religion* (New York: Doubleday, 1972); Lawrence W. Levine, *Black Culture and Black Consciousness: Afro-American Folk Thought from Slavery to Freedom* (Oxford: Oxford University Press, 1977); David E. Swift, *Black Prophets of Justice: Activist Clergy before the Civil War* (Baton Rouge: Louisiana State University Press, 1989); Hans A. Baer, *The Black Spiritual Movement: A Religious Response to Racism* (Knoxville: University of Tennessee Press, 1984); C. Eric Lincoln and Lawrence H. Mamiya, *The Black Church in the African American Experience* (Durham: Duke University Press, 1990); Hans A. Baer and Merrill Singer, *African-American Religion in the Twentieth Century: Varieties of Protest and Accommodation* (Knoxville: University of Tennessee Press, 1992); Robert Gregg, *Sparks from the Anvil of Oppression: Philadelphia's African Methodists and Southern Migrants, 1890–1940* (Philadelphia: Temple University Press, 1993); Evelyn Brooks Higginbotham, *Righteous Discontent: The Women's Movement in the Black Baptist Church, 1880–1920* (Cambridge: Harvard University Press, 1993); Charles Taylor, *The Black Churches of Brooklyn* (New York: Columbia University Press, 1994); Ingrid Overacker, *The African American Church Community in Rochester, New York, 1900–1940* (Rochester: University of Rochester Press, 1998). For examples from the Birmingham context, see Andrew M. Manis, *A Fire You*

Can't Put Out: The Civil Rights Life of Birmingham's Reverend Fred Shuttlesworth (Tuscaloosa: University of Alabama Press, 1999); Eskew, *But for Birmingham,* 15–16, 20, 87, 137–39, 335, 384 n. 1; Kelly, *Race, Class, and Power,* 105–6.

9. Marcus Garvey, *Philosophy and Opinions of Marcus Garvey,* ed. Amy Jacques-Garvey (New York: Arno, 1969), 239.

ABBREVIATIONS

ACIPCO   American Cast Iron Pipe Company

ACMHR   Alabama Christian Movement for Human Rights

BCRI OHP   Birmingham Civil Rights Institute Oral History Project

NAACP   National Association for the Advancement of Colored People

SCLC   Southern Christian Leadership Conference

TCI   Tennessee Coal and Iron Company (originally the Tennessee Coal, Iron, and Railroad Company)

UAB   University of Alabama at Birmingham

CHRONOLOGY OF EVENTS FROM
APRIL AND MAY 1963

April 3   The ACMHR and the SCLC led sit-in demonstrations at down-
          town Birmingham lunch counters. Twenty participants were
          arrested at Britt's lunch counter. Kress, Loveman's, Pizitz, and
          Woolworth's closed their counters.

April 4   Dr. Martin Luther King Jr. led a march to City Hall. According to
          the *Birmingham News,* the march "fizzled with only a handful
          of Negroes following him."

April 5   Ten sit-in demonstrators were arrested, including six at Lane Drug-
          store (First Avenue and Twentieth Street) and four at Tutwiler
          Drugstore (Fifth Avenue and Twentieth Street).

April 6   Protesting the previous arrests and the status quo, Rev. Fred Shut-
          tlesworth led a march toward City Hall. The march began at the
          A. G. Gaston Motel. Police halted the march at Eighteenth Street
          and Fifth Avenue, arresting thirty-two participants.

April 7 *(Palm Sunday)*   Revs. A. D. King, Nelson Smith, and John Porter led
          a march beginning at St. Paul Methodist Church (Sixth Avenue
          and Fifteenth Street). Though they intended to reach City Hall,
          the marchers were stopped, and twenty-six people (ranging in
          age from seventeen to seventy-eight) were arrested after a prayer
          near the Henley School (Sixth Avenue and Seventeenth Street).
          Nine of those arrested were female. Police dogs were used to
          disperse black onlookers. Leroy Allen, a nineteen-year-old dem-
          onstrator, was bitten and knocked down by a police dog.

April 8   The *Birmingham News* reported "hit and run sit-ins staged in sev-
          eral locations downtown."

April 9   Seven blacks and one white man from Illinois were arrested for
          picketing in front of Loveman's. According to the *Birmingham*

News, "The largest crowd to assemble at any of the racial demonstrations since they began last week gathered on sidewalks in the vicinity of the pickets." Blind entertainer Al Hibbler vowed that he had come to Birmingham to be arrested with other demonstrators. The Birmingham Police Department refused to arrest him. He was assisted into a paddy wagon by two other demonstrators who had been arrested. Hibbler later was released without being charged.

April 10   Sit-ins were attempted, but lunch counters were closed. Police arrested twenty-seven protesters in the 400 block of Nineteenth Street. Thirteen Miles College students sat in briefly at the Main Library downtown. They left before being arrested. Three people were arrested at Britt's (Second Avenue and Nineteenth Street), and nine people were arrested at the Bohemian Bakery (1804 Fourth Avenue).

April 11   Twelve demonstrators were arrested after appearing in three groups between Second and Fourth Avenues on Eighteenth Street. Dr. Martin Luther King Jr., other leaders, and those persons previously arrested received a court-ordered injunction against "boycotting, trespassing, parading, picketing, sit-ins, kneel-ins, wade-ins, and inciting or encouraging such acts."

April 12 *(Good Friday)*   Dr. Martin Luther King, Rev. Ralph Abernathy, and Rev. Fred Shuttlesworth led a march starting at St. Paul's in defiance of the injunction and were arrested within yards of the site of the Palm Sunday arrests. During his incarceration for this offense, King wrote his "Letter from Birmingham Jail." The *Birmingham News* printed "A Statement by Some of the Negro Leaders of Metropolitan Birmingham," which pled with Birmingham's city officials immediately to appoint "a biracial committee which would be charged with the responsibility of looking objectively at the problems in this community where race is involved." The statement continued, "The current struggle in our community is an expression of the uttered or unexpressed deep yearnings of the heart of every Negro in this community. This struggle is not one of strife, but of striving to say to our friends and neighbors of whatever race and creed, 'Let us live together in human dignity as American citizens and Sons of God.'" Sixty-two names were listed with the statement.

April 13   Six picketers were arrested at Atlantic Mills (1216 Eighth Avenue North).

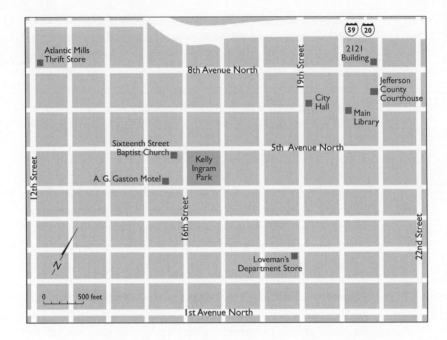

April 14   Four African American women and one African American man
            attended white worship services at the First Baptist Church. Two
            African American women attended services at the First Pres-
            byterian Church. African Americans were turned away from
            several other churches. Approximately a thousand people at-
            tempted to march to City Hall but were stopped by police, and
            thirty-two were arrested, including Revs. John Porter, N. H.
            Smith, and Frank Dukes.

April 15   Five people were arrested at a sit-in at Britt's, and four picketers
            were arrested at Sears.

April 16   Five protesters were arrested outside of an unnamed variety store,
            and two others were charged with trespassing at the Bohemian
            Bakery (1804 Fourth Avenue North).

April 17   Rev. Henry Crawford and fifteen black women marched from the
            Sixteenth Street Baptist Church to the courthouse to register to
            vote but were arrested in the 1600 block of Sixth Avenue.

April 18   Demonstrators staged two sit-ins at lunch counters. One of the fa-
            cilities was closed; at the other, the demonstrators were ignored
            and not served. No arrests were made.

April 19 Eleven protesters were arrested at the 2121 Building lunch counter.

April 20 Seven picketers outside Pizitz were arrested. Seven protesters were arrested at a sit-in at Britt's. Four people were arrested inside Atlantic Mills. Seven people were arrested at Tillman Levenson.

April 21 Fifteen African American worshippers attended white church services at the First Baptist Church, the First Presbyterian Church, and the Episcopal Church of the Advent. African Americans were turned away at First Methodist, First Christian, Woodlawn Baptist, Southside Baptist, and Highland Methodist Churches.

April 22 Sit-ins took place at Woolworth's, H. L. Green, and Britt's. Demonstrators were not served, and no arrests were made.

April 23 Three girls and two boys were arrested for picketing at Atlantic Mills.

April 24–May 1 Sporadic demonstrations. Protesters spent much of their energy in the courtroom, fighting the injunction and contempt-of-court charges. Mass meetings continued at various churches.

May 1 Judge William Jenkins handed down sentences of five days in jail and fifty-dollar fines for eleven leaders held in contempt of court for ignoring his April 11 injunction.

May 2 Children demonstrated en masse against the Birmingham Police Department and Commissioner Bull Connor. Nearly one thousand children were arrested, most in groups of between thirty and sixty as they moved east on Sixth Avenue between Seventeenth and Eighteenth Streets. Ten groups converged on City Hall from all directions. Nearly 40 percent of the student body was absent from Parker High School.

May 3–4 Demonstrations involving children continued. Bull Connor responded with police dogs and water hoses, infuriating the demonstrators and the onlookers. African Americans retaliated against the police and fire departments. Sixty were arrested in the first wave of demonstrations in or near Kelly Ingram Park. Several demonstrators were bitten by dogs, and several dogs were struck with bricks. A white man was arrested when he attempted to run his car into demonstrators. Twenty-seven demonstrators knelt and prayed at City Hall and then were arrested and charged with loitering. Fifty demonstrators were arrested at Twentieth Street and Second Avenue, and thirty were arrested at a church on Seventh Avenue. By May 4, more than three thousand demonstrators had been arrested. Jails in Birmingham and Jefferson County were filled, so many of those arrested were taken to the Alabama State Fairground, also known as Fair Park.

May 5 Kneel-ins were held at twenty-one white churches. A mass rally was held at the New Pilgrim Baptist Church (Sixth Avenue and Tenth Street South). The rally culminated with a march to the Southside Jail and a massive demonstration in Memorial Park across from the jail. Firemen refused to use hoses on the demonstrators.

May 6 One high school, presumably Parker, reported 1,339 children absent and 87 present. The principal, R. C. Johnson, attempted to stop the youth from leaving, but according to the *Birmingham News*, "On each side of the principal, a stream of black youths flowed out through the two open doors onto 8th Avenue North, believing they were going to change the world today." Arthur Williams, a star athlete, said, "We wanted to get out and he was trying to keep us in. A bunch of us were shouting, 'Freedom,' and some of us were singing, 'We Shall Overcome.' Then a chant started building up as one by one it spread through the group until it was pounding across the lobby, 'Gotta go, Mr. Johnson gotta go.'"

Comedian Dick Gregory arrived in Birmingham and within four hours was arrested with the first of several groups of children and adults that had assembled at the Sixteenth Street Baptist Church. Police sealed off Kelly Ingram Park to prevent demonstrators from entering. According to the *Birmingham News*, "Negroes crowded the sidewalks in all directions around the church," and at least six groups of demonstrators emerged from the church in just the first fifteen minutes of the demonstrations. Many of those on the sidewalks joined in the marches to the downtown area and to City Hall. Massive arrests resulted, with demonstrators loaded into police wagons and school buses and taken to Fair Park and to the Southside Jail.

May 7 Children continued to demonstrate. Rev. Fred Shuttlesworth was hospitalized with injuries inflicted by high-powered water hoses on the steps of the Sixteenth Street Baptist Church. Demonstrations flared in the downtown area from Sixteenth to Nineteenth Streets and from Second to Seventh Avenues. Groups assembled at Woodrow Wilson Park, City Hall, and various stores, including Loveman's, Pizitz, and Woolworth's. The *Birmingham*

News reported that "a vanguard of about one hundred first trotted along 3rd Avenue. . . . This proved to be just the first wave. Pouring East on 3rd Avenue came another singing army." More than thirty-five hundred demonstrators were arrested between April 3 and May 7.

May 8   Demonstrations were suspended. Movement leaders said white business leaders were acting in good faith to settle issues of concern.

May 9   The *Birmingham News* printed an article, "Both Sides . . . and Human Side," by Relman Morin of the Associated Press. Most of the article reported a conversation between Juvenile Court judge Talbot Ellis and Grosbeck Parham, a fifteen-year-old arrested for demonstrating. The judge lectured the young man on freedom, restraint, and the necessity for nonviolence. The boy replied, "Well, you can say that about freedom because you've got your freedom. The Constitution says we're all equal, but Negroes aren't equal." The judge replied, "But your people have made great gains and they still are. It takes time." Parham replied, "We've been waiting over one hundred years."

May 10   Leaders of the demonstrations, represented by Martin Luther King Jr., and the white business community, represented by Sidney Smyer, reached an agreement. Provisions included an end to demonstrations, a cooling-off period, the desegregation of downtown lunch counters, the removal of signs designating "Colored" and "White," the hiring of African Americans as clerks in downtown stores, and the release of those demonstrators still held in jail. Bull Connor denounced the agreement and applauded the police and fire departments "for the wonderful job they have done to save segregation in Birmingham." Newly elected mayor Albert Boutwell said the agreement was not binding on him and the City Council. According to the *Birmingham News,* incumbent "mayor Arthur Hanes called the agreement hogwash and said he would order the arrest of any person violating the city's segregation codes."

May 11   The A. G. Gaston Motel and the home of Rev. A. D. King were bombed, and the African American community responded violently, burning buildings and overturning cars. Police and firemen were prevented from entering the area, and chaos reigned.

May 13   Federal troops were brought in.

The Sixteenth Street Baptist Church, bombed September 15, 1963. Four little girls were killed.
Copyright 1978 Matt Herron/Take Stock.

James Armstrong and an un-
identified child, September 1963.
Copyright 1978 Matt Herron/
Take Stock.

A teenage girl hit with a water hose during the children's demonstrations, May 1963. Courtesy of the *Birmingham News.*

Whites demonstrating against school desegregation. Courtesy of the *Birmingham News.*

Children being arrested and taken to jail in a school bus. Courtesy of the *Birmingham News*.

A teenager attacked by police with a dog. Courtesy of the *Birmingham News*.

Demonstrators being loaded into a police paddy wagon. Courtesy of the *Birmingham News*.

FOOT SOLDIERS FOR DEMOCRACY

EMMA SMITH YOUNG

BORN IN CAMDEN, ALABAMA, in Wilcox County, in 1902, Emma S. Young and her generation of activists linked the ACMHR-SCLC period to a much older tradition of African American resistance. Her mother, a woman old enough to have observed African Americans' struggles to define their freedom in the wake of emancipation, left Camden rather than submit to the exploitative practices of the town's white farmers, saying that she was "going someplace where she could do better and not let white folk take all she had labored for."

Young and her new husband initially remained in Camden, but she soon joined the migration of black job seekers to the city. Young's new job as a laundress made her and her family dependent on her wages, especially after her estrangement from her husband. Yet, Young, like her mother, refused to be treated like a servant by her white employers. When one of these employers included another person's clothes with her order, Young left the job rather than work under conditions imposed without her consent: "I'm not going to wash them other people's clothes. If they want me, let them hire me."

Such open defiance of white authority carried the possibility of physical danger, a fact that constantly forced Birmingham's black men and women to weigh the costs of resistance against the satisfaction of asserting their humanity. All too familiar with the specter of white violence in Alabama, Young refused to allow her son to intervene against hose-wielding firemen during the mass demonstrations in 1963. "Dave wanted to buck against me and go out there anyway," she remembered. "I told him, 'Don't you go out there and let that man kill you, because I couldn't take it. I couldn't stand here and let him shoot you down.'"

Young died in 2004 at the age of 102, after having outlived all of her children.

THE MOVEMENT WAS ABOUT FREEDOM

I lived in Camden until I was between seventeen and eighteen. Then, [around] 1921, I left there to come to Birmingham. I had one sister. She died several years ago. Her name was Lola McGraw. I have three children, one boy and two girls. The two oldest ones, Dave and Eula Mae, were born in Camden. Mamie, the youngest, was born in Birmingham. Before we moved to Birmingham, I wasn't doing any work. I went to school but only got to the fifth grade. I lived with my mother because my daddy was gone. I was age four when he left. I moved to Birmingham after I got married. My husband did farm work while we were living in Camden. When we [first] moved to Birmingham, my husband did cement work.

My mother decided to leave first because she got tired of Camden's white people. At the end of the farm season, they took out too much pay. That year, Mama didn't make but two bales of cotton, and they took those two for their pay. They left her with nothing. She said she was leaving there, going someplace where she could do better and not let white folk take all she had labored for.[1]

I married my husband before she left. After Mama left, my husband and I decided to leave. My husband checked with my stepdaddy in Birmingham about a job at the cement plant. When we came to Birmingham, at first we lived with my mother. Soon afterwards, my husband and me got a two-room house. We lived in a community called Hillman Station. We became affiliated with Hopewell Baptist Church. My husband left the cement plant and worked on many different jobs. He was eventually hired by Woodward's iron-ore mine. We rented a house from the company. Then we moved down to Cairo, back in[to] Hillman, and eventually we moved to Grasselli Heights, bought our house, and stayed. It was in our Grasselli home where my husband retired from the ore mine and later died. Grasselli Heights was a move up for us.[2] Mama was getting social security payments. They did not call it that back then. They called it a pension. We lived together. I joined another church called St. Luke in Cairo after my mother joined.

In Camden, I was a housewife. When we got to Birmingham, I started to run ads for jobs. I would get maid jobs, or I would be a cook, something like that—housework. Later, I started doing hand washing on the rub board.[3] During that time, we used the rub board to wash because that was all we had. At first, I would go to the private home and do the laundry. Once I got enough money to buy a washer and dryer, I started taking it into my home. I would wash and iron for all the people, black and white. Once I worked at the Snow White Laundry before moving to the Gary Hotel in Bessemer. I also worked in a hotel in Birmingham. I could always get a job because I could iron shirts so good. I could fix the collars like men like them. I could keep that crease on the collar from bunching. I could handle a shirt so well [that] everybody wanted me to wash and iron for them.

I went to work for a lady named Miss Florence. I quit because she was trying to make a fool out of me. I overheard her say to a friend, "Oh, my girl just work. She can iron a shirt like nobody's business." The friend said, "Oh, I wish she could iron one for me." Miss Florence then said, "I'll put two or three of your clothes in with mine and let you see how she can iron." She put them in my basket. I knew the clothes and asked her, "Why do I have more clothes this week?" I said, "I don't like you adding more clothes than I been washing." She said, "All those were your clothes." Well, I found out they were Miss Daniels' clothes. I just walked off and left them there. I didn't finish that job. She had the clothes spread out on the ground when I got there. She had a fire made up and everything ready.[4] I decided that I was not going to iron for somebody and not get paid. I said, "I'm not going to let her make a fool out of me." I say, "I'm not going to wash them other people's clothes. If they want me, let them hire me." Before I left, she told me, "Emma, where can you get another job? You can't do without another job." I said, "Oh, yes, I can."

I wasn't making but three dollars [a week] at that one. Yet I said, "Well, I will do something with those three dollars." I could take one dollar and put it on a layaway and put that other dollar on another layaway. When the end of the month came, I would have all my dollars get together and get all that stuff out. I had plenty. I was usually pretty well dressed. They wondered, "Where that woman get so much of something? Where she get so and so?" They couldn't tell where I was getting it. I worked to get it. But it wasn't their business. I said, "I work and get what I got. I'm entitled to use what I have, and that's what I'm going to do."

I was working for my three children and myself. My husband was gone over to the bootlegger's house. I didn't have a close relationship with [my husband]. As a matter of fact, I didn't take up with him at all. I just let him be there. I didn't take up with bootleggers. He said I thought I was better than them. Well, I didn't take up with what I didn't like, and I didn't like that kind of stuff. I wanted to go to church every Sunday or every other day I wanted to go to church, and I did. I left my husband because he wanted to know why [I didn't] go with him sometime. I said, "Why don't you go with me sometime?" So we both were doing different things. He went to the bootlegger's, and I went to church. His being in and out of the home affected my children very much. He would live with his stepmama, then come back and live with me, and then move back with her. We did that for a long time. But altogether we stayed together for fifty years. Some folk see that as being remarkable, considering people can't stay together fifty minutes or two hours these days.

· · ·

Before the movement, I was having a hard time. I remember most about how I related to whites and how whites related to me. I used to ride the buses downtown to shop all the time. I remember a double-length streetcar. The front end belonged to the white people, and the back end belonged to the Negroes. We had to get back there. If we're sitting on one part when the white folks get on, we had to get off the bus and go around to the back to reenter. If there wasn't any room in the back, you just stood up until you could find yourself a seat. If a white person came in and wanted to sit there, sometimes you had to get up. The man driving the streetcar would get out of his seat and come to the back. He would ask you, "Would you please let so-and-so have this seat?" We had white folks' seats. We had to get up and let them have the seats. But I got so I would refuse. I wouldn't get up.[5] Sometimes when I refused to get up, nothing happened. The driver wouldn't try to make you do anything. You would pay the [white] rider no attention. They were riding just like you. But if the driver came back and moved the board, that was an indication. If the board is sitting behind you and he moved it back further, then the driver wanted you to move back. If he didn't come back, we could ride on.

Before the movement, we wouldn't refuse. We'd get up from our seats, get in the back, and stand up until we heard Martin Luther King say, "You're a fool. Don't you know you paid your money just like they paid theirs?" He said, "Don't get up. Sit right there and let them know that you paid the same thing they paid." That's what we were talking about, fighting about, and praying about during the meetings.

In 1963, the movement was going on—well, even before then. But at that time, I attended all the mass meetings and had a fine time. We would sing and pray and take up money to pay [the legal fees] for the [NAACP] cases before the Supreme Court. We told them that we want our freedom, and we want it now. While others were saying, "You can't get it now, you have to wait," we said, "We don't want to wait. I want my freedom now." We helped to get this freedom that we have now. The movement was about freedom. Sometimes we had so many people [that] we could fill two or three churches. We had the little walkie-talkies so we could hear everything that was being said in the other churches. Some folk had them in their homes.

We were trying to get a chance to sit on the buses without being interrupted or having to go to the back. "When you get on a bus, just sit down," Rev. Martin Luther King would tell us. "You have a seat right there in the front. Don't go back there in the back. If they tell you to get up, don't get up." We didn't. I got a kick out of sitting there. I sat right up front. When the whites got on the bus, they would not sit beside me. Sometimes when we sat up front, they would put their books down to keep you from sitting next to them. I'd move the book and put it anywhere. I'd just sit right where the books were. Martin Luther King had told me what to do, and I was doing it. One lady came along and said, "Don't bother that nigger. That's one of them old Martin Luther King niggers." I said, "Yes, I am." I wasn't arrested. Martin Luther King told me, "Don't say a word. Don't you hit them. Just don't hit them. And let them hit you, but don't you hit them. Just sit there and don't say a word and don't move." I would sit and not move.

I took part in all of the demonstrations. Every time we marched up to City Hall, I marched. I went everywhere they wanted to march. We marched to Selma; I marched down there with them. I was there at Sixteenth Street Baptist Church when [Fred] Shuttlesworth was hit with water and knocked off the steps of the church. My son, Dave, tried to go across and pick up Shuttlesworth, to keep them from killing him. Bull Connor was sitting across the street yelling, "Put that water on the nigger." He had them put the water on him, making Shuttlesworth go farther, farther, and farther down the sidewalk. They were just wetting Shuttlesworth. Dave got so mad, he wanted to go out there. I pulled him back. I said, "Don't go out there. That man say for you not to come out of there." Dave wanted to buck against me and go out there anyway. I told him, "Don't you go out there and let that man kill you, because I couldn't take it. I couldn't stand here and see him shoot you down."

My son was very active in the movement. He was the reason why I was there. I got started on account of him. He was going, and his wife wanted to go, then I wanted to go. When he said, "Let's go, I'm going to the movement," we couldn't get ready soon enough. He would ask me, "All right, you ready, Mama?" I'd say, "I'm ready."

My husband didn't ever go. He didn't pay any attention to the movement. He thought nothing of it. He said, "Them folk going to kill y'all out there acting a fool." That's all he would tell us. The children called him an Uncle Tom. My son would say, "All old folks ought to be dead," because his father would not participate in the movement. I asked him, "Why you think all old folks should be dead?" I said, "Your mama and your papa both is old." [He responded,] "I can't help it." [He continued,] "Because if all of them old folks were out the way, these young folks can get something done." I said, "I tell you what, if these old folks could get themselves down there, I'll tell you, they would. Because you young folk want to do whatever you want to do, and they can't get it done like that." I didn't agree with that statement. I loved to get out there with them. When they would say, "Ain't gonna let nobody turn me around," I was right there, singing, "Ain't gonna let Bull Connor turn me 'round, turn me 'round, turn me 'round. Ain't gonna let Bull Connor turn me 'round. I'm gonna keep on a walking, keep on a talking, walking up to freedom land." I was right there.

All my grandchildren were there marching for freedom. All of them went to jail. They filled up the jail so fast [that] they had to put them in the [jailhouse] yard. One of my grandchildren was jailed at Fair Park. She started calling back to her mother, saying that she wanted to get out of that place. They had her out there in the rain. They didn't have anywhere else to put them. They put them out there in that [jailhouse] yard with the high fence. Up so high, they couldn't get over the fence. My grandson was already in jail. They carried him off in the paddy wagon. Martin Luther King went at that time. My son was also in jail. He stayed in jail about two weeks or a month. One point, Martin Luther King refused to come out. They was trying to not give him any water, not feed him, and all that stuff.

There was a situation once where some white ministers, rabbis came from Oklahoma or somewhere. They came down to help us because we were in trouble. They wanted to sit in the meetings and hear how they were treating us. Bull Connor told his people to go in there and get them "damn niggers" out of there. He called the white rabbis "niggers." He took all our rabbis out of the church. They came in with their Gatling guns on and their guns hanging on their shoulders. They came and said, "Get up, and let's go." And [the rabbis] followed. We went on with the meeting. Then the man in charge of the meeting told us, he said, "All right. Bull Connor done come in here and got our people that come to help us and visited us and have disturbed our meeting. We, the whole church, will go down to City Hall. That's where we are going to preach at today. We are going to have a meeting down there, with our company that had come with us." Now, these people that they took out were all white. It was decided. The entire church went down to city hall.

Bull Connor had a crowd. He got up in his paddy wagon and said, "Hey y'all people, go back home." He wouldn't call us "niggers" then. He said, "All y'all people go on back home, back to your church." We replied, "You didn't let us have no peace in our church. We're going down to City Hall and do just what we were doing at the church." I was right along there with them. Bull Connor began putting the water on us as we went, wetting us up. We went down anyway. We kept going, stepping over the water. Everybody was going on just praying and singing. Singing that song, "Ain't gonna let nobody turn me around." We said, "We going on, Bull Connor ain't gonna turn us around." They hosed us out there, putting the water on us, following us. All of a sudden, the pipes stopped running. All the water run out from somewhere. Bull Connor said, "What's the matter with y'all? Why don't you put that water on them? I said put the water on them!" One man, a fireman, told him, "I'll tell you where I'm going: I'm going back home and eat breakfast with my wife." He started talking about "God done stopped the water." He said he was scared to mess with the water. He said to Bull Connor, "Well, won't no water come out." The water just stopped. We stepped over the line, went on and kept singing, "Ain't gonna let nobody turn us 'round." We didn't let anybody turn us around until we got to City Hall. We preached, prayed, shouted, and sang. We did everything we were going to do at the church down at City Hall.

I remember when the Sixteenth Street [Baptist] Church was bombed and those little girls were killed. I wasn't there. I just heard about it. They were at Sunday school. I didn't go to Sunday school there. I went to St. Luke Baptist Church. I went to the funeral, at Sixth Avenue Baptist Church. I remember that day. We had a gang of rabbis there. We had the whole back of the church filled with rabbis that day. Then they rolled the bodies in, one by one, one by one, and one by one. I was right there looking down on them when they rolled the little girls in. The church was packed to capacity. That's what I wanted to see.

The Supreme Court and *Brown v. Board of Education* changed the school system. The Court gave a ruling on "separate but equal" and said it was illegal. Bull Connor and George Wallace didn't like that at all. No black and white children were going to go to school together. They didn't like colored children going to white schools. George Wallace said it wasn't going to happen: "No blacks were going to any school with white folks. Segregation now, segregation forever." He stood in the schoolhouse door and said, "You ain't coming by here." When some black children tried to go to the University of Alabama in Tuscaloosa, George Wallace got in that door. A man much taller than he said, "Would you step aside?" Wallace was scared of that man, he said, "Oh, yeah, I'll do this." And he stepped aside. I remember him saying, "Any nigger come in here he going to go over my dead body." But when that man came there, he didn't say anything. He looked up, got something, and stepped aside. This man's name was Katzenbach, and he represented the federal government.[6] He was so big and tall. Wallace was just a show. Trying to bluff somebody to make them do like they wanted them to do. He didn't fool around with that man. He didn't mess with that man. That man just told him to step aside. Katzenbach went on into the school, right through the door.[7]

I have had a wide and varied experience in the civil rights movement. During the '63 demonstrations, I was in my sixties. Now I am in my nineties. I feel good about the changes that I lived through. Being the age that I am, I just wonder, how did I come through? How did I get through all that stuff I had to come through? What these people are going through now, I've been through. I've come through what they're going through. I thank God I'm here. All I can say now is, "Thank you, Jesus. Thank you, Jesus." We used to have a woman at the movement who used to say, "Thank God for Jesus." One day, she shouted so much they came and got her. It took six men to take her out. I spoke to her one day when I saw her outside the church. She was on her way in, and I was on my way in, and I said, "Oh, God, there go that old shouting lady." What did I say that for? She said, "You better wish you were a shouting lady." I said, "Oh, I wasn't talking about you." She was old, just not as old as I was. There were so many people there, but I was one of the older ones. It seemed that just about everyone you could find was there, unless he was a drinker or he loved to run around and drink and didn't care anything about anything, just drinking and having a time. [People like that] didn't pay the movement any attention.

My church was very involved. All the deacons and members of the church were involved. They could have the meeting at our church any time. I remember many people who fought during the movement. Rev. [John] Porter of Sixth Avenue Baptist Church was real nice. He really loved the movement. He was always there, although his church didn't want him involved. They figured since Shuttlesworth had gotten his church bombed that the same folk would come over to their church. They told him they didn't want them there and to stay away from our church. Rev. Porter said, "Yeah, they coming all right," and he stayed with the movement. Porter allowed the movement to come to Sixth Avenue Baptist. The girls who were killed wouldn't have had their funerals there without him. He stopped the talking about they weren't coming there, because Rev. Porter was all for it. He was with them at every meeting. He said, "My people don't want me over here, but I'm over here."

I also remember the Woods brothers. They were active in the movement, the daddy and the two brothers. Calvin Woods, Abraham Woods, and I don't know the daddy's name, but all of them were preachers. Another man was Carlton Reese. He was the piano man that wrote a lot of the songs. He played the music for us, and he would do all the singing. He would just sing whatever he wanted to sing. He could just make up a song and sing it. He would sing something about Bull Connor and we would go right along with him.

I enjoyed going to the movement meetings so much, I couldn't be afraid. I wouldn't be afraid when the white folks would come in with all those machines and lights and things in your face. They were taking pictures and all that kind of stuff. I didn't have sense enough to be scared of that. I was so enthused over Martin Luther King and what they were doing, until I didn't pay them any attention. But they were back there, catching every word they said and everything else. Martin wouldn't pay them any attention. He told them, "I want my freedom, and I want it now." That became sort of a slogan for the movement.

Toward the end of the movement era, they were following Martin Luther King. They were trying to keep up with him for a long time to get a chance to kill him. He said something or other about seeing the mountaintop, where "I might not get there with you, but I want y'all to keep on going. Just keep on going."[8] He said, "Walk. If they won't let you walk, crawl." He said, "If you can't crawl, slide on in there, just so you keep going."

I remember the day when Martin Luther King was killed. I was standing at the ironing board. My husband said, "That must have been your man, you carrying on so." I said nothing about him being my man, I just love him so because he was teaching us so much. I said, "Oh, God, that couldn't be Martin Luther King. That's the main man. They killed the poor man." I had a fit. I couldn't iron any more. I threw those clothes away. I was just sick. I said, "Well, Jesus, what are we going to do now?" But I knew Shuttlesworth and Rev. Gardner and all those guys were still here. We were going to keep on going, just like Martin said. So we did.

NOTES

BCRI OHP, vol. 10, sec. 4 (September 29, 1995). Edited, annotated, and abridged by A. Michelle Craig, Horace Huntley, and John McKerley.

1. In the wake of emancipation, many former slaves viewed sharecropping as a means by which to eventually claim independence through landownership. These black men and women looked forward to directing their own labor (or at least having it focused on their own families) outside white control. On the whole, however, racial discrimination and disfranchisement produced conditions in which black southerners paid the most and gained the least from the cotton economy's cycles of boom and bust. Even after two decades of relatively stable growth between 1900 and 1920, more than 60 percent of white farm operators owned their property, compared to only 22.4 percent of blacks. At the other end of the scale, almost 40 percent of blacks were croppers, compared to only 11.1 percent of whites. See Gavin Wright, *Old South, New South: Revolutions in the Southern Economy since the Civil War* (New York: Basic Books, 1986), 121. On the lives and labors of black women in the cotton South during this period, see Jacqueline Jones, *Labor of Love, Labor of Sorrow: Black Women, Work, and the Family, from Slavery to the Present* (New York: Vintage, 1995), 79–92.

2. Many iron-ore miners and their families suggest that moving out of the mining camps, where workers rented housing from the company, and buying homes in neighboring communities represented upward mobility.

3. A "rub board" was a rectangular, ridged instrument, approximately twenty-

four by thirty inches, that laundresses used to clean clothes by hand. After placing the board in a tub of soapy water, the laundress vigorously scrubbed a single piece of clothing (a shirt, dress, etc.) against the ridges. For more on the lives and labors of black laundresses in the postemancipation South, see Tera W. Hunter, *To 'Joy My Freedom: Southern Black Women's Lives and Labors after the Civil War* (Cambridge: Harvard University Press, 1998), esp. 74–97.

4. Water was boiled in a big kettle and clothes were placed in the boiling water and agitated with a long stick.

5. Andrew M. Manis, *A Fire You Can't Put Out: The Civil Rights Life of Birmingham's Reverend Fred Shuttlesworth* (Tuscaloosa: University of Alabama Press, 1999), 115–16. For an in-depth discussion of black resistance to segregated busing in Birmingham prior to the 1960s, see Robin D. G. Kelley, *Race Rebels: Culture, Politics, and the Black Working Class* (New York: Free Press, 1996), 55–100.

6. Nicohlas Katzenbach was deputy U.S. attorney general during the Kennedy administration.

7. Taylor Branch, *Parting the Waters: America in the King Years, 1954–63* (New York: Simon and Schuster, 1989), 821–22.

8. Young is referring to King's final sermon, "I See the Promised Land," delivered on April 3, 1968, the day before his assassination, as part of his efforts to aid striking sanitation workers in Memphis, Tennessee. For the full text of the sermon, see Martin Luther King Jr., *A Testament of Hope: The Essential Writings and Speeches of Martin Luther King, Jr.,* ed. James M. Washington (New York: Harper San Francisco, 1991), 279–86.

EVA LOU BILLINGSLEY RUSSELL

EVA LOU BILLINGSLEY RUSSELL was born on a plantation in rural Perry County on May 5, 1919. Like many interviewees, she and her husband, Edward, moved to Birmingham in search of employment. After working as a cashier to earn money to help support her son's education at Morehouse College, she took a job at the Fraternal Café, a restaurant in the Fourth Avenue district. By 1959, Russell had bought the restaurant and turned it into a vehicle for serving the movement. "Some people referred to me as being the breadbasket for the movement," she recalled. "There was a lot of people who ate there [and] didn't pay." Later in life, Russell became known as the Rapping Grandmother for her rhymes about the importance of religion and black history. She died on December 14, 2001.

BREADBASKET FOR THE MOVEMENT

Simon Billingsley was my daddy. I was born on the Billingsley plantation, [and so were] my two older sisters. My mother had two sets of twins. I am the third child. My mother, Ethel Moore, had eleven children, and they are all gone except about four or five of us living now. I'm the oldest living. We lived on the Billingsley plantation until my mother had her first set of twins. Then we moved down on a white man's plantation. We grew up with the white children. During those days, it wasn't like it is now. The children got along. We played together, and we ate together. We laid down and slept on pallets together. No one ever thought anything of it.[1]

In Perry County, I had to walk so far to school. We walked to Perry County School, which was two miles or more. I remember my first elementary school teacher. She was a Morris. After her I had Miss White. I found a seventh-, eighth-, and ninth-grade book out of a ditch and carried that book back to my last county schoolteacher, and he taught me independently out of that one book for three years. When I started high school, I was three years advanced.

I went to [Lincoln] High School in Marion, Alabama, [in] Perry County. In high school, I was president of my class every year. Students always elected me as president of my class because I was a little older and knew a little bit more than the [other] ones that were there. I was already prepared when I went to high school. We had white and black teachers there then. I was at this school during the time when Coretta Scott King attended. Her sister, Edythe, and I were classmates. We all boarded together. Coretta was younger than Edythe. I used to comb her hair in the morning time when Edythe didn't want to comb it. Marion was a pretty affluent school at that time. It was very, very, very good. It had a rich history. Alabama State Teachers College [in Montgomery, now Alabama State University] grew out of [Lincoln] High School. It still carries the colors, and when I see the colors, I just say, "That's my school."[2]

I married out of high school. I didn't graduate from high school. I didn't go higher than the tenth [grade]. I was old then, and I got married. When a man said they wanted to marry you, you just went on and married him. I went to a mining camp after I got married. I didn't know anything about a mining camp. It was U.S. Pipe and Foundry out in Adger, Alabama [a mining camp outside Birmingham]. My husband was a coal miner, but he used to work on the top. I lived in Adger about two years. Evidently it was 1942 because I had my oldest son, who was born shortly after I moved over.

When I moved to Birmingham, we rented a house on Sixteenth Street and Twentieth Avenue North. We lived right in the front of a packinghouse.

It was right in front of our door. They killed hogs, cows, and sheep. It was miserable. I had seven children. I also raised my husband's son.

I began writing when I was in high school. I would write little poems. I didn't get credit for it, but I just loved to write. We had a teacher who could recite poetry: "I shot an arrow into the air, it fell to earth."[3] It just went all over me. Her name was Grace Lewis. She was a white woman, and she was good with that poetry. My two favorite poems that I have written are "Black Sons Come Forward" and "Mother's Love Cannot Be Measured."

I was very active during the movement. I met Dr. [Martin Luther] King, and he ate in the restaurant that I owned, called the Fraternal Café. My restaurant was next to the Masonic Temple right on Fourth [Avenue] between Sixteenth and Seventeenth Streets. Andrew Young married a girl from Marion. I think he used to pastor a church in Marion at some time. But, anyway, they would meet there to eat, and we would cook. I had two sets of cooks— one to cook dinner, and I had two short-order cooks and four waitresses. Half of the time, we didn't have what we should have had. But thank God, we had what we had and shared it with the civil rights movement people. I had every one of the names of the people that were marching. I would keep their names, put down the date, and then we would send that to Atlanta or wherever the [SCLC] headquarters was. They would then send me a check to pay for their food. I just had to keep up with what they ate.

What I remember about Birmingham before the movement was that it was kind of rough. Half of the time, we were afraid to be caught out anyplace. You would go places, but you didn't feel free to go about visiting and traveling around at night like you did after the struggle. You had some thugs out there then. You were just afraid. I would have to go out places at night and didn't know what might happen to me. I had a lot of little children to take care of. But after all, the movement did bring about today. It brought about change.

My first job was in 1959. I had a son go to Morehouse College. He got drowned out there. My only son got drowned at Morehouse College. He had been there three weeks and got drowned. But, anyway, he was getting ready to go to college, and I went down to Wilkerson School [in East Thomas, a black neighborhood in Birmingham]. It was right below my house, and I went there to see if I could apply for a job for the fall of the year. The principal, Mr. John Norman, was there, and I asked him if I could apply for a job there. First thing he said, "What you in here for? How come you want to work?" I said, "Well, I have a son going to Morehouse, and I want to try to get him his spending change." I wanted any job they had for counting money because I could count money. I could always count money. He had a little job for a cashier, and I applied for it. He paid me twenty dollars a month—a dollar a day—and I was just so happy. I worked there until I put in for the Fraternal Café.

The café was already opened, and I got a job as a cashier. That's how I got to be the owner of the Fraternal Café, by applying for a job. I did so well for the two sisters that were there that when they got ready to move out, I inherited it. I didn't necessarily inherit it, but I paid for it. I can't remember their names. I worked there two years before I bought it. They found somebody that could run it, and that was me. They decided to come out of it because they had gotten old. So, I got that and did the best I could with it. Anybody said they needed a job, I hired them and paid them a little bit, just like they were paying us a little bit until they moved on. My children would walk from Parker High School down to the café to work. It was the younger children, because my older children were already in college. I just thank God for that café. That café gave me two lawyers, two counselors, a hospital administrator, a speech therapist, and a businessman, and I just thank the Lord for that café. I was blessed. The Carver Theater [Birmingham's most noted black theater] was right across the street from my café.

When they started marching, I saw them turn the water hose on Carlton Reese and knocked him as high up as a field is long.[4] When he came back down, he hit the ground singing, "I ain't gonna let nobody turn me around. I'm gonna keep on walking, I'm gonna keep on talking, marching up to freedom land."

I was right in the middle of all that tension. I had to drive to work every day, but I made it, and I have been missed twice. I was taking a shortcut, going a back route one morning, and a piece of iron come right across in front of my car and didn't touch me. Somebody threw an iron pipe at me but missed. Another time, a piece of an iron pipe fell down off of my café. I was coming out of the restaurant to get in my car, and it fell, just missing me. God is good.

I didn't get a chance to attend the mass meetings because I would be busy all day trying to get the groceries to serve for the next day. I had to prepare to feed the movement. Some people referred to me as being the breadbasket for the movement. There were a lot of people who ate there [and] didn't pay. But God knows I give what I get. Whenever Dr. King came into my café, I didn't come so close in contact with him. He and some of the other leaders would come in, and they would mostly have these little meetings where nobody could disturb them. I was never a person who would stand over people to see what they were talking about.

I owned the Fraternal Café from 1959 until I got tired and just walked away. I didn't sell it. I just left everything in there, just walked out, and went on. I had got tired, and I just went home. I don't know what become of that store. All the equipment from the store was mine. The stoves and refrigerators, icemakers, and whatever else that was in there, but I just got tired, and I just walked out of there. I retired and rested a while. I was old enough. I have just been enjoying life since then. I did a lot of traveling. God is good.

Birmingham has had a history of being a really hard-core segregated city, and over time it really has changed some. White folks and black folks just didn't get together before the civil rights [movement]. If [whites] saw a black man with a white woman or something, they would throw him out. There were maybe one or two white people that came to my place once or twice. Before you knew anything, the police were right there. They asked them to leave. But I didn't bother them. I was raised under white folk. Down there where we were raised, white and black folks got along together. Before integration, a white woman told my mama one time, "Ethel, they tell me when we all get to heaven, we all just going to be the same." My mama said, "Yes, Miss Maggie, that's what the Bible say." Then she called my mama again. "Ethel?" My momma said, "Yes, Miss Maggie." She said, "But you know we aren't going to like that." My mama said, "Yes. You got nothing to worry about, because you won't be there." My mother said it directly to her: "You don't have anything to worry about, because you won't be there."

I dream about that place right now. We used to make a shortcut across this pasture and go right on about and go in our backyard. But, she said, "Don't make no shortcuts." So I got right from that point. Ain't no shortcuts to glory. Stay in the middle of the road.

• • •

I now have a new name. I have been termed the Rapping Grandmother. Most people think this rap thing is something new. It's not new. It's old. They were rapping when I was a child. They just didn't call it rap.

> Ham bone, ham bone, have you heard?
> Mama gonna buy you a mockingbird.
> If that mockingbird don't sing,
> Mama gonna buy you a diamond ring.

Now, that was a long time ago. I tell them that rapping ain't anything new, it's just a fast tongue that people got, and [it gets] your attention right quick. And the reason why they call me the Rapping Grandmother is because I like the children. I say,

Listen everybody I can tell you from the start,
You better get Jesus in your heart.
You don't believe God does what he mean.
Read your Bible, John 3:16.
Because in the Word that he sent his son,
That you should know his will must be done.

And have the children say, "Get Jesus in your heart." After all, you got to have some God somewhere. And I go on to tell them,

You don't believe God meant for you to live clean.
Read your Bible, Matthew 5:16.
Jesus said to let your light shine,
So you watch my light, and I'll watch thine.

Get Jesus in your heart.

And then I tell them how hard I had to work:

I worked on a farm from sun to sun
The work on a farm wasn't ever done
You get up in the morning and make my bed
Go to the kitchen and cook the family's bread.
I went to the barn, had to milk the cow
Put a little weeds to feed the hogs their chow.
I poured water from a pump from a spring
Children nowadays wouldn't think of such a thing.
I went to the woods and caught bees for honey,
In those days there wasn't any money.

And then they [say], "What you talking about, Grandma?" I got my mike. I tell them a whole lot of things that I've done on the farm:

I went to the vines, I picked blackberries,
I climbed up trees, picked wild cherries.
Picked up potatoes by the bushel and peck.
I picked cotton and didn't leave a speck.
It made no difference how hot the sun,
You had to keep on working until the task was done.
It made no difference how hard you had to work,
You had to get up every Sunday and you walked to church.

[They say,] "Now, what are you talking about, Grandma?" [I say,] "I'm talking about folk like you and me." And then I go through my little reading spell again.

Know this is a fact:
We pulled little peanuts, we put them in a stack.
We shelled corn until our fingers got sore.
Before they got well, we had to shell some more.
We pulled watermelons from the watermelon vine,
Then they pick them and preserve them from the
    watermelon rind.

Now, that's history and it's true. I thank God for that. They always say, "How can you find something to rap?" I say, "Well, that's not anything new. They had rap songs when we were coming up."

The children love it. There's a lot of things, children think this is something new come along, but all of this had been done before. When I am rapping, I am rapping about life—real life. I learned to do that, but I learned to rap without doing that twisting and going on. I don't do that kind of rapping. That ain't my style of rapping. I stand where I can stand in place and tell you everything I want you to know. I don't rap about anything but the truth.

I haven't made [a rap] about the movement yet. I have done some on religion. The children relate well to me. They just go crazy about it. They just say, "Oh, Granny." I'm thinking they are just listening to the tune, I bet you they couldn't tell you a word I had to say. When I get the mike, and I'm breathing, and the kids say, "Ah, go Grandma." I perform whenever they invite me. I start off by saying, "Listen everybody, I can tell you when to start. You better get Jesus in your heart." Now, they don't talk about Jesus in school anymore. A lot more of them need to hear it, but they don't want to hear it.

I don't know what kind of dancing they're doing. I reckon I did anything that a child could do. We would make those shoes talk. I know I can do anything. I never sat in the background, in the back row. I moved to the front, because I feel like that's where you're going to learn something. You can't stay on the back and keep your head down. You have to come from back there and get out there and see what the world is about. I did the best that I knew how to do.

NOTES

BCRI OHP, vol. 17, sec. 3 (May 28, 1996). Edited, annotated, and abridged by Horace Huntley, A. Michelle Craig, and John McKerley.

1. Adults taught black and white children the meaning of race at an early age. White southerner Harry Crews recalled of his black childhood friends: "'There was a part of me in which it did not matter at all that they were black, but there was another part of me in which it had to matter because it mattered to the

world I lived in.'" "When Crews referred to a respected black man as 'Mr. Jones,' Crews's aunt quickly corrected him. 'No, son. Robert Jones is a nigger. You don't say 'mister' when you speak of a nigger. You don't say 'Mr. Jones,' you say 'nigger Jones'" (Edward Ayers, *The Promise of the New South: Life after Reconstruction* [New York: Oxford University Press, 1992], 132). In response to this culture of white supremacy, black parents designed strategies to insulate their children from segregation's degradation and taught them the skills necessary for preserving their dignity in the face of the constant threat of white violence. Ralph Thompson, who grew up near Memphis during the 1930s and 1940s, recalled, parents "tried to keep you away from things that would be embarrassing when they couldn't fight back" (William H. Chafe, Raymond Gavins, and Robert Korstad, eds., *Remembering Jim Crow: African Americans Tell about Life in the Segregated South* [New York: New Press, 2001], 5).

2. Unlike most schools for black students during this period, Lincoln had an integrated faculty. There were several other black boarding schools in Alabama's Black Belt, including Summerville in Pickens County and Linden Academy in Marengo County. On Coretta Scott King and the Lincoln Institute, see Papers of Martin Luther King Jr., http://www.stanford.edu/group/King/about_king/details/270427b.htm (accessed April 25, 2007). See also "Coretta Scott King Dead at 78," *Atlanta Journal-Constitution,* January 31, 2006.

3. Henry Wadsworth Longfellow, "The Arrow and the Song" (1845).

4. For Reese's description of the incident, see Carlton Reese, BCRI OHP, vol. 15, sec. 2 (May 16, 1996).

JIMMIE LUCILLE SPENCER HOOKS

JIMMIE LUCILLE SPENCER HOOKS was born in Eutaw, Alabama, in Greene County, on January 10, 1923. She grew up in Birmingham. Her mother was a domestic, and her father worked in the ore mines. Hooks recalled how Birmingham's culture of white supremacy influenced daily interactions both between and among the city's black and white residents. Describing her days as a student at Parker High School, she noted that opportunities were often connected to skin color: "[T]he light-skinned children had a better break than the dark-skinned kids. It's true. Everybody that worked in [the school] office was very fair." On the street and even in her home, she confronted racism through the power invested in representatives of the white-dominated state, such as streetcar operators and police officers. Still, even in Birmingham, some kinds of interracial alliances were possible. The wife of a liberal white employer helped Hooks vote, but she never fully trusted the woman: "They would ask me things" about the movement, she recalled, "but I didn't know anything." "I was at the movement just about every day, but I didn't know anything when I got to work."

I JUST KEPT MY MOUTH CLOSED

My mother and father were farmers. I had two brothers, no sisters. I was in the middle. I was two and a half years old when my parents came to Birmingham. After coming to Birmingham my mother worked for Dr. [John] McTier for years as a domestic. My daddy worked at the ore mines—TCI ore mine in Ishkooda. We lived in Travellick and he walked to work. He was a member of the union, but I don't remember the name of it.[1]

I started first grade at Wenonah. It was the original Wenonah High School built by TCI. I left Wenonah in the ninth grade and went to Ullman High for ninth and tenth grades. And then from there, I went to Parker High. I would ride the streetcar. It was just exciting, wanting to ride the streetcar. I always wanted to go to Parker. I knew if I went to Ullman first, then I had a better chance of getting in Parker. I loved it. The teachers were great. The principal, Mr. [R. C.] Johnson, dearly liked me. I played basketball at Wenonah, and when I got to Parker, the first thing I heard was Mr. [Major] Brown [saying], "Where's Jimmie Spencer?" From then on I just made it real good at Parker. I was a cheerleader, and I was in one play there. I was a fairy in this play. I was just all over the school as the Fairy Jimmie Spencer. It was a lot of fun. I was really a person to go after something. I didn't let [anyone saying] "You can't do this" stop me. From a young kid, I was always aggressive.

I hate to say this, but the light-skinned children had a better break than the dark-skinned kids. It's true. Everybody that worked in that office was very fair [in their complexion].[2] I was fortunate enough to get there. Mrs. [Myrtis] Thompson, Mr. Johnson's sister, she was crazy about me. I was kind of an open child. I was a smart child, if I have to say. And I mixed well. So, my color really didn't keep me back. But some of the kids it definitely did keep back, because if you were not light-skinned, you didn't get a job or you didn't go to school—I mean, you didn't work in the office.

[When it came to whites], well, as we used to say, you knew your place. You knew what you could do and what you couldn't do. The things that blacks didn't do, you just accepted that. You'd go to the back of the streetcar. You'd go in the stores—you would be the first one in and the last one to get waited on. We just adjusted to that. I remember when I was a girl, they had boards on the streetcars and they read "Colored" and "White." It didn't matter how many blacks were standing, you could not move that board if it was just a half a dozen whites on the streetcar. We just had to stand up. I never did see anybody move the board. You stayed in your place, standing up and reeling and rocking until you got to your destination. You couldn't go in the front of the bus and walk down the aisle. You had to put your money in the front and walk around to the side or the back of the bus, and they would open that back door and let you in. They had plenty of seats up there. Now you may get a good motorman and he would move the board up once or twice, but very seldom. When I was going to school, we would just be like sardines in the back. You couldn't come up to the front.

Also, when I was a child, we were just as scared of the police as you were of a snake. If the policeman came to your house, oh, it nearly scared you to death. I remember one time they came to our house. Me and my brothers got up under the bed. We'd heard so much about how they'd beat you and mistreat you—arrest you for anything. It was, "Yes, sir" or "No, sir," and if you didn't say it loud, you don't know what would have happened.

When my brother came home from [military] service, he said, "Yes" [instead of "Yes, sir"], and the policeman said, "Nigger, what did you say?" He said, "Yes, sir." They slapped the daylights out of him. My brother-in-law came and got me. They had [my brother] in the [police] car when I got there. I never was afraid of them after I got old. I told [the policemen] that my mother worked for Dr. McTier and that we weren't reared up like that. I said we were reared up in their yard almost. So he told me, "Well, I'm going to go on down with him, and you come down in about two hours, and you can get your brother. That's the only way." They had a pistol lying on the backseat where he was sitting. I'm sure they thought he was going to pick that pistol up. If he had got his fingerprints on that pistol, we wouldn't have ever seen him no more. So it was hard, but we adjusted to it.

My neighborhood was nice. It wasn't the best neighborhood, but it was nice. We all knew each other, and we loved each other. We got along real well. The neighbors looked out for the children. In my mother's time, she worked, and we had to stay in the yard because she just didn't allow us to run the street. There really wasn't anything to do but stay in the yard and play with your homemade toys. Blacks and whites in the neighborhood got along fine. If Miss Polly liked you, she was in your corner.[3] And if she didn't, she could call the police. She could make a citizen's arrest. She had that much authority with the policemen. She could call them and get them [when] nobody else could. That was directly behind [my house]. On the side was Cowden's

Grocery Store. My mother had a bill there. We got along real well. They were poor whites when they first got there. I remember when I was a younger lady, they had a gristmill. My mother would take corn there, and that's how they got their mill. Then they had a little bitty store, and they kept adding and adding until it became a grocery store. They built that store. They lived in the back. There was a little house there. Mr. Cowden kept adding and adding. He built it himself, because he worked out at the cement plant. When he wasn't working, he was just building. They lived in the back of there, and they made the little store in the front.

Back toward Bessemer, there were two or three white families. They had children, and you would be scared to death because they were mean. They were poor whites, very hard to get along with. Those boys would stand on the side of the road, and when we were coming from school, they would throw rocks and all that. My older brother and myself, we were just about as tough as they were, because I popped one upside the head once. They came there and said that they were going to have me arrested. Evidently they changed their mind. We heard no more. Mama assured them that I would not be on that side of the street. She would always tell us to walk on the other side of the street, so I never had any more trouble out of them.[4]

After high school, I got married and started my family. After the fourth child was born, I went back to school and finished my education. Most of the men worked at TCI and Fairfield Steel. A lot of the mothers were domestic workers. My husband worked for TCI, at first the ore mines. He was transferred to Fairfield Steel when the ore mines closed.

Oh, goodness, that's when I slipped down there. I left my job and slipped down to the courthouse and voted. I was working for Dr. [Alston] Callahan, and his wife [Evior H. Callahan] was in accord. She just said, "You just go." She told me what to expect and what to do. She was in favor. They would do a lot of nice things for you, but they would keep it a secret from the other whites. I worked for [that family] for twenty-three years. At first they lived at [Crest Road]. I had no difficulties with them. I didn't know I was black, working for them.

The movement was one thing I stayed away from talking to them about. They would ask me things, but I didn't know anything. I was at the movement just about every day, but I didn't know anything when I got to work. I was helping my husband raise our children, and I needed to work at that time. So to keep my job, I just kept my mouth closed. It might not have made a difference too much with them, but they got so much [trouble] from their neighbors that they didn't need to know. I just kept it to myself. I was getting what I wanted to, also.

My oldest son had an encounter with the police. He was coming from work. It was a hamburger place. I don't remember the name. Anyway, him and his friend were coming from work. The police stopped Sherman, which was the friend, and they beat him up. Ernest took out running and made it home in the car. When he was knocking and banging [on the door] so hard, I ran in there with my [night]gown on, and he said, "Mother, open the door, open the door." By the time that he got in the house good, the police were there. I had shut the door, and they told me to open it. I said, "Just a minute. Let me get my robe." They pushed that door open and came on in. They would not let me get fully dressed or get a robe on. They carried him to the car. I talked with them, and I told them, "Let me call the doctor that I work for and see if he can be responsible for him until daybreak." I didn't want them to carry him away that night. When I told them who I was working for, I didn't have trouble. They released him in my custody. They didn't take him away. He said every time they would see him, they would ask him, "Ernest, you still being good? You better be good to your mama." That's what they would tell him. Evidently they knew Dr. Callahan, because he was one of the biggest doctors, Dr. Alston Callahan, and he carried a lot of clout, I'm sure. He worked at the Eye Foundation.

I could never get [my son's encounter with the police] out of my mind. I said that one day it was going to get better. The minute that I heard talking about the civil rights movement, I was ready, because I never forgot that. I never forgot hearing other people talking about how they had been taken advantage of. White men came in your house and didn't have to knock on the door. People used to have bill collectors come around to your house to collect the money. They would just open the door and walk in. And you never were "Mrs." or "Miss"; you were always by your first name, boy or girl. Clara was my mother's name. I never heard one [white person] address her as "Mrs. Spencer" or "Miss Clara." It was always "Clara," and she was old enough for a grandmama. When they were talking abut the civil rights movement, I was ready, too much ready to get involved. To this day I don't regret it one bit.

I first got involved in [1963], I believe it was. It was during the time when we sent all the kids out to the hotel to integrate. We filled the buses up going to jail because they put every one of them in jail. I had two in the bus that we sent out from the church. I worked at the church, the Sixteenth Street Baptist Church. We got [the students'] names. We gave them food, drinks. We lectured them on what to do and what not to do. We would tell them, "If they go to arrest you, don't resist." We would say, "Say 'Yes, sir,' and 'No, sir.'" I said, "You may not have to say it always, but to keep them from going upside your head, you don't mind saying 'Yes, sir,' and 'No, sir.'" I always taught them that. I was always in the front one way and the back the other. Now, I had to try and stay away from [the all-night strategy meetings] in the motels, because I had to get up and go to work. I'd stay away, but I would always call. They would tell me what happened and all that.

I was right there working every day. I didn't march. I was the one always getting them together to march. I would have been seen, and the next thing I would have known, I would have been out of a job, maybe. I'm not sure, but I didn't take the chance. I stayed and did the work inside, didn't march. I would go in the car alongside of the marches, but I never did march with them. I encouraged my children to be involved. I told them what was happening. I said, "Someday, this will make it much better for you." I said, "It may be hard now. Your tears you shed now, later on may be tears of joy. When your children come along, they won't have to experience what you had to experience, because every generation will probably get better." They were ready.

[My children] were in high school. We were fortunate to have a car. My husband would take them and then pick them up. That's the way the kids got back and forth. We had a lot of children out there, their friends and their boyfriends and girlfriends. They all went to jail together. Once the news [about the children's marches] got out, Sixteenth Street [Baptist Church] couldn't hold them. They just poured in. They had more then enough. [The police] had a rope where they weren't going to let the kids come across from the church. Those kids broke that rope, and they all just took off in different directions. They went to this part of downtown and that part. My son went to, I believe it was Holiday Inn. He was in that group. They took them to Southside [Jail] first, and then they got carried from there to Fair Park. They had some to go to the Juvenile Court. The younger ones were there. We had them in all ages: elementary school kids and high school. Children weren't in school because everybody had heard about it and were ready to join in with us. I was there to see the dogs when they held them. I have one daughter that was almost bitten by one of those dogs. I had to go to Atlanta. When I got back, they said the kids had to stand out all night in the storm. My daughter was in that. They said that the neighbors would throw cookies, apples. The jail was full, and they put [the children] in the back of the jail out there in the open, in the yard, so they didn't have any shelter. They had to stand in the rain. When I got back and I heard about that, I was furious. They carried them to Fair Park. They carried some down here to Tuscaloosa Avenue, to Juvenile Court. I had a son there. So I was just into it. I had one in one place and one in the other.

I said, "I've got to get them out of there," because at that time they said that they were taking those black girls and having sex with them. When I found that out I just—oh, goodness, I went over. [The police] said that I had to be a property owner before I could get her out. So me, being just not afraid of nothing, I said, "Oh no. When I leave today she's going." So I got real loud, and they sent for her, and they brought her out. I said, "Come on, Baby. You're going home." I didn't sign no papers. That's the way I got my daughter out. [We] left there and went down to Tuscaloosa Avenue to the Juvenile [Court] and got my son the same way. I didn't put up a dime. This lady asked me who I was. "I'm Mrs. Jimmie L. Hooks." She said, "Who?" I said, "Mrs. Jimmie L. Hooks." She said, "I mean are you Mary, Jane, Sue, or Sal?" I went wild then. I said, "Listen, bring my son to this door, and if you don't, me and you both are going back there, and I'm going to be leading you." So that was just the kind of attitude that I had. They brought my son, Malcolm, out. He was a nervous wreck. This guy with him said that they were beating those kids down there. They didn't get nothing [to eat] but a bologna sandwich. All of that still didn't discourage me from working in the movement. It worked. It really worked, but when they got grown, [the children] were ready to leave Birmingham—or as they say now, Bombingham.

When we were in church, when Dr. [Martin Luther] King walked in the church, policemen would be all around. Do you know that you could hear a pin fall when he walked in the church? You could hear a pin fall. I enjoyed every minute of it. Dr. King was a very good speaker. He would speak to the people. He would talk. Rev. [Fred] Shuttlesworth was a good speaker. He would talk and tell you the dos and don'ts. Jesse Jackson was a good speaker. I admire his preaching. I was there the Sunday he preached. We thought it was going to be trouble, but it wasn't.

I traveled a lot in my life, and I'd stop to eat or go into different places when I was out of town. They would ask if I was from that place, Bombingham. It made me so hurt. I said, "No, Birmingham is one of the nicest places you want to live." "Well, do they still kill people and put the dogs on them?"—those are the kinds of things you would get when you'd go outside of Birmingham. A lot of them were scared to come here, and a lot of them said they would never come to Birmingham. I said, "No, we live good. If you come to Birmingham, you would see that it ain't what you think it is." I would always speak up for Birmingham because that's my home and I had to come back here and live.[5]

But, really, if it had been left up to me, I would have left Birmingham forty years ago. My family and my husband never wanted to leave. By being a homeowner, I guess he thought he could never get another home anywhere out of Alabama. I didn't want to go back south. I wanted to go north. If I had the choice, that's where I wanted to go. I never regretted not leaving because it has been good to me. I can't complain. At one time I never thought I would have a chance to be free or have a car, could own a home. My mother was a working lady. She got a home when I was about sixteen [or] seventeen years old, their first home they bought. I said, "Well, if my mother can do it, I can do it." So we just started our roots here, and we're still here. I love leaving—going and coming back. Once I leave [to visit my children in Atlanta, Seattle, and Portland, Oregon], I stay a month, but I'm ready to come back. There's nothing like coming back home.

I was active in electing the [first black] mayor of Birmingham [Richard Arrington, in 1979].[6] I worked with all of that. We put Mayor Arrington in, and we want to keep him in until he's ready to come out. The first night we were there at the Parliament House, we rocked it. You could actually feel it rocking. They had to ask some of the people to get out on the street. As many were in the street as were in the inside, because we were so happy to get a black mayor for Birmingham. So I lived to see the first black mayor and helped elect him. He has served his purpose. He has proved to the world that he could make a contribution to Birmingham. Now he can sit back and reap some of the good that he has done—enjoy his older life, let a youngster come in there and get a taste of Birmingham. Now you're just praying for it to get better. You notice now that a lot of black kids, as soon as they finish college, they leave Birmingham because of [jobs], and white people just really are not ready. I think when all of the older [whites] leave, it will get better. It's getting better. It's a lot better than it used to be.

So I've shared some of this business that I've never shared with anybody but my family. Now that they can't hurt me, I want them to know that I worked. I'm not ashamed of it anymore, and I'm not afraid anymore. I met so many friends when I was working at Sixteenth Street Baptist Church. Names I don't remember now, but faces I do. There were a lot of women involved, but not out from my area. I had some friends, and we were all working. We just had to do it hush-hush. My husband and my oldest son, we all would go every day, but I didn't see many people from the area. Mostly people had jobs, and they were afraid to go. At times they were even afraid to talk about it. It's just so much. I never shared this because I didn't want to be—I don't know what. I always had a good job, and I didn't want to lose my job. I wanted to keep my pride. I said, "I can do all of this and don't have to talk." I think I did more that way than I would if I had been out in the front to be seen. It was just a lot of fun in a way, and it was a lot of tears in a way.

So that's just the way we do. We just go. I don't regret it one lick.

NOTES

BCRI OHP, vol. 36, sec. 2 (May 27, 1998). Edited, annotated, and abridged by Laura Anderson, Wayne Coleman, A. Michelle Craig, Horace Huntley, and John McKerley.

1. Hooks's father was most likely a member of the International Union of Mine, Mill, and Smelter Workers.

2. On the link between color and class in Birmingham's black community, see Lynne B. Feldman, *A Sense of Place: Birmingham's Black Middle-Class Community, 1890–1930* (Tuscaloosa: University of Alabama Press, 1999), 133.

3. "Miss Polly" was the white owner of a neighborhood service station and store. Black residents believed she was a member of the Ku Klux Klan.

4. Company policies, whites' enforcement of customary segregation, and black residents' need for protection from white violence contributed to the spread of residential segregation in Birmingham during the late nineteenth and early twentieth centuries. Between 1926 and 1951, a racial zoning ordinance further concentrated black residents in neighborhoods around commercial and industrial development. Since these areas were often zoned for either black or white residence (most often in multifamily units), blacks and working-class whites sometimes lived in relative proximity to one another. When blacks attempted to move into formerly all-white, single-family housing units after the U.S. Supreme Court struck down the ordinance in 1951, violence often resulted. During this period, the North Smithfield neighborhood earned the moniker Dynamite Hill. On the relationship between race and housing in Birmingham before 1926, see Henry M. McKiven Jr., *Iron and Steel: Class, Race, and Community in Birmingham, Alabama, 1875–1920* (Chapel Hill: University of North Carolina Press, 1995), 55–76, 133–52; on the racial zoning ordinance and its aftermath, see Charles E. Connerly, *"The Most Segregated City in America": City Planning and Civil Rights in Birmingham, 1920–1980* (Charlottesville: University of Virginia Press, 2005).

5. Black interviewees often reported finding themselves defending the city despite their experiences with its culture of white supremacy. As they explained, their defense was not of the Birmingham of Bull Connor and his dogs and water hoses but of the Birmingham where a single mother of four provided her children with higher education, though she was illiterate and worked for three dollars a week. It was the Birmingham where a mother and father raised eleven children in a five-room home and never missed a meal. It was the Birmingham where teachers went the extra mile to nurture their students and provide the foundation for adult life. It was the Birmingham where black parents insulated their children, the best they could, from the debilitating racist society that was so all-encompassing.

6. The electorate split along clear racial lines, with only 10 percent of white voters casting their ballots for Arrington. As whites fled to the suburbs over the next decade, Arrington consolidated black influence over the traditionally white-dominated city government through a powerful, black-led political organization, the Jefferson County Citizens Coalition. Although Arrington and the coalition came under attack for his alleged corruption, authoritarian leadership style, and regressive tax policies, Arrington continued to receive considerable support among black voters for his desegregation of the police force and the dismantling of other key elements of the city's white-supremacist infrastructure. When federal authorities began investigating alleged fraud in connection with the construction of the Birmingham Civil Rights Institute during the late 1980s, Arrington and many other prominent members of the city's black community argued that the proceedings were racially motivated. When Arrington was briefly jailed for refusing to turn over records to federal investigators in 1992, approximately seven hundred supporters, including Shuttlesworth and many other prominent civil right activists, staged a protest march through downtown Birmingham. Arrington was never charged with any wrongdoing. He served as mayor until 1999. See *New York Times,* November 4, 1979, January 24, 1992, July 18, 1999, December 18, 1999. For a useful but largely uncritical biography of Arrington, see Jimmie Lewis Franklin, *Back to Birmingham: Richard Arrington, Jr., and His Times* (Tuscaloosa: University of Alabama Press, 1989).

NIMS E. GAY

NIMS E. GAY was born in Choccolocco, Alabama, in Calhoun County, on January 25, 1923. Gay's father, a railway brakeman, brought the family to Birmingham when Gay was a baby. He grew up in Greenwood, in East Birmingham, a black neighborhood separated by a railroad track from its white counterpart, Inglenook. When his parents moved on to Cleveland, Ohio, during his early teens, Gay remained in Birmingham, supporting himself through his own labor and the generosity of friends and family. Looking back on his experiences during the 1930s and 1940s, Gay recalled finding few organizational outlets for black activism in the city. Distrustful of the city's cadres of communist organizers, he turned to the NAACP but found it largely powerless in the face of white employers willing to pressure their employees into silence. After the state government outlawed the NAACP in 1956, Gay joined the ACMHR and served the organization in a variety of capacities, including as one of the original codirectors, with Mamie Brown, of the ACMHR Choir. Like many interviewees, Gay stressed the central role of religious faith in his activism. When fire hoses unexpectedly failed to douse him and other praying activists at one point during the 1963 demonstrations, Gay believed that "God kept that water from coming."

WE KNEW THE POWER OF PRAYER

I came to Birmingham when I was one year old with my parents. I grew up the youngest child with an older brother who is now deceased and a sister who presently resides in Cleveland, Ohio.

My mother was a housewife, and my father attended Tuskegee. Coming off a farm and looking at big words, when he got to Tuskegee, he saw the word *agricultural* and he thought that is what he wanted to do. But after he found out the word meant "farming," he decided that wasn't for him. So he came on to Birmingham and became a brakeman on the Louisville and Nashville Railroad. Then he brought his family to Birmingham. He was later laid off and migrated to Cleveland, Ohio, and started working for Pharaoh's Foundry there. When he became retirement age, he came back to Birmingham.[1]

I primarily grew up in the Greenwood, East Birmingham area, near Stockham Pipe and Fittings. During that time, Greenwood and Inglenook were separate. On one side of the track were blacks, and on the other side were whites. My education consisted of elementary school and some high school. I attended Shields [Elementary] in East Birmingham. I later attended Ullman High School as one of the first students there. I stayed there until the tenth grade and then went over to Parker High. Ullman at the time only went to the tenth grade. I lacked two months graduating from Parker. I didn't graduate because of financial difficulties beyond my control.

I was putting myself through school from the age of thirteen because my mother became ill and had to go to Cleveland, where my father was. I stayed behind because I didn't want to leave Birmingham. My aunt eventually came over to stay with me. I was able to support myself in school because I worked and received help from friends. There were two men who were especially instrumental in helping me. They encouraged me to go to school if I wished to go. Their names were West Scruggs and Johnny Norris. They said, "We will give you fifty cents a day if you go on and complete your education." I also worked for the Birmingham Country Club as a caddy on the weekends and afternoons to support myself. I was able to keep a place to stay, and my parents would send money from Cleveland to help pay the rent. Rent was inexpensive in those days when compared with today's standards. You could get a house for as little as six dollars a month.

After high school, my first job was at WJLD Radio. I was the first black announcer they had, and that was about fifty-two years ago. At the time, Bob Umbach was the chief engineer. He did some of everything there. He told me, "Well, you have the voice of radio." When he started me, he had me bringing on the best big folk and all the big quartets. He had me doing it so frequently, I said, "Now wait a minute. What kind of money do I get?" He said, "Well, I'll give you ten dollars [a week]." I said, "No, I can't do that." So they raised it to seventeen [dollars] a week, and I stayed there for three and a half months.

The radio station was located directly above the courthouse in Bessemer at the time. I, along with other blacks, was consistently harassed by the police officers coming in and out of the courthouse. The environment was as prejudiced as you could find. Jeff Bryant owned the station, and he and other whites didn't want a black man to even wear a tie at that time. He told me, "You on the radio. You gonna wear a tie? We cut niggers' ties off when they wear it here." I said, "Yeah, and I am going to cut yours off, too." He said, "Well, now wait a minute. I thought you was a Christian." I said, "So was Peter, but he cut the man's ear off with Christ standing there." I said this to make sure I got respect from the very beginning.

I eventually left because the money wasn't enough. I was nineteen years old and married with kids at the time. The railroad was paying twenty-five dollars a week, so I went to work for [the Louisville and Nashville] Railroad. Most of the occupations for people in the Greenwood community were domestic work. Black women would mostly go out and work in white people's homes. The men would work at Stockham, McWane, and Vandiver Furnaces, and places like that. They thought it was a blessing when you worked on the railroad like my father did. They looked at his job in the same light as a firefighter or some other job like that. My wife never worked. She stayed home with the kids. My wife and I had eight children, but the oldest one drowned when he was seven.

I started first as a hostler helper [servicing locomotive engines]. We had what was called a roundtable down there. You would put that engine on that table and revolve it around as you worked. Our job was to carry [the locomotive] down to the roundtable. Then they decided to transfer me downtown, where I was a coach cleaner. We fueled up diesel engines that replaced coal engines. Our job was to ice up those cars [providing blocks of ice for use on the train]. Around this time, the war broke out, and they deferred me there to stay and work, helping to prepare the cars for the soldiers. The soldiers used the cars to go back and forth to Ozark, Alabama, because that's where the German prison was. My job was to prepare the engines by coaling them up. I say "coaling them up"—that is when you had those old steam engines, and you would run the engine up under a chute. That chute would let the coal come down and fill up the hopper back there. This is where firemen would get the coal to fire the boiler up so the engine could run. When I went downtown, I didn't have to do that anymore. All we did was see to it that the coaches were serviced for the troops.

The Birmingham Police Department's relationship with the community can be described as peculiar at best. The police functioned just like insurance salesmen. If you owned a shot house, a gambling place, or a prostitute house, he would drive through there, and you would pay him off. Some very prominent men in Birmingham now in high positions used to go and collect money, just like a policy agent, from people who participated in illegal businesses like these. This is why we used to say [that] when you see that sign "MUN" [for *municipal,* on police cars], that stood for "Murder U Niggers." That's what we felt it was. You couldn't have any respect for people that didn't have any respect for their own self. We did not look at police as being protectors and servers of the community, only as enemies of the community.

As a community we had certain kinds of recreation. There were baseball and gospel choirs. We would go play ball mostly at Stockham Park. When we weren't at Stockham, we went to a big old cornfield in our community where the boys and girls would go and play. I managed the girls' and boys' ball club. One disadvantage we had was not being able to play under the lights like white ballplayers down on Tenth Avenue. The park then for the white people was on Tenth Avenue and Thirty-fifth Street. So I went on my own down to City Hall and talked to [public works commissioner James T.] "Jabo" Waggoner to complain. They decided to let us play under the lights. I had always been told that if you wanted something done, you had to do it yourself. We were the first [black] community that played under the lights.

[Black people] would come from Ensley and everywhere to play under the lights. Friday and Saturday nights were our designated times. The teams we set up all around Birmingham would come over there and play. Some of the girls who played for our teams would become part of East Birmingham in order to get a chance to play under the lights. I had some girls out of Ensley who played with my girls' clubs, so we became united, and other churches and clubs would come over to play us from ACIPCO and different places. They got the chance to come over there and play under the lights, which we saw as something very interesting at the time. [Still], baseball and gospel choirs were the ways that white people pacified blacks to distract their attention from real issues. They were just putting a pacifier in your mouth like you put a pacifier in a baby's mouth. Businesses sponsored singing groups and baseball teams. The [Louisville and Nashville] Railroad had a choir with W. W. Whetstone directing. Reverend Sherlock and myself were both part of this choir. ACIPCO and Stockham had choirs. This was all a part of the pacification process. The white man thought that giving you different activities would keep you satisfied. They also thought that if you were in church, you were a good person, meaning you would not get involved in the movement. They thought if you sang spirituals, you were not going to harm [them].

I sang with the choirs and had some initial training from Dr. Henry over at Parker High School. He taught us the Negro spirituals and music as it was supposed to be. Then I went with [John] Streeter, and he taught us whole notes and note singing. The rest of it was just a gift from God. After singing with Parker High School Choir, we went with the Singing 40s at the [Louisville and Nashville] Railroad. We were singing with Dr. Whetstone, and after him we started singing with Dorothy Love Coates out at Evergreen Bottom. After the Gospel Harmonettes was organized, we listened to their style, which they adopted from the original Roberta Martin Singers. With the influence of groups like these and our background, we formed the Gay Harmoneers. People thought we were really good and we should travel. However, it was not my desire to move, so we stayed right here in Birmingham. We sung together for about twenty-nine years. We would go out of town to various places like Birmingham; Andalusia[, Alabama]; and Tennessee, but we never wanted to migrate any further. Everybody seemed to appreciate the style of music that we were doing. Some of the music we were doing, others started recording nationally. Our group was in the forefront of the development of gospel music. The Original Gospel Harmonettes were the first, and Dorothy Love Coates came on the scene later.

The first person that attracted national attention in Birmingham was William Blevins. He was the first black that ever sang on the radio in Birmingham. He worked for the *Birmingham News* and WSGN, [which] was [owned by the newspaper] at the time. But all blacks had to come up the freight elevator to the studio. So even though people all over everywhere were listening to him, he had to come up the freight elevator. Anyway, the Gospel Harmonettes, with Odessa Edwards, Willie Mae [Newberry], and Mildred Howard and all of those, became the Gospel Harmonettes. Vera [Cobbs], Odessa, and Willie Mae were the originals. Dorothy Love Coates joined them later, and then they became a powerhouse. They went all over the world singing, but all of them came back home here to Birmingham.

As far as community organizations were concerned, at the time there really wasn't any. The only thing that you had at that time was the Communist Party. The Communist Party was trying to come in and take over and get the black people to be with them. The Ku Klux Klan was already raging. Our parents would tell us all the time, "You know what's over here, but you don't know what's over there in the communist countries." They would tell us not to sell out because the communist people would come over, and they would try to get us. One time, my father was working around different men at different plants. [Communist organizers] would come to me, and they'd say, "Now, what you got to do is help blow these places up." But the black people would not go for it. The Communist Party was attempting to overthrow the government. They tried to fool us by telling us what communism was and how good it was for us, but in the end they wanted to really control America. That's the way I saw it.[2]

The Communist Party was also involved in the labor organizations. Some of them were undercover. The main thing was the communists really began to get a hold over here was the Scottsboro case—when the Scottsboro boys were taken off a train and accused of raping two white women [in 1931].[3] This incident gave the [Communist Party] a better view of what was going on. During the 1930s, Birmingham became sort of the southern regional headquarters for the [Communist Party].[4] Also beginning to organize at this time were the [Steel Workers Organizing Committee]; United Mine Workers; and the International Union of Mine, Mill, and Smelter Workers.[5] The [communists] were obviously good organizers. Mr. [Gus] Hall, who ran for president on the Communist ticket, stayed at my uncle's house so many times. Anytime he came to Birmingham, he stayed with us. My uncle worked for Vandiver Furnace, and he claimed not to be involved with the [Communist Party], but I believed he was. This all took place during the 1930s and [1940s]. A whole lot was not happening with civil rights at this time in history.

Most people felt that the NAACP would give us a chance to really move out. [But] many people that worked for these different white organizations would say, "Well, if you work for that [organization], you can't work for me." In other words, they always tried to hold you down through some kind of monetary way, where they figured you couldn't make it. I was a member of the NAACP in 1956 when Robert Durr was over it, and then later [W. C.] Patton and all of them came along.[6] In 1956, the state of Alabama outlawed the operation of the NAACP. When they outlawed it, Rev. Fred Shuttlesworth came along and founded the [ACMHR]. Shuttlesworth was very displeased that the NAACP was outlawed. When Dr. Patton told Shuttlesworth what was happening and the state outlawing it, Shuttlesworth said, "The hell with y'all!"

The ACMHR was started to fill the void that came about with the absence of the NAACP. We had a lot of people at the time. We didn't know exactly which way to start because we were trying to start a voters' drive. [Attorney] W. L. Williams came on to help us get the voters' rights set up among the people where they could become qualified voters.[7] When I became a voter, you had to pay a poll tax. This was one of several ways to try and keep you from becoming a voter. When I first went in to register, they told me, "Boy, what you want to vote for?" I said, "[So] I'd have a right to protect myself from taxation without representation." One thing about it, I knew how many questions they were going to ask me. When they were talking to me, I said, "I tell you what. I want to ask you a question because I know smart white folks like you know it." So I told them, I said, "I heard about Paul Revere and the Midnight Riders and all of that, and I hear about the British was coming." I said, "Would you mind telling me a little something about that?" I said, "I've heard where Patrick Henry said: 'What is it that gentlemen wish? What would they have? Is life so dear, or peace so sweet, as to be purchased at the price of chains and slavery? Forbid it, Almighty god! I know not what course others may take; but as for me, give me liberty or give me death.'" I said, "Were white folks ever a slave?" He said, "I ain't got time to talk to you. Go on. You pass." This was the way I was able to register and vote. It was my first try. My wife went the next week, and she did not have a problem, either. This was in the 1950s, around the time that the movement was starting to develop into what we knew we wanted to do.

At this time, Mamie Brown and I were directors of the ACMHR Choir. After that, Bernard Sneed and Carlton Reese came on the scene.[8] We always wanted to be able to have the best-qualified person for the job. That is what we trained to do in the beginning of the civil rights movement. Our motto was to let the man who could do the job do it, and we'd be followers, so Carlton took over as director of the [ACMHR] Choir. But, in the beginning, it was Nathaniel Lee, John L. Frazier, and Mrs. [Ophelia] Palmer as the musicians, and Mamie Brown and myself were the directors.

The mass meetings would take place every Monday night. We would meet every week, and we could not wait for Monday night to come. When something happened, we got to where we would call the meetings in the middle of the week. You couldn't get into the churches. Some of the churches wouldn't accept you. In my community, the Forty-sixth Street Baptist Church, where I was a member, was the only one that would let you meet there.[9] Rev. [Emanuel] Hester was the pastor at that time. We had a chairman of the deacon board who didn't want to meet. In later years, I became the chairman of the [deacon] board. At that time, I was a minister of music, working with the choirs.

Rev. Hester feared there would be repercussions for the church's involvement and said, "They gonna blow our church up." He would say, "Well, it just be blown up." There was some dissension in the church, maybe one or two, but everybody else was in accord. A typical mass meeting could be described as very hyped up. You still had a lot of nervous Nellies and Uncle Toms, however. When Dr. Shuttlesworth would come in and speak, he was speaking the facts. Anytime you are telling the truth, the people have to accept it. Then of course, you had policemen who would come in and sit in the back of the meetings, but that didn't scare anyone. They were there to try and find out what was going on so they could carry reports back to City Hall.

There are some things that stand out in my mind when I look back on the events of the movement. One in particular was when they burned the buses of the Freedom Riders in 1961 at Anniston. Rudolph Bailey and myself were one of the first to get up there. If [whites] had been thinking, all they had to do was to go through Pell City and block that road, and we would not have been able to get through. Joe Hendricks was also there, but I don't know who was in the car with Joe. When we all got up there, the police and the highway patrolmen said, "We can't go on the highway with you, but we will take you here in the city." They wanted to know who was going to take us. We had some protectors to carry us. They didn't know we were talking about the Lord and Savior Jesus Christ. That's the person we were talking about. Joe Hendricks put [the Freedom Riders] on the floor of his car. These were black and white [riders] that we picked up. They had quite a few whites in there. They got through even with those smoke bombs they threw in there. They were about as black as we were, but they were white. After we got the Freedom Riders back to Birmingham, we brought them down to Rev. Shuttlesworth. Bull Connor came and told Reverend he was watching them to protect them. Brother Hendricks carried them over to his house, where they stayed. During that time, you had to be very careful what you let anybody know. You had people come to the sessions just for that.[10]

Another thing that stands out in my mind is when they even put the fire hoses and dogs on us—out there on Sixth Avenue, when the firemen turned the hoses on, and Bull was telling them to turn the hose on them. We prayed and [Rev. Charles] Billups was sitting down there praying. Only God kept that water from coming. The firemen were trembling more so than we were because the water would not come out of those hoses although they turned them on. When we got through praying and went back across the street, the water went everywhere. I know it had to be someone bigger than you and I to keep the water from running.[11]

I would go to a lot of the marches, and I participated in the ones downtown. I never went to jail and was never arrested. A lot of the times, when they said, "Let's go!" I'd be the first to stand up. They never put me on the line; I never knew why. Eventually I found out later on. I had two children go to jail as a result of demonstrations. My children were school-aged at the time. They left school. One thing about it, the kids would leave school anyway. A lot of the teachers were afraid, and they didn't want to let the children out. I always told my kids, "A scared person never won anything." We would sometimes go get the children out of these different schools and bring them over there so they could demonstrate. This was not a problem because [SCLC organizer] James Bevel needed help.[12] One thing about it, the communities were more together then. You find more people today who are afraid of losing their jobs than at that point of time. Nowadays, in many establishments, you find us selling each other out for a higher position or for money. I feel as though you should always stand on right and reach out and touch somebody's life. That same favor will come back to you.

Other members of my family were in accord with the children's activity. My daddy said that riding those buses was going to get everybody killed, [but] eventually he came around to see what it was all about. I witnessed my oldest son, Cardell, being washed down the street with a hose. This was one of the hardest things to accept. This is the time when you really have to control yourself. I would not have thought twice about hitting one of those firemen or policemen. I figured we could have won that battle with violence, but there is a hereafter, and you must stand before God to be judged. They were putting our children in jail and discriminating against us in every way. We knew the power of prayer, because if it had not have been for prayer, a lot of us would not have made it.

NOTES

BCRI OHP, vol. 4, sec. 3 (April 6, 1995). Edited, annotated, and abridged by A. Michelle Craig, Horace Huntley, and John McKerley.

1. For an examination of the migration of black Alabamians to Cleveland during this period, see Kimberley L. Phillips, *AlabamaNorth: African-American Migrants, Community, and Working-Class Activism in Cleveland, 1915–45* (Urbana: University of Illinois Press, 1999).

2. On communist organizers in Alabama and the party's relationship to Birmingham's black residents, see Nell Irvin Painter, *The Narrative of Hosea Hudson: The Life and Times of a Black Radical* (New York: Norton, 1994); Robin D. G. Kelley, *Hammer and Hoe: Alabama Communists during the Great Depression* (Chapel Hill: University of North Carolina Press, 1990).

3. On the Scottsboro case, see Dan T. Carter, *Scottsboro: A Tragedy of the American South* (Baton Rouge: Louisiana State University Press, 1979).

4. As Kelley notes, "The Central Committee of the [Communist Party] chose Birmingham, the center of heavy industry in the South, as headquarters for the newly established District 17, encompassing Alabama, Georgia, Louisiana, Florida, Tennessee, and Mississippi" (*Hammer And Hoe*, 14). Communist organizers were active in the city as early as 1929.

5. On labor organizing in Birmingham during this period, see Horace Huntley and David Montgomery, eds., *Black Workers' Struggle for Equality in Birmingham* (Urbana: University of Illinois Press, 2004), 5–12.

6. W. C. Patton was the president of the Birmingham branch of the NAACP during the early 1950s. Like most leaders of Birmingham's established black professional class, Patton supported voter registration and legal challenges to Jim Crow, but he was suspicious of the ACMHR and the politics of mass protest (Glenn T. Eskew, *But for Birmingham: The Local and National Movements in the Civil Rights Struggle* [Chapel Hill: University of North Carolina Press, 1997], 78, 127).

7. W. L. Williams, BCRI OHP, vol. 46, sec. 3 (May 13, 1999).

8. On the ACMHR choir, see also Carlton Reese, BCRI OHP, vol. 15, sec. 3 (May 16, 1996).

9. The Forty-sixth Street Baptist Church was one of a handful of churches that allowed the ACMHR to use its facilities during the movement's early stages. On initial resistance to the ACMHR from within the black community, see Eskew, *But for Birmingham*, 125–27.

10. For Hendricks's account of these events, see Joe Hendricks, BCRI OHP, vol. 8, sec. 1 (June 23, 1995).

11. For other interviewees' accounts of this seemingly miraculous event, see Almarie Billups, BCRI OHP, vol. 8, sec. 2 (June 28, 1995); Charlotte Jernigan, BCRI OHP, vol. 7, sec. 3 (June 14, 1995); and Emma S. Young, BCRI OHP, vol. 10, sec. 4 (September 29, 1995).

12. On Bevel's role in the Birmingham demonstrations, see Eskew, *But for Birmingham*, 242, 254, 261–66, 272, 280, 313.

JAMES ARMSTRONG

JAMES ARMSTRONG was born in Dallas County, Alabama, on April 27, 1923. After high school, he was drafted into the U.S. Army. During his training at Camp Shelby in Hattiesburg, Mississippi, tensions arose between assertive black soldiers and local whites, and after members of the Hattiesburg police force "killed one of our black boys." "The black soldiers got a little rowdy, so they shipped us away." After the war, Armstrong moved to Mobile and later Birmingham, where he used the GI Bill to obtain training as a barber. Armstrong subsequently became a founding member of the ACMHR and a loyal supporter of Rev. Fred Shuttlesworth. Armstrong took part in numerous demonstrations and protest actions, and he and his children were central players in the effort to desegregate Graymont Elementary School. "It was just like when I was in the army," he remembered: "You go through so much in the army, especially when I left off of Normandy Beach. Fear leave you. You think about what you are trying to do, and you just move forward filled with faith. That's the way I took it."

JUST LIKE WHEN I WAS IN THE ARMY

My father and mother were born [and raised] in Dallas County. [They were] originally farmers. They had very little schooling. I doubt if they went through the sixth grade. You didn't get much schooling back in those days. They owned a farm. The land is not still in the family. That's been sold and done away with for years.

I attended Morelet Junior High School in Dallas County. Then I went to Emmanuel Brown Training School in Richmond, Alabama. After high school, I went to the army. I was drafted at eighteen.

When I left Alabama, I went to Fort Benning, Georgia, where I was inducted. When I left Fort Benning, I went to Camp Wallace, Texas. I was in the infantry. When I left Camp Wallace, I was brought back to Gadsden, Alabama, Chemical Warfare Service, Camp Cypress. And then we left there and went back to Camp Shelby, Mississippi, and the quartermaster. I spent a short while at the quartermaster in North Carolina.

When there was trouble between black soldiers and townspeople, they would ship the soldiers out. During that time, the troops had a conflict with the police down in Camp Shelby in Hattiesburg, Mississippi. The police killed one of our black boys. The black soldiers got a little rowdy, so they shipped us away. A police officer killed one of our soldiers about a black girl. They quarantined us for the trip to New Jersey and for overseas.[1]

I spent maybe two years and about six months in Europe. [I] never encountered the enemy, but I remember delivering gas about seven miles from the front line, and it sounded like I was right in the midst of it. So that's the closest I got to the front line. When we returned, we were greeted by bands playing music when we got off the ship in New York, and I was so glad to be home. It is hard to explain that feeling. When the train was loaded to come south, I remember I was a sergeant, and I was in charge. I was charged with the black and the white. We were mixed, then, coming back south. And the closer we got to the South, the less the white boys wanted to stay in the coaches with the black boys. You could see the changes made with them when they come back to America.

I went back to Dallas County but didn't stay there too long. I went to Mobile and worked at a laundry, a Chinese laundry. I learned how to do laundry work—starch shirts and iron, things of that nature. I learned how to run washers and things of that nature. I was there maybe a year. I met my wife in Mobile—married in Mobile. Her father had a home out here in Pratt City [in Birmingham]. They were down there because he worked at the shipyard in Mobile. So after we married in Mobile, we moved to Birmingham and lived in their home while they were in Mobile.

My first job in Birmingham was at a service station. I also worked where they make tires. Eventually I got a job at TCI. I worked TCI at the track company—ES [maintenance] shop. I stayed there until the strike began in [1956], I believe.[2] It would be about nine months. I stayed in Pratt City maybe two years. When I left there, I came home and I went with my uncle in Smithfield for a short while until I got an application for a [housing] project. Then I moved into Southtown Projects.[3] It was a move up because when you get out on your own, the first time you have been on your own as a man in a family and children will be born. I had four children, and all in Southtown Projects. Then I left Southtown Projects to where I'm living now on College Hills. I've always liked Smithfield. When there were a lot of homes in College Hills for sale, we just went out house looking, and we found a house in Smithfield that we thought we would like, and we planned for it. That was in '57, '56, or something like that.

The people that lived in Southtown Projects had low-paying jobs, because people that lived in the projects didn't have much, wasn't making no money. That was why they were living in the projects, because of low income. And far as the recreation, well, they had things out there—you could play ball. They had a field out there where you could play ball and whatever exercise you wanted to do in the Southtown Projects.

Well, when the strike hit, I was going to school. I was going to barber school [and getting] on-the-job training. [I was] working in the daytime and then [going] to school at night. I was going to Lincoln [annex to Parker High School] on the GI Bill for barbering.[4] When I finished, I worked. I stayed at the shop where I was working for a while, and then I ventured out on my own. I was still living in Southtown when I started.

I became a registered voter during the time when I was in veterans' school. I went to register about three or four times before I passed the test, because they had a long sheet you had to study. But when you get down there, they asked you nothing that was on that study sheet. I went in one day, and [the registrar] asked me how many seeds are in a watermelon. And I couldn't tell him, so I was turned down. So he told me to go and come back. So when I came back, he asked me how many windows are in the courthouse. So I didn't know how many windows were in the courthouse. So that's the second trip. When I went back again, he wanted to know how many steps from the courthouse to the City Hall. I couldn't answer that question. So the next time I went, he asked me to name the senator of Alabama, and I named John Sparkman. He wanted to know where he lived. I told him Mobile. Then he wanted to know his address. I told him I didn't know his address. Fourth time I was turned down. So what passed me, I really don't know. But I never [will] forget that he asked another young man that was with me to recite the Constitution of the United States. This young man recited the Gettysburg Address, [and] he passed him. When I went back to veterans' school, my teacher would tell me to go right back up there. The registrar told me, "Don't come back in the next six months." But my teacher sent me back within a week or so, and I was willing to go back.[5]

Well, back in those days, the police department was the boss in Birmingham. You never got out of place in Birmingham with police in those days because that was it. You couldn't stand on the corner back in those days and talk with more than three people because of the Birmingham Police Department. You had to move off the block. I never had any problem with the police as far as that was concerned. I knew them, and I never wanted to be arrested doing nothing, because back in those days you could get arrested for vagrancy if you didn't have a job.

• • •

I was there the first night the movement was organized [June 5, 1956]. I was one of the members that stood up for Shuttlesworth to be president at Sardis Baptist Church on that particular night. There was some controversy, but Shuttlesworth was elected the first president of the [ACMHR]. I remember that well.

A mass meeting was a meeting of information. [Organizers told] you about your responsibilities as a citizen and putting prayers into action. We would be concerned about one another, caring, voting, and all that—what a vote would do for you if you use it. All these kinds of things. We had different people to speak [on] different things—about what a struggle mean, what you have to do, why you might lose your life and might lose your job, which they did. Anything could have happened during the struggle, and a lot of things did happen during the struggle.

I participated in most of the marches. Greyhound Bus Station—I integrated that. I went to jail out of there. I had a ticket in my pocket to go to Gadsden [Alabama], and they put me in jail for integrating [the] Greyhound Bus Station. And I didn't go to jail with transit, but I tried to get in jail. I rode 6–Pratt [bus] to Ensley, and they wouldn't arrest me. I played Red Skelton and got on another bus.[6] I got off the front and come back in town, and they still wouldn't arrest me. So I named a lot of things now—[the] golf course, and I went and I [sat in] out at the airport and the lunch counter at the airport, and different other things. I went to jail at the lunch counter in Newberry's. I was looking at things yesterday at the [Birmingham Civil Rights] Institute where I was in jail thirty years ago on Easter Sunday [1963], marching. I went to jail so many times until the man wanted to know when I was going to stop coming over here—he had my fingerprints so much. I said, "Well, [if] you get things straight, I don't have to come."

[Jail] was a hard experience. I went to jail at least five or six times. I remember the last time I was in jail with A. D. [King] and [John] Porter. Smith stayed in there a while—N. H. Smith and Carter Gaston, Calvin Woods. About eighteen of us were in the cell. And I will never forget that night in that cell when A. D. was asking a question. He wanted to know where he was going to sleep, and somebody told him "You standing in your bed"—nothing but a concrete floor. Later on that night, everybody started to lie down, and we had the newspaper, and most of the preachers had their robes. They made a pillow out of that robe, and they put the robe under their head. And so later on, about twelve or one o'clock, all the toilet tissue was used up. See the toilet sit in your cell, and you have no privacy at all. Later on that night, somebody used some newspaper and that stopped up the toilet so everybody had to stand up the rest of the night.

My wife went to jail, and my children went to jail. My daughter was out at the fairgrounds because she was a teenager. My boys were under teenage, so they went to Juvenile Court. Most of the kids left Parker [High School] in the demonstrations. But my kids, I kept them out for the demonstrations. I didn't let them go to school that day [May 2, 1963]. I had family that was frightened and afraid for me, and I had another part of the family who was with me. I know my aunt, my daddy's sister, told me that if I had any problem of paying my house note [that I should] let her know. So that gave me a little more strength to keep going.

I had a lot of customers quit coming because they were afraid of what was going to happen at the [barber] shop. The word got out that [Klansmen] would stop in front of my door and take a picture of the shop and take off. All those kind of things happened. And a lot of things [happened that] I couldn't tell my customers because I didn't want to lose business. And then I have had Carol W. Hayes [supervisor of Birmingham's black elementary schools]—he tried to discourage me because the superintendent had got on to him, and he let the superintendent know I was his barber. And so when he found out that I wasn't going to change, then he got on my side.

Being threatened was just an every night thing. I have had calls all night long, and I've had trucks come to my house. A man pulling one of these big hole diggers—I don't know what you call them. But anyway, I don't know if it was a gas company or another company—I never did pay any attention what the company was. But they came to my house around one o'clock at night and say somebody called them that I needed some plumbing work unstopped. I said, "Well, I didn't need [a] machine this large to unstop any plumbing." I have my own plumbing. So what they were doing is trying to keep you awake all the time. And so the next night I had the fire truck to come, the big fire truck with the man on the tail end with that long trailer on it. It came that night and shined the lights all through the house, and he'd say someone called that the house was on fire. And I told them, "No house on fire here." Another night, here comes the ambulance. All of them came late at night to disturb you, asking if somebody got hurt. They came, but nobody was hurt. So the next night, the police came, which the police were always running up and down Ninth Court, and they wanted to know what was going on. They got a call that a disturbance is going on at this house. I said, "Not this house, everybody back here is in the bed." I was on the front. My family stays in the back. At the same time, I had guards outside watching them. That didn't work, so I started getting letters from the Holiday Inn in Pascagoula, Mississippi, [saying] that I had lived in the hotel down there and never paid my bill. I never been in a hotel in Pascagoula, Mississippi. So that didn't work [to make me stop]. I had to go clear that up. Then I got a bill from the newspaper because somebody had put an ad [saying] that I had a late-model Chevrolet that I wanted one thousand dollars for. I never owned a Chevy in my life. They would call you at night and anytime—late at night to keep your family upset.

We got used to a tragic thing like that. You get used to it. And I would answer the phone, nobody answer. They would call and [ask] how would I like to see my kids in a casket. Well, I told him, "I feel the same way you feel if yours was lying in a casket. We all are human." I had men to guard my house every night for two years. They were men [who] come to the mass meetings. They were men that lived out on the suburbs of Birmingham, from Pell City [and] out on these mining camps. I have had to go to Rev. Shuttlesworth's house to guard his house, and I would guard Smith's house at night. At that time, I was a member of New Pilgrim Baptist Church. N. H. Smith was pastor, and he was the secretary of the [ACMHR]. Most members were very supportive, and he preached strong sermons to give you the courage to do things. Mrs. [Ruby] Shuttlesworth would call and want to know if I had any guards. I told her yes, I had guards. She said she didn't have anybody over there. So to keep Fred from knowing he didn't have any guards, I volunteered to go and spend the night over there guarding his house while somebody [was] guarding my house.

I wasn't attacked—only handled rough by the police department. Birmingham police were big fellows then. They would pick you up and throw you in the paddy wagon, not put you in the paddy wagon. You had to protect your head. They would throw you in the paddy wagon and ride you four or five hours at night on the roughest streets in town. Driving as fast as they could go, throwing you from side to side of the paddy wagon rather than just carrying you on to jail. I don't think I suffered financially. I ran short on some things, but I was supported by my people and a lot of folks came to me more because of my stand. [They] gave me strong support, and that gave me courage to keep going.

Well, one thing I can say [about] the benefit [of the movement was that] I was able to move [into] a place where black folks wasn't allowed after the sun go down. Because you'd work up there, you'd cut grass [in the spring] and get out before dark. And you would rake leaves in the summer and wintertime, and get out before dark. I live there now. I benefited from that. When we moved into Collegeville, it was a white neighborhood. Whites lived next door. The reception was good until I applied for [Graymont Elementary School]. When I applied for the school, they started moving. And I had neighbors lived behind me—whites lived behind my fence. That's how my dog got poisoned, I believe, from them back there. I had a dog. He was poisoned over the fence because my fence ran into the apartment where they lived.

• • •

In 1957, Shuttlesworth decided to take his kids and enroll them in Phillips High School. Fred told Abraham Woods, myself, and three or four others to meet him that morning at the east end of Phillips High School. Woods was in charge of the detail.[7] When we got there, we heard that they had jumped on [Shuttlesworth] around at the south door. We rushed around there, [but] they had beaten him up and somebody had carried him on to the hospital. I went around there, and I assisted one of his girls to take her to the hospital because one of his girls got her hand mashed in the door. Somebody slammed a door on her hand. Reverend [J. S.] Phifer was driving the car. We walked all through the mob. One of them stuck Shuttlesworth's wife with an ice pick. They didn't make any attempt towards us.[8]

Fred was a man. He has always said, "Never set a hen on one egg. You waste the hen's time." He said, "Set on a bunch of eggs." So he started protests at schools, lunch counters, buses, and whatever. When he called for families to come forward with our attack [on] segregated schools, ten families came forward—my family and nine others. But the other nine fell out for various reasons. So I carried the ball. Lots of them got fired from their jobs, and different things happened to them. People were fired from their jobs because they signed a petition. Some of them left the city because they lost their job. Well, I thought it was a thing that had to be done, and I asked myself a question: "Why not me?" I guess I said I was self-employed—I could handle it much better, so I just stuck with it.

I had talked with my wife. Women during that time, they were on the fear side. She signed the petition, but she was still afraid. When we started, she went out and spent the night with her mother out in Pratt City and left the kids and I holding the bag. But she eventually came back home. The paper never knew about that because they would have blown that out of proportion. It was just like when I was in the army. You go through so much in the army, especially when I left off of Normandy Beach. Fear leave you. You think about what you are trying to do, and you just move forward filled with faith. That's the way I took it.

My kids took it with a smile, and they gave me courage watching them, how they acted. They had a lot of problems, but they gave me the courage. We went through the process for six years. When I first filed the case to desegregate Graymont School, it was with my oldest kids, [Denise and James Jr.]. The journey through the court was a long process. By the time it came up, they were gone on to Parker High School, so I had to use my two younger boys [Floyd and Dwight] to carry out the case. So that's how the two younger boys got on the school case.

We first filed in 1957. They got in the school in 1963. We had fireside chats, and I told them—well, my kids went to the movement. When you go to the movement, Shuttlesworth or whoever speaks builds your courage. So they had courage from going to the movement with me every night. My whole family attended the mass meetings every Monday night. This had a lot to do with them building their courage. When they got into the school, they knew how to handle it.

The first day [September 4, 1963], there were about 250 hecklers. Prior to going to school that morning, my lawyers, [Ernest] Jackson from Florida and Constance Motley, came to the house early.[9] Shuttlesworth and I think Oscar Adams, Charles Billups, and myself—we [all] went down that morning. There were hecklers around on the entrance side of the school, in the front, so we went in the east side. [Alabama governor George] Wallace had state troopers, about thirty-five, planted all around the building to keep us from entering the school. So we had to go back and get another court order.

We got in the school on [September 10]. We didn't even need a lawyer that morning to go down there.[10] So we went in there, and we went in that morning, and everybody was accepted that went into the principal's office. And from that day on, I would go to school every day [at] about ten [and] three—the school hours—to see them safely home. And the agonies and headaches I got whenever a fire wagon passed my door going that direction, I got a loaded stomach. Anytime a siren going that way, for thirty or forty minutes you got a heavy stomach because you don't know if they were going to Graymont School or not. So those were the heavy problems. For a whole year, I had to go along with that. Especially when the boys came home in the evening and Dwight would tell me about his lip was busted where he had made an attempt to drink water out of the water fountain. Some white boy hit him behind his head and kind of bust his lip a little bit. And then I taught them that you have to stand behind one another to get a drink of water; you don't just go up there by yourself. So that's the way they would drink water, one standing by the other to get water. And when they go out to play ball, the white boys had an act of turning the bat loose. So I taught them how to stand behind the crowd: "If your time come up to bat, just stay behind one white kid. Protect yourself that way." That's the way they had to do it. And for two or three games of football, they wouldn't throw my boy the ball. So eventually things changed and eventually they started throwing Floyd the ball. So things got better. Each day the things got better.

They were down there for two years before any other blacks came to the school. The first year I taught them not to fight because I didn't want them to get expelled from school, so they laid quiet. I knew my boys. The second year, I turned them loose, and they had fewer problems. I told them to protect each other: "Whatever happens, you take care of yourself." They did not get into any fights the second year because they were ready to return or retaliate.

Superintendent Rice asked why did I want to send my kids to Graymont School. I said "Well, it's close to home." Wilkerson [the closest school for black children] was about five or six blocks, plus you had to cross Eleventh Court, which is very dangerous traffic. Graymont was actually a block and a half, and I wanted them to be near home. And I found out they had some books in that school they didn't have in Wilkerson. The white kids had schoolbooks that we didn't have at our school.

They went to Ensley High School the first year, but the following year they went to high school in Boston, Massachusetts. My oldest son was in Boston on a French program—the same program that Angela Davis had attended.[11] My oldest son lived with the Roche family. And they find out that he was brother to Dwight and Floyd in Birmingham that integrated Graymont School. So the Roche family wanted them to come and live with them and go to high school in Boston. So that's how they got to Boston with the Roche family. If they remained here in Birmingham, they would have probably finished at Ensley.

Boston was a great experience [for them]. They learned twice as much because they had the South experience and they went with the North experience. So there was a whole lot that they could offer those children, and they learned from those children up there. After they graduated from high school, Dwight went to Tufts University in Boston. And Floyd, when he graduated, he went to Boston College. Dwight lives in Louisville, Kentucky. He has a job with General Electric. Floyd lives in Maryland, right on the border of Washington, [D.C.]. He just got discharged from the navy as a lieutenant commander.

I remember a whole lot about Dr. [Martin Luther] King. He was one of my idols. I cut his hair several times, and he was a man that—I don't know how to really say it, but I had a lot of faith and confidence in him. The same as Shuttlesworth. Fred Shuttlesworth and Dr. King were two persons that if the average black person had met Dr. King, they wouldn't be what they are doing today. That is one of the greatest mistakes we made, not meeting Dr. King and those who were around in that area. If they had only met Dr. King and knew what he was about, Birmingham would have been a whole lot farther. We would have been better people than we are today because we would have had his dream. I wonder sometimes what would he think if he was living today, if we walk around and say "I got a dream." Dr. King was a strong man, and God sent him for America, not just for black folks.

NOTES

BCRI OHP, vol. 4, sec. 5 (April 10, 1995). Edited, annotated, and abridged by Horace Huntley and John McKerley.

1. In 1943, according to historian Timothy B. Tyson, "the War Department reported . . . there was 'general unrest' among black troops all over the country and the imminent danger of revolt." Often concluding that northern blacks and other "outside" agitators were to blame for such "unrest," southern whites attempted

to prohibit the sale of northern black newspapers to African American soldiers during the war. According to the *Chicago Defender,* "In Hattiesburg, Miss., near Camp Shelby, one of the largest camps in the country, salesmen of northern Negro newspapers are reported to have been told by police that no further sales of the papers would be permitted in Hattiesburg" (*Radio Free Dixie: Robert F. Williams and the Roots of Black Power* [Chapel Hill: University of North Carolina Press, 1999], 37; *Chicago Defender,* July 24, 1943).

2. In April 1956, the Brotherhood of Locomotive Firemen and Enginemen began a strike against TCI that shut down six steel plants in the Birmingham area. For more on the brotherhood, especially its discriminatory practices toward black workers, see Eric Arnesen, *Brotherhoods of Color: Black Railroad Workers and the Struggle for Equality* (Cambridge: Harvard University Press, 2002), 28, 67, 120–26, 148, 195–96, 204–19.

3. On black residents' transition to public housing, see also Washington Booker III, BCRI OHP, vol. 1, sec. 2 (January 5, 1995); Gwendolyn Gamble, BCRI OHP, vol. 12, sec. 1 (January 24, 1996).

4. On the opportunities and limits of the Selective Service Readjustment Act (or GI Bill of Rights) for African Americans during this period, see Ira Katznelson, *When Affirmative Action Was White: An Untold History of Racial Inequality in Twentieth-Century America* (New York: Norton, 2005), 113–41.

5. On the various means by which white registrars limited black voting rights in Birmingham, see also Nell Irvin Painter, *The Narrative of Hosea Hudson: The Life and Times of a Black Radical* (New York: Norton, 1994), 258–60.

6. Richard Bernard "Red" Skelton was a comedian who built his career on playing confused and dimwitted characters (Richard Severo, "Red Skelton, Knockabout Comic and Clown Prince of the Airwaves, Is Dead at 84," *New York Times,* September 18, 1997).

7. For Woods's account of these events, see Abraham Woods, BCRI OHP, vol. 35, sec. 3 (April 30, 1998).

8. On September 9, 1957, Fred and Ruby Shuttlesworth accompanied their daughters to Phillips High School in an attempt to integrate the school. Members of a white mob beat Fred Shuttlesworth and stabbed Ruby Shuttlesworth. For a detailed description of this event, see Andrew M. Manis, *A Fire You Can't Put Out: The Civil Rights Life of Birmingham's Reverend Fred Shuttlesworth* (Tuscaloosa: University of Alabama Press, 1999), 147–52.

9. Constance Baker Motley was an NAACP Legal Defense Fund attorney from New York (Eskew, *But for Birmingham,* 252, 254).

10. Armstrong and his sons did not need a lawyer because earlier that morning, President John F. Kennedy had federalized the Alabama National Guard, which Governor Wallace had ordered to replace the state troopers. See Glenn T. Eskew, *But for Birmingham: The Local and National Movements in the Civil Rights Struggle* (Chapel Hill: University of North Carolina Press, 1997), 319.

11. Angela Davis is a civil rights activist and professor of history of conscious-ness and feminist studies at the University of California, Santa Cruz. She grew up in Birmingham but left the city in her early teens through an American Friends Service Committee program that allowed black students to attend integrated northern high schools (Angela Davis, *An Autobiography* [New York: Random House, 1974], 103–13).

JOE HENDRICKS

JOE HENDRICKS was born into a farming family in Boligee, Alabama, in Greene County, on March 22, 1927. In rural Alabama, Hendricks re-called, community members would pool their resources to pursue com-mon objectives, including the education of children, who were then expected to return to serve the community.

Like many of his contemporaries, Hendricks migrated to Birming-ham in search of work. After first becoming active in the NAACP-sponsored voter registration drives, he made the leap to the ACMHR in 1956. Hendricks described how ACMHR activists structured mass meetings to mirror church services: "It was based on prayer. Someone would speak. The pastor got a musical department, and we had a choir, mass choir, and those kinds of things. That's what it was based on, and they would take up collection, and this is the forum that we used to fight the cases in court."

I GOT ARRESTED BECAUSE I SAT ON A BUS

It wasn't very much education going with my parents because my parents' daddy and mother were under slave masters, and out of that they had to get whatever was pretty well left, and they was under the Hoover days. Back in that day, there wasn't anything very much to do, especially on a farm. And they didn't have anything to get an education with. As a matter of fact, even after I got up, it was left to a community to educate a child, not a family.

When they met like we meet on Sunday now, they would raise money to send that girl off to college so she could continue her education along with the community.[1] [There] wasn't enough money for most families to send a kid to school. It first started by the churches and the community getting involved with a kid when you found a good student. So out of that it wasn't any chance for very much education, because under the slave master it wasn't allowed. Farming is the only thing that they had, and maybe go out to cut timber in the winter to do something like that. And that's about all they had to do.

My father was a farmer. At that point, there was no such thing as nobody worked at home. Everybody farmed in our house. My mother went to the field, daddy went to the field, and the children went to field. They put me in the field when I was five years old, and I been there ever since.

I went to Jane Wood Junior High, and I went to the ninth grade. After that I came to Birmingham. I came here and started to work. Going to school there, they had teachers who were very smart. At that time anybody who finished high school seemed to have been teachers because it was in the area where very few people went to college. Our teachers were twelfth-graders to a [bachelor's] degree. And that [is] what more or less that they had to offer. My schooling was very scarcely done because I went to school like three months out of a year. Most other times until I got fourteen years, I was out of school. I only went about three months because everything was real bad, and we didn't have the sufficient clothes and things to attend, as we should have. So those kinds of things made it kind of rough. But after fourteen, then I started going pretty regular after that.[2]

There wasn't any money there too much. In 1946, I felt that I could come [to Birmingham] because I had some brothers here. They had left and had done pretty well, and I decided I would come here, too. I came here and went to Jim Dandy and stayed there for thirty-eight years.[3] [I] worked there until they closed. I left there, and I went to Lumberjack Meats, where they kill and prepare meat for market. And I left there and went to Hayes Aircraft, and that was about it until I started working some for myself.

I was involved with Mr. [W. C.] Patton before the movement.[4] And when the [ACMHR] started, I thought that was the biggest thing that really helped our people, so that's what I did. I got with them and tried to do whatever I could. I lived on Fourteenth Street between Third and Fourth Avenues, across from Edward Chevrolet [automobile dealership]. That's really in the civil rights district now.

As soon as we could, I became a registered voter. We had a lot of hassle with it. They gave us a real hard time. We had an application to fill that included questions about the senators and congressmen that we had in Washington, all of the officials in Montgomery, our Birmingham district, all those kinds of questions we were to answer before we could vote. And they started asking questions like how high is height, how far is distant, [and] how many bubbles in a bar of soap—those kinds of questions.

I didn't hold office in the [ACMHR], but I did go to the meetings. I was active from the day that it started because everything went well, I thought. And I thought that was the biggest thing, the best thing that had ever happened on my part. So I gladly started taking part and stayed with it as long as it was seemingly doing something worthwhile. I think the first days of the movement, they said they were going to meet somewhere, and they finally ended up meeting at Sardis Baptist Church. And they organized there. I believe that was something like '56. Later on, they started every Monday night, you would have mass meeting. Everybody was looking forward to Monday night. The mass meeting was set up on mostly what we know. It was based on prayer. Someone would speak. The pastor got a musical department and we had a choir, mass choir, and those kinds of things. That's what it was based on, and they would take up collection, and this is the forum that we used to fight the cases in court. They would have a speaker every night. It was based on the same operation as a church service. That's what it was, and we would have a minister and the choir and devotion with prayer and those kinds of things.

The police were present at the mass meetings. We didn't feel that they were there for the right purpose, so we had our own guards along with the policemen on the outside. We didn't look at the police being there as protection. We didn't feel like that was the purpose of them being there, and we would tell them sometimes, "We appreciate you all being here, but we don't feel comfortable with you."[5]

I was going to guard duty out to Rev. [Fred] Shuttlesworth's house when I was stopped by the policemen. So there were about fifteen cars of policemen in a dark place, you couldn't see anything. And they said to me, "Give me your driver's license." There was no courtesy at all, and they were using the word *nigger* and this kind of thing. I was kind of shook up. I gave them my [ACMHR membership] card because I couldn't see anything. [When] I went to my billfold, the movement card was hard like the driver's license. The driver's license had hard plastic, and I just felt something hard, because there wasn't any light. And when he shined the light on it, he said, "Alabama Christian Movement for Human Rights" rather than a driver's license. I was afraid at that point. The way they surrounded me, I knew it wasn't a good sign. They just pulled around me and stopped real quick. I knew it wasn't a good sign. And where they stopped me at, it was real dark, no light at all. So they seemed to meet, and they said to one another, "What we going to do with this nigger?" And the other one said, "If we kill him, then what are these other niggers going to think that belong to this movement?" So at that point, I said, this is just it. And when they finally made their suggestion, one of them asked the question, "If we kill him, and if it beats back to us, then what these others going to think?" So they finally said, "We better let him go, because if it leads back to us then we are going to have to answer to the call." So they let me go. I think the card worked in my favor. But sometime God has a way that you don't have to get things done. That's my feeling. That's what I really ended up saying afterwards.

I got arrested because I sat on a bus.[6] I was the first case. I came through town and they—white brothers—were on every corner. White people had congregated on the corner. They had chains and billy clubs and sticks, and they said to one another, "What time Shuttlesworth going to get here?" That's what they called him. And I go to the next corner, and they were asking for him. So I then turned and went on out to Rev. Shuttlesworth's house. And I said to him, "This is the wrong day for you." I said, "You better give me that pass and let me go to town." He said, "Well, what about your job?" I said, "Well, the job won't mean as much as your life or whatever those [whites] planned. This just ain't the right day for you." So I pursued to go and follow through with whatever he had planned and what I felt was best to [do], that I should do rather than let him walk into that kind of situation. I was planning to go with him anyway. And after it seemed they were going to make a problem for him, then I was willing to do whatever was necessary to do on my part. We had like fifteen to twenty people. We went and sat on the bus, and the bus driver say, "Move to the back." And we said, "We [are] comfortable where we are. [We] don't see any reason why we should go to the back. We paid our fare, and we feel that we are comfortable where we are sitting." And we stayed where we were sitting. I caught a bus going to Ensley. Instead of them taking me to Ensley, they took me to the bus terminal and pulled us up in between some more buses there and called the policemen before we left town. They called the dispatcher, and they were the ones that ordered them to not go on the route but to take us down to the bus terminal. And from there, they called the paddy wagon to take us to jail. I spent five days and six nights in jail. But the worst part of it was they sent us to court. Then the judge turned around and said, "Send them back." That night, they sent us back to jail for the respect he had for another judge. They then decided to bring us back to court the next day, which I never did understand. Then we had to come back to court the next morning before that other judge, and he released us. I don't think I was arrested any other time.

I took part in the protest at the airport. They didn't arrest us at the airport. At the airport it was a matter of trying to be served as any other citizen in the airport restaurant. And they refused to serve us for a whole week. We set up three groups. The first group would go on when they opened. The second group would come on at ten o'clock. I was a part of that group: Mamie

Brown, Jim Hendricks, me, and I believe Hattie Felder—I think that's right. I think it was a ham sandwich and a drink is what we ordered. It was $1.85. But the manager came out and instructed them to charge us $5.85 for [a] $1.85 sandwich. Some of them didn't want to pay it. So I offered to pay for whoever didn't want to pay. I just wanted a receipt. So she said that she would give me one. We were special guests, so she charged us $5.00 extra. So we paid it and we took it on to court. Constance [Baker] Motley represented that case, and she did real well. She knew the law. She used that sandwich, that $1.80 sandwich that I paid $5.80 for, as evidence in that case. We won.[7]

In 1961, we had a group of people called Freedom Riders who started their trip in Washington, D.C., and was headed to New Orleans.[8] When they arrived in Alabama, some things took place. After these people had been in Anniston, Alabama, for something like a week or three or four days or something, I felt that they were trapped there. I consulted [Shuttlesworth] about it, and he said if I felt that way or if we felt that way, we should go. He thought somebody should go check on them, that's the way he put it. So we pursued to go there. And those people were vicious, seemed to be mad about something—I don't know what. And they had formed the white people on the street out there to stand over us with guns and intimidate us.

We formed a car pool to go there to pick them up in cars. And we went there to pick them up. We carried one person per car, not more than two, because we left space for the people who were there in Anniston, in case we could bring them back. In getting them back with us, we had difficulty out of the sheriff's department. They had them in the basement at the hospital. They had been beaten up. They were downstairs in the basement at the hospital, and we couldn't get in there until these sheriffs deputies let us in. They made us stop out on the lot before we got to the hospital. We had to communicate with them, so I asked the other people to stay back because the tension was so high. The people were so brutally mad, and they had all those guns. So I asked the other people to not go and let me go up and see if I could get them released. So, he finally said to me, "If you want to take the chance, I wouldn't do anything to help you. I won't protect you even if something would happen to you on this hospital yard. You are on your own." There were other whites on the street before we got on the lot. They had stopped us and stood over us with all kinds of guns. I had a flat [tire], and they stood over me the whole time I was fixing my flat. And they ran me out of the service station. They wouldn't let the people in the service station fix it. So we pursued to go ahead and get my spare out the trunk and fix it that way. They just stood there with the guns, as if they were out there hunting for us, like we were animals or something.

We knew [that the Freedom Riders] were stranded because it was on the news. By me being active in the movement, we knew that they were there and had the location of where they were. The people who were stranded were both black and white. We had even four white ladies in the group. The men who were with me were actually afraid to let them ride back because it was so much animosity and so much bitterness there. And I just took the initiative to load them in my car, the white ladies, and into my best friend's car, which was Forest Washington. And we got them back to town. But no one wanted the white ladies in their car because of the guns and the way the people were acting and the way they was treating them. By them being white ladies in a black man's car, riding down the street, by these guns and all these people, that was the reason. And you had sixty miles of rural route to get between Anniston and Birmingham.[9]

So they came back to Birmingham. And when I got here, I had the same problem. No one wanted to deal with the white ladies. When nobody would take them, I said, "Well, then all white ladies load back in my car and come and go home with me." They hadn't had a bath. They hadn't had anything of that sort. So I took them home and my wife made a way for them to take a bath and give them some clothes. She gave all of them something to put on and change in. They put the clothes on, wore them back home, and mailed them back. We lived over in Titusville, Honeysuckle Circle.[10]

I was [also] one of the guards for [the] Shuttlesworth home and [Bethel Baptist Church]. The next-door neighbor to Rev. Shuttlesworth had a screened-in porch where you could see off the porch all the way around. We would sit straight across from the church, and we could see on the side and all way on both sides of the church and the front. We had a fence on the back. So that's where we would sit in. And we could stay there if it was raining or whatever and be able to see. We were close enough to the church to see anything that goes on. We had a few shotguns hid out. We didn't have to use them. We had an occasion where maybe someone might have thought that we had bombs brought there, and the man said he wanted to get into the church so the preacher could pray for him. He had a five-gallon can of dynamite under a raincoat. [He was] a white male. When we moved in his direction, he became evasive. He dropped the can and it blew up in the street. I was on duty that night that it happened. I believe a fellow named John L. Lewis did the closing in on him. And it blew the windows out the church and a big hole in the street.[11]

NOTES

BCRI OHP, vol. 8, sec. 1 (June 23, 1995). Edited, annotated, and abridged by A. Michelle Craig, Horace Huntley, and John McKerley.

1. On black southerners' communal approach to education during the late nineteenth and early twentieth centuries, especially for girls, see Stephanie Shaw, *What a Woman Ought to Be and to Do: Black Professional Women Workers during the Jim Crow Era* (Chicago: University of Chicago Press, 1996), 1–108.

2. For more on the experience of black students in the Jim Crow South, see James D. Anderson, *The Education of Blacks in the South, 1865–1935* (Chapel Hill: University of North Carolina Press, 1988), 148–85.

3. The Western Grain Company was a Birmingham-based firm that produced the Jim Dandy brand of dog food (History of Savannah Foods and Industries, http://www.referenceforbusiness.com/history2/65/Savannah-Foods-Industries -Inc.html [accessed April 24, 2007]).

4. W. C. Patton was the president of the Birmingham branch of the NAACP during the early 1950s. Like most leaders of Birmingham's established black professional class, Patton supported voter registration and legal challenges to Jim Crow, but he was suspicious of the ACMHR and the politics of mass protest (Glenn T. Eskew, *But for Birmingham: The Local and National Movements in the Civil Rights Struggle* [Chapel Hill: University of North Carolina Press, 1997], 78, 127).

5. Indeed, the police attended ACMHR mass meetings to monitor their activities, not to provide protection. For examples of the police reports of the meetings, see "Alabama Christian Movement for Human Rights, 1963," Eugene "Bull" Connor Papers, Reel 268.13.2–13.5, Birmingham Public Library, Department of Archives and Manuscripts, Birmingham.

6. In the wake of the successful bus boycott waged by the Montgomery Improvement Association, ACMHR members attempted to draw attention to segregated busing through direct action. On December 26, 1956, twenty-one ACMHR members were arrested for breaking the segregation ordinance (Manis, *Fire*, 115–16).

7. Constance Baker Motley was an NAACP Legal Defense Fund attorney from New York (Eskew, *But for Birmingham*, 252, 254).

8. On the Freedom Riders, see Raymond Arsenault, *Freedom Riders: 1961 and the Struggle for Racial Justice* (New York: Oxford University Press, 2006), xi–xii.

9. The greatest racial taboo in the Jim Crow South was interracial sexual relationships between black men and white women. Even its suggestion (as in the case of white women riding in the car with a black man) could result in violence. For an example of white men's willingness to use violence to police black men's behavior with regard to white women (and thus the actions of white women

as well) as late as 1970, see Timothy B. Tyson, *Blood Done Sign My Name* (New York: Crown, 2004).

10. Titusville is a black middle-class community southwest of downtown Birmingham. On Titusville, see Lynne B. Feldman, *A Sense of Place: Birmingham's Black Middle-Class Community, 1890–1930* (Tuscaloosa: University of Alabama Press, 1999), 64.

11. There are several versions of this incident, which took place on December 13, 1962. See LaVerne Revis Martin, BCRI OHP, vol. 19, sec. 3 (July 17, 1996); James Roberson, BCRI OHP, vol. 18, sec. 2 (June 25, 1996); Colonel Stone Johnson, BCRI OHP, vol. 1, sec. 3 (January 6, 1995). Neither Martin nor Johnson, who were also present, recalled the "evasive" white man that Hendricks describes.

JAMES SUMMERVILLE

JAMES SUMMERVILLE was born in Greene County, Alabama, on March 30, 1928. After a brief stint in the military during the Korean War, Summerville moved to Birmingham with his wife in 1956. A movement activist and labor organizer at ACIPCO, Summerville described the need to protect himself and his family through anonymity: "There wasn't any effort by my people to deter me from my involvement because I wasn't in the public eye. Things such as going to jail, I had to distance myself from. I would be in the crowd and wear things so that I couldn't be recognized." Summerville suggested that the movement's relative success also contributed to greater factionalism within the black community, especially between men and along class lines: "You see a huge difference when we come together to make a stand. Now we kind of got some distance between each other. Sometimes I hear, 'I have mine. I got a good job.' All they think about is these material things, and that is only putting us further and further back."

ONE OF THE ONES THAT GUARDED

My daddy was a farmer. As I was growing up, I can remember that he was a farmer, and he also did construction work. In those times, especially the boys, we had to do most of the work out in the fields. On our farm we had cotton, corn, peanuts, sweet potatoes, and sugarcane. We call it ribbon cane. My parents didn't own that property. We rented it from a black man named

Frank Wilder. He rented a lot of land from white folk and would then rent it out to farmers that were around that area. There were four of us who lived on that plantation. My mother was a housewife. There were six of us siblings. We kept them pretty busy. While in Eutaw [in Greene County], I went to Eden High School.

As soon as I finished Eden High School, I had to go into the service for two years. This was during the Korean War. When we first got in there that night, a plane flew over and they had all of us hit the dirt. That was the only action that I saw. They had just about ceased fire when we got there. I was over there just about a year.

I enjoyed making that transition from Greene County to the military. That helped me to stand on my own two feet. That experience gave me a whole lot of discipline. Being in the army was different. As a matter of fact, I saw a lot of things that I had never before seen in my life. It helped me decide what I wanted to be or what I would like to be.

When I got out of the military and came back to Greene County, there wasn't any work to be done. I tried the sawmill, and I tried construction work. I [also] hauled coal. I eventually moved to Birmingham. The transition from rural Greene County to the city was a little difficult. I had to learn where I was going, what street to go on. I had to learn about that way of life. As my wife and I grew together and learned the area, we began to stretch out and find a lot of friends. I started work at the ACIPCO plant on April 1, 1956.

I had never been involved in civil rights work before I came to Birmingham. I was one of the ones that guarded the community of Titusville. There were three guards on each shift. We had a guard on the corner of McCary [Street]; we had a guard at the corner on Goldwire [Street] and a guard on Center Street. We had three shifts, and a car usually parked in my driveway. I would normally take the first shift because of my job. We would alternate often, and I think that gave us a lot of courage. We needed the protection after the bombing down on Center Street. It gave our neighbors a lot of concern, and when you get concern out of neighbors, you begin to do things that would protect them.

There wasn't any effort by my people to deter me from my involvement because I wasn't in the public eye. Things such as going to jail, I had to distance myself from. I would be in the crowd and wear things so that I couldn't be recognized. I knew that it was necessary for me to be involved when I saw things, and I knew that they were not the way I would have liked it to be. If you want to be somebody in life and to be respected in life, you've got to help others to improve their lives and also your life, too.

We were not exactly told face-to-face that if we were caught participating in the movement we would lose our jobs.[1] They would send out a memo. I was aware that I had children to raise, and the movement made me look at that. What really encouraged people was the opportunity to go into places they were not able to go into before. While I was in Birmingham, my parents would say, "Y'all be careful and watch out for yourself. If you need some help, take it to the Lord and you pray." They would always say, "You know who you are and what color you are." [The movement] was an experience for them and also for us.

There were many incidents of racism at ACIPCO. You would be working on one job for years and years and never get a promotion. You also would have to get the dirtiest job. After the movement, we saw some changes. We began to move to a lot of electrical work and going to different classes. The racism didn't end, though. Even though we had the training, they would never let you wire up anything. We made efforts to get a union. We tried it, and it came down to a vote. Everybody wanted it, [but] when it came down to a vote, as always, white people have the ways to get to some blacks. They got to a few, and that put it off. I have to give it to some white people; they understood. They kind of stepped around it, and then they started giving you a little bit more opportunity to do different things. In a way we had it rough, but we found out that [the movement] did benefit.[2]

The most important thing that happened because of the movement was the buying power. There were certain areas you couldn't go in. There was a certain amount of money you could borrow. When the movement came, that gave you the opportunity to go to these places, and it gave you the opportunity of buying power. It also gave an opportunity for the young that were getting their first job. That's what impressed me, because we couldn't even do these things. We couldn't even go to a decent park. We had a different park we had to go to, and you could look around and see the difference in the equipment we had versus what was in the park that the whites had. That empowered us a lot. It empowered us because we were taxpaying citizens, and there were places that we were not allowed to go to.

People say now that because we don't sit at the back of the bus anymore and we can go to the hotels downtown, there is no need for the movement anymore. I have to react to that differently. I have to say this: black people and black men don't have the respect for each other anymore. The love and care for each other is not the same—especially men. What I'm saying here is that we fell asleep, or we have committed ourselves to something else, to material things. We feel like, "Now I have what I want, but I never look at the consequences of what is in front of me." When you find men with their families, [with] the churches and schools coming together, you see the difference in your community. You see the difference in the schools. You see a huge difference when we come together to make a stand. Now we kind of got some distance between each other. Sometimes I hear, "I have mine. I got a good job." All they think about is these material things, and that is only putting us further and further back. Because we are reaching for it because we've got our children reaching for things that they can do without. We don't have time enough to come together as a family to even say a prayer or grace at a table like a family used to.

I have to say I give thanks to the Lord for my wife. We can look around and see where we came from. I know where I came from. I know what I have, and I know that she has helped me to realize it. She has made me realize that there are things that we can do, and it made me realize that I have to take a stand to do things. She does things that I feel like I should be doing, but she wants to do it. She looked out for the family, and she had love for the children. I thank God as I look and I hope that the children and people can look and see that it's not where I'm going but how I'm going to get there. If you find yourself in a happy marriage life, don't take on any more. Don't tell your wife, "This is your goal, and this is mine." Be together. The family is the center. It's the center in life. Always have blessing with the family, and then you can sit down and talk. Let your children communicate with you, let them ask you questions, you ask them questions. Let them help you.

NOTES

BCRI OHP, vol. 21, sec. 2 (Sept. 13, 1996). Edited, annotated, and abridged by A. Michelle Craig, Horace Huntley, and John McKerley.

1. On the fear of job loss at ACIPCO, see Henry M. Goodgame, Sr., BCRI OHP, vol. 20, sec. 1 (July 31, 1996). Goodgame described much more direct tactics of intimidation on the job.

2. On the efforts of black workers to use new federal antidiscrimination legislation to challenge the segregated seniority system at ACIPCO, see Horace Huntley and David Montgomery, eds., *Black Workers' Struggle for Equality in Birmingham* (Urbana: University of Illinois Press, 2004), 22, 110, 204. See also Harvey Lee Henley Jr., BCRI OHP, vol. 7, sec. 5 (June 21, 1995); Jimmie Louis Warren, BCRI OHP, vol. 16, sec. 4 (May 17, 1996); Henry M. Goodgame Sr., BCRI OHP, vol. 20, sec. 1 (July 31, 1996).

HENRY M. GOODGAME SR.

HENRY M. GOODGAME SR. was born in Hollins, Alabama, in Coosa County, on November 4, 1930. He came to Birmingham as a child when his parents migrated to the city in search of work. After graduating from Parker High School, he attempted to attend college in Chicago before starting work as a laborer in Birmingham. Goodgame was a member of the NAACP and ACMHR, but, he remembered, "we had to be extra careful about being associated with these various organizations. I can recall many, many times when we would have our mass meeting, police would come around and take tag numbers off your cars so they could harass you." ACIPCO officials also attempted to intimidate movement activists: "On my job at ACIPCO, all the blacks had been called into the auditorium and told that if you're ever caught in a demonstration or if you were ever arrested because you were demonstrating, you're automatically discharged. [It was] another fear tactic."

YOU STILL HAD THAT DRIVE

My mother was from Talladega, Alabama. She was born there. And my father was from Hollins, Alabama, where I also was born. I was brought to Birmingham as a baby, and that's where I was raised in a neighborhood called Kingston. I have one brother who's older than I am, and I have a sister younger.

I think my mother had a third-grade education and my father—I believe it was about seventh [grade]. He did more maintenance work for various companies. He would work one place, finish that job, and go somewhere else. My mother did nothing but domestic work outside of the house. As a matter of fact, this white lady she was doing this work for lived about three blocks from where we lived, so she was able to walk to work. This lady had two children. We were about the same age. We played around somewhat until we were told as to what we could do and how far we could go into the house. But generally we played outside. Most of the men in Kingston worked at Stockham [Valves and Fittings Company]. Then there were people at ACIPCO, Conner Steel, and Virginia Steel.

The community itself was like family. It was mostly homes, not apartments. The house I was raised up in was a duplex, but there were very few duplexes around in that community. We had a lot of fun because we manufactured our games: spinning tops, hopscotch, and that type of thing. We all were like family and skeptical of outsiders. You had to know someone in Kingston in order to be allowed to stay. You know how kids are. If they see something or someone they don't know, and if they don't like their answers, we would run them out of Kingston.

I started school at Kingston Elementary and stayed there until the sixth grade. From the sixth to the eighth grade, I went to East Avondale School. And after graduating the eighth [grade], I went to the ninth and tenth [grade] at Ullman and then the eleventh and twelfth at Parker High School.

Parker was great fun. It was the most exciting place to be. Wearing uniforms—it just made you feel proud. Up until your junior year, you wore blue and white, or the boys could wear khaki pants and a white shirt. The girls always wore blue and white. When you got to be a senior, then you were something then. Then you had the option to wear khaki or black pants and white shirts. You could wear a tie. You felt important, you really did. And I think it's a good thing.

I wanted to play football, and [Parker coach] Major Brown said I was too small. I was weighing about 160 pounds. We had these huge people there then, and I wanted to play right tackle, and he wouldn't permit it. It was rough during those days. He wanted me to be a quarterback. I told him, "No." I told him I wanted to hit, not get hit. And so I decided I just wouldn't play football, so I joined the choir under Mr. Henry. At that time, my girlfriend was already in the choir, and she could sing well, too, so that was one of the reasons I wanted to be in the choir. Of course, later on we got married. That was my first wife. But I made the grades and the honor roll. I was vice president of the senior class. It was during the time when all of us hated to graduate. Oh, everybody was in tears. They didn't want to leave school. They knew that after graduation, we wouldn't see each other. They had become your friend.

I finished high school in 1949. I left and went to Chicago. I wanted to go to college at Chicago University and wasn't able because I did not have the financial support.[1] My parents could not afford it. So I was there for about three months before I came back. In 1950, I decided to get married. I had already considered volunteering to go into the service. After deciding to get married, I decided I wouldn't go into the service. So I decided to get me a job. I worked at TCI out in Fairfield. And I worked there two years until I got laid off. I was just a laborer, working on construction. I was buying my home. Two coworkers, Will and Scarbrough, had signed the note for me to buy the house. I assured them that I would pay my debt at the credit union. So in the meantime, I was going over the mountain cutting grass, trying to make out until I could find a job. And then finally, after about two weeks, I got hired at ACIPCO. With my first paycheck, I paid the credit union off. I paid three house notes out of that money. My notes were only $49.50 per month.

When I first started at ACIPCO, I worked as a laborer. I worked there, and I was instrumental in trying to get ACIPCO integrated. We had formed an equal opportunity committee. And that was back in the early '60s. I worked with them and was instrumental in being one of the thirteen individuals who filed suit against ACIPCO at the time.[2] I went from a laborer to what is known as a craftsman job, as an annealing oven operator.[3] I had guys working under me, and from there, in 1975, I was promoted to supervisor. Of course, now, all of this was due to the fact that I had previously filed suit so that when these positions opened, I would be one of the ones that was chosen.

Every black man was a laborer. Whites—it didn't make any difference about age, whether they were eighteen or nineteen years old—if they were hired there, they were your boss. So you had to do whatever they said do. There was no work for a white man to do except certain jobs. They watched the blacks work. Blacks did all the heavy work. It was manual labor. It wasn't automatic nothing: pushing wheelbarrows, shoveling sand, and using a pick to dig ditches and things of that nature. I was there thirty-eight years.

• • •

I remember when the NAACP was outlawed. My understanding is that the state wanted the records of those individuals who were members. I was a member, and the state was denied the membership list. So they decided they wouldn't permit the NAACP to operate in the state of Alabama. This is when the Alabama Christian Movement for Human Rights was formed.[4] I was one of the initial members when Rev. [R. L. Alford] was the first president for a short period of time.[5] It was exciting, really, in the sense that we now [had] something or some leaders that could support us and announce what to do as far as Jim Crowism and that kind of thing. We were pretty proud about that. As far as fear was concerned, yes, everybody was afraid. That was a time when Ku Klux [Klan], the White Citizens' [Councils], and Asa Carter were on the scene.[6] They were threatening organizations, and Carter was a fanatic.

But [they were] really no more troublesome than the police. We had to be extra careful about being associated with these various [civil rights] organizations. I can recall many, many times when we would have our mass meeting, police would come around and take tag numbers off your cars so they could harass you. I remember one Sunday, my wife and I were getting ready to go to a movie. I was stopped, and my wife and I noticed the police had been trailing me, but I knew I hadn't been speeding. I had just bought a brand-new '56 red-and-white DeSoto. I remember he was trailing me, but I wasn't in any violation or anything. So he finally stopped me around Thirty-fifth Street, and I sat in the car. He came to the car and asked me to get out. I asked him, "For what?" He said, "You were speeding." I said, "No, I wasn't speeding." He said, "You disputing me, Boy?" I said, "No, but I wasn't speeding. Ask my wife. She'll tell you. She's sitting right here. She can tell you." So, he said, "Well, I said you were speeding." I said, "Okay, if you say I was speeding, I was speeding." He said, "Well, I ain't going to give you no ticket this time, Boy, but I better not catch you driving back down here again." I said, "Well, okay." And we drove on off.

That is just one of several incidents in North Birmingham. My next-door neighbor asked me to pick him up from work one night. My cousin was here, and he worked at ACIPCO. He was new in the city, from Gainesville, Alabama. He had just finished high school. I let him drive the car. We arrived to pick my neighbor up and were parked waiting for him. There were two policemen that were bystanders. They came up to the car while we were parked and asked my cousin where was his driver's license. He's a country boy, and he couldn't hardly talk [because he was] afraid of what might happen. [One of the policemen] said, "You from Gainesville? What you doing way up here?" [My cousin] said, "I work up here. I live with my cousin, and I work up here now." [The policeman said,] "Where you say you from?" He said, "Gainesville, Alabama." "Who your folks?" [the policeman asked]. He began to tell him John Scott and Lena Scott were his grandparents. That's who raised him. They just kept agitating and irritating him. I said, "Officers, if we haven't done anything wrong, leave us alone." "Oh," [I thought,] "What did I say that for?" [The policeman] jumped up. He told the other policeman—there were two of them—to pull me out of the car. I said, "You're not going to pull me out. I'll get out of my car." So I got out of the car and stood up. I had a hat on. [One of the policemen] said, "Boy, don't you interfere with me." I said, "We were sitting here, bothering nobody, and you came up, and you've asked him several questions, and he's answered them, and you just keep irritating him about the same thing." "Boy, you interfere with the police," he said. "Anybody ever tell you when you talk to a policeman, you're supposed to pull your hat off?" I said, "No. I've never heard nothing like that in my life." [He said,] "Pull your hat off." I said, "I'm not going to pull my hat off." So he took his flashlight and knocked my hat off, and then he wanted me to pick it up. I said, "I'm not going to pick it up. I didn't knock it off, and I didn't pull it off. I'm going to leave it down there." [He said,] "So, you just want to be a sassy nigger, now, don't you?" I said, "No. I'm just being frank with you. We were just sitting here. We were waiting on this man to take him home." By that time, Charles Breeding came around. I was standing outside, and they had me hemmed in. He said, "Goodgame, what's wrong?" I said, "These police got me held up talking about we interfering with them." Charles said, "Them the same son of a bitches that stopped me last night." So it appeared [the police] got afraid when he said that. There were four of us. There was my cousin and myself and Charles and another guy that came out. So it appeared this frightened them. [The policeman] told me, he said, "Come out to the back of the car. Boy, I ought to beat your brains out down here." By that time, Charles said, "Come on Henry, let's go." So they told me, "Boy, if I ever catch you coming through here again, I'm going to kill you." I told my cousin, "Let me drive." I wanted to drive, because if I see [the policeman], I wanted to run over him. But he didn't let me drive. After we got home, he told my wife, "Henry wanted to kill a policeman. He was going to hit him." She said, "Well, I'm glad you were with him, because he would have." And I would have during that time. Because he told me don't ever come back through there, I decided I would. I came back through there the next night, and nothing happened.

· · ·

At twenty-one years of age, I went down to register to vote, and the questionnaire had seventy-five to one hundred questions. They asked me questions about state and national elected officials. So, this little man—he was nasty—was the [registrar]. When I finished filling out the form, I walked right up, gave it to him. He said, "Well, Boy, you missed one question." I said, "I missed one? Which one did I miss?" "I'm not going to tell you," [he said]. "You just go on back and come back in six months." So I didn't pass. When six months came around, I went back, and the strangest thing happened. When I got there, this same man was there. He said, "You missed one question." I said, "Yes, that's what I was told." He said, "Do you know the answer?" I said, "Yes, I know the answer." He said, "Okay." He never asked the question. He wrote me up, and I became a registered voter. He didn't ask me one question. That's all he said, and I became a registered voter. During that time, you had to pay the poll tax, too. So I paid my poll tax, and I became a registered voter and been one ever since.[7]

You had that fear that something was going to happen, but you still had something else beside that fear that pushed you forward. It overrode fear and the inferiority complex. It was that drive that you had to express yourself. You said to yourself, "I don't like it, and I want to do something about it." And so you get at those marches. Yes, you're afraid, but you still had that drive. You still had that incentive to go on in spite of what might happen. On my job at ACIPCO, all the blacks had been called into the auditorium and told that if you're ever caught in a demonstration or if you were ever arrested because you were demonstrating, you're automatically discharged. [It was] another fear tactic.

In my first demonstration, I had my twelve-year-old daughter with me. I had recently had a hernia operation and was still sore. I knew I couldn't keep up if anything happened. So I was near the back. We were attacked with the dogs, and we all dispersed and ran. On another one I was involved in, one of my coworkers was accused of hitting a policeman with a brick. He was arrested, but it could never be proven that he threw the brick. He denied that he ever participated in the march, so the company couldn't fire him immediately. They harassed him, and after about a year he was fired. A Rev. Grier that worked out there got fired because he was an activist. They found him out and fired him.

One of the last demonstrations, we left New Pilgrim [Baptist Church]. They had a fire hose when we got to the corner, and of course I'm way back in the back, so I couldn't hear everything that was going on. I understood that Bull Connor had ordered them to use the hose. They just refused to use the hose. The fireman just refused. Eventually, I noticed that we were moving. So we were going across Sixth Avenue South, and at that time it was known as Ellsberry Park. We went over there, and we knelt down and we prayed. Of course, they wouldn't allow us to get any closer, but we knelt down there and prayed.[8]

It is obvious that some progress has been made in the area of hotels, motels, and eating establishments. However, racism is still a problem.

NOTES

BCRI OHP, vol. 20, sec. 1 (July 31, 1996). Edited, annotated, and abridged by Horace Huntley and John McKerley.

1. Goodgame is probably referring to the Chicago Undergraduate Division of the University of Illinois, which later became the University of Illinois, Chicago (Office of the UIC Historian, History of the University of Illinois at Chicago, http://www.uic.edu/depts/uichistory/index.html [accessed August 18, 2008]).

2. In 1966, Goodgame and other ACIPCO employees filed a class-action suit under Title VII of the Civil Rights Act of 1964, charging that the company used a variety of discriminatory tactics to limit African Americans to low-level, poorly paid jobs. In 1974, the U.S. Court of Appeals for the Fifth Circuit found in favor of the plaintiffs and ordered the company to end the illegal practices and to provide back pay to all workers who had experienced discrimination (*Rush Pettway Et Al., Etc., Plaintiffs-Appellants, v. American Cast Iron Pipe Company, Defendant-Appellee, U.S. Equal Employment Opportunity Commission, Intervenor*, 494F.2d 211 [5th Cir. 1974], http://bulk.resource.org/courts.gov/c/F2/494/494.F2d.211.73–1163.html [accessed April 10, 2009]).

3. An annealing oven is "a special furnace, or chamber, that controls the cooling process of glass by slowly lowering the temperature to prevent the glass from breaking into tiny pieces" (Florida State University Museum of Art, Trial by Fire: Contemporary Glass, Glossary of Terms Related to Glass, http://www.fsus.fsu.edu/SchoolInformation/SchoolRelations/Partnerships/Exhibitions/trialbyfire/glossary.asp [accessed April 23, 2007]).

4. The state's injunction against the NAACP included a one hundred thousand dollar fine and a demand that the organization turn over its membership records.

5. Shuttlesworth was elected as president and Alford was elected first vice president (Glenn T. Eskew, *But for Birmingham: The Local and National Movements in the Civil Rights Struggle* [Chapel Hill: University of North Carolina Press, 1997], 125–26).

6. Asa "Ace" Carter was a Birmingham radio personality who became an influential anti-integrationist militant during the 1950s. For a brief account of Carter, his affiliation with the Klan and White Citizens' Councils, and eventual fall, see Eskew, *But for Birmingham*, 114–18. See also Diane McWhorter, *Carry Me Home: Birmingham, Alabama: The Climactic Battle of the Civil Rights Revolution* (New York: Simon and Schuster, 2001), 125.

7. For a description of black efforts to organize voters in Birmingham during the 1940s and early 1950s, see Eskew, *But for Birmingham*, 76–78. On white registrars' attempts to limit participation by black voters, see also James Armstrong, BCRI OHP, vol. 4, sec. 5 (April 10, 1995).

8. There are several versions of this encounter. See, for example, Emma Young, BCRI OHP, vol. 10, sec. 4 (September 29, 1995). See also Andrew M. Manis, *A Fire You Can't Put Out: The Civil Rights Life of Birmingham's Reverend Fred Shuttlesworth* (Tuscaloosa: University of Alabama Press, 1999), 373–74.

JOE N. DICKSON

JOE N. DICKSON was born in Montgomery, Alabama, on March 5, 1933. After Dickson's father, a worker at a cotton mill, died of pneumonia in 1938, his mother brought him and his siblings to live in Birmingham with her sister and her family. Like many of the children of his generation, he remembered his mother's struggles to make ends meet as a domestic worker. "Black people didn't want you to give them anything," he recalled, "so they would work, work any number of jobs."

After a brief stint in the military, Dickson returned to Birmingham, where he attended Miles College, a historically black college founded in Fairfield, a suburb of Birmingham, in 1905. At Miles, he became active in the student-led voter registration drives and antisegregation campaigns of the late 1950s. Although the school's administrators supported the registration drives, they took a cautious approach to more direct forms of student-led protest, citing the need to raise money in the white community. For Dickson, this attitude offered proof of the need for community self-sufficiency, a principle he had learned as a student and later promoted as an employee at A. G. Gaston's Booker T. Washington Insurance Company and as an organizer during the selective-buying campaign initiated by Miles College students against white-owned downtown stores in March 1962. Although he worked for a black-owned firm, Dickson still confronted the tension between employment and the potential for arrest that came with nonviolent direct action. While Gaston came to support the movement financially, he also feared that mass protest could harm the community and the respectable image that he and other local black leaders strove to maintain. One of Gaston's associates told Dickson that Gaston had "put his money in." "He's with us, but we have to have men who are working. We don't want you to go to jail anymore."

WE DIDN'T OCCUPY THE LAND

My mother was born in Hope Hull, Alabama, a few miles outside of Montgomery. My father was born in Fort Deposit, over in Lowndes County. Each of them migrated to Montgomery, and they got married there. I was born in Montgomery in 1933, the third child in my family. I have one younger sister and three brothers now, but there were six of us. I had one older sister who died in infancy. We lived on the west side of town.

Montgomery had few schools at that time. I started school at Catholic kindergarten and left there and went to Loveless School. Mr. [A. H.] Loveless was an undertaker, and they built a school on the west side and they named it Loveless School. It went from elementary through high school.

My mother worked in the white folks' house, and my father worked at a cotton mill in Montgomery. He died rather young. He caught what they called "eight-day pneumonia." Back then, if you caught pneumonia, they didn't have penicillin and all this other stuff to get the fever down. If you made it through the eighth day, you would live. If you didn't, you died. Now, of course, they've got that under control, but in 1938 he died. I was five years old.

Black folk at that time weren't getting the health care they needed. Immediately after my father died, my mother's sister died. She had four children, and her husband had died with tuberculosis, [and] my mother had her five children, too—my daddy died in May of 1938 and my brother was born in June. About nine months after my mother's sister died, their oldest sister, who was living in Birmingham, came to Montgomery. She decided that my mother, who was the youngest, was overwhelmed. She said, "Rachel, you can't take care of these children. You're nothing but a child yourself." She brought all of us back to Birmingham, out to Fairfield, to live with her, her husband, and one child. My mother raised me, my older brother, and my other two brothers and sister by herself here in Birmingham. She was a domestic.[1]

It wasn't hard then to find employment, because if you could clean up the house—wash, iron, cook, and sew—you could get a job. I remember my mother having two or three different jobs. When my father died, we didn't qualify for social security because the Social Security Act was just really coming into effect. Welfare was just unthinkable. Black people didn't want you to give them anything, so they would work, work any number of jobs. They didn't call it welfare. They had another name for it. You could not, back during this time, go to anybody else's house to eat. I don't care how hungry you were, you had to refuse. If [your parents] found out about it, then you had a reckoning coming.

One of the things I guess all children grapple with is how to relate to other children around you. I can remember our trying to associate with the other children around us. We were from Montgomery, and Birmingham was a larger city. Montgomery was more rural than Birmingham was, so we were from "the country." My uncle and aunt were kind of protective. They didn't want us to go out in the yard because they knew we were new in the city, and they didn't know how we would mix in with people. I remember that being a problem.

When I was in the third grade in Montgomery, I had gotten to skip a grade because my oldest brother was a good teacher and he taught me well my ABCs. I could read. One of the most distressing things to me when we got to Birmingham was that they put us back a grade. I just couldn't understand why they would do that, but they were doing that with just about everybody. I never understood that to this day. It didn't hurt me, but it was kind of tough.[2]

When we got to Birmingham, we went to Sixty-first Street School, which is now Robinson Elementary School. It was a good school. The teachers were very interested in the students. Mrs. [Esther] Robinson was an older lady, and you really had strict discipline there. You didn't play around. You had to get your lessons. I guess one of the most memorable things was that my mother had to be over the mountain to serve breakfast for the people she worked for, which meant she had to get up early. Everybody rode the bus; nobody had a car. She would get up and cook, and my oldest brother would see to it that we would have food to eat. When Mama came back, the dishes and everything had to be clean, so we washed the dishes before we left for school, and we got the other children ready to go. As a consequence, I would be late every morning. George Albert's mother taught me in the fifth grade. One day I got to school crying, and Miss Yarbrough came to the desk, patted me on the back, and said, "Son, just get here. Just get here." I've never forgotten that.

Even before I left [elementary school], I got one of the best lessons of my life. We had spelling matches within the school. One day I intentionally sat down and wouldn't spell a word. I thought I was smart, just frolicking and trying to show the teacher what I was going to do. Our class lost the spelling match because I wouldn't do anything. I was clearly the best speller, but I was devilish and didn't want to be a team player. They couldn't win without me, and I showed them that they couldn't win without me, which only showed that I wasn't a team player. It didn't make sense. I looked at Mrs. Moore when I sat down. She just shook her head. She said, "Joe Nathan, come back. I want to see you." She called a word out to me and I spelled it. She took a strap, and she beat me and told me one thing that I've never forgotten. She said, "You take too much for granted. You play too much. Do not take things for granted. You got to get serious about yourself." I guess the strap got me on business. I've been serious ever since then.

I was anxious to get to high school. I wanted to go to high school, but I had this proclivity to take up other folks' burdens and get into trouble. I guess the thing that saved me was the fact that I had to get my lesson. At Fairfield [Industrial] High School, you had to get your lesson. If somebody were fighting, they would come and get me to fight for them. If someone were fighting my brother, they'd come get me. If my brother wouldn't fight, I'd get mad and fight. When I look back at it, I think I had a chip on my shoulder. It might have been I was mad because my father was dead or my mother couldn't put in any time with me. Back then you had the "high yellows" and the "black" ones and all this other stuff, and you'd think people were picking on you. It was just a situation where I was not mature and didn't understand what was going on. And I was really strong. I could wrestle anybody.

I was just the guy that you'd get to solve a problem. Somebody told me once, "If you were in New York, you'd probably get a job with the Mafia because of what you try to do." But I guess I was just a confused youngster.

The thing that I think saved me was that the teachers took a lot of interest in me. The fact that Mrs. Moore took that time out with me to tell me about taking so much for granted was a blessing. When I got to high school, I was always the leader of the class. I was the president of my class from the time I was in the first grade until I was a junior in college. Kids liked me. I don't know why, but I could get along with people.

I was a paperboy. While I was going to the fifth grade, I had a job. I fed the hogs in the morning [before] I left home, and I fed them in the evening when I came back. I started throwing papers when I was in the sixth or seventh grade. I worked for Mr. [George] Burt, who had the route for the *Birmingham Post-Herald*. You'd graduate to working as a news carrier. You'd sell the *[Baltimore] Afro American*; you'd sell the *Pittsburgh Courier*; you'd sell the *New York Amsterdam News,* the *Birmingham World,* the *Birmingham Mirror,* and you'd make two pennies. I didn't have any problems then because I was making money. I always had to take the money I made home because my mama needed it. When I graduated to the white folks' paper, I began to work with Wilbert Hughes and Edwin Hicks. Wilbert had the largest route, and Edwin had the next-largest route, and Wilbert would put the different sections of the papers together. When I got to about the ninth grade, Wilbert was graduating from high school. That meant that I was the big man in Fairfield then because I had that big paper route. I hired my brother and other people to help me sell the paper, and I got to be known. I was popular. I was elected president of the senior class. It's not so much that I was smart, but people knew me and liked me, and they would vote for me.

I guess the other thing that kept me all right in school was that I made the honor roll every six weeks. The reason I made the honor roll was that my oldest brother was on the honor roll. Mr. [E. J.] Oliver would parade us across the stage in front of everybody and he'd say, "Joe Dickson, honor roll, junior 3–C, second six weeks is maintaining." He'd tell how long you'd been on the honor roll. So, I said to myself, "I'm not going to let my brother beat me." That is why today I am against magnet schools. I'm against separating different types of students from one another because you take away competition. When I was in school, whoever was the smartest had [one] seat. The next smartest had [the next] seat. Everybody was trying to outdo the other one and get their lesson in order to be recognized in the community. That was the thing that saved me—that and the fact that every time the man put you out of school, you had to bring your mama back. You'd get the punishment from him before you left, and if your mama couldn't go to the white folks' house and work because of you, she'd tell you, "Boy, I don't know what I'm going to do with you! Come on. Let's go on up there."

Finally, in the eleventh grade, I got into trouble. I was suspended from school. Mr. Oliver called me to come back, and he did something for me that stuck with me. I'd use it for my family. He made Robert Lee Taylor and me come across the stage, sit down in assembly, and apologize to all of the students at Fairfield Industrial High School for my behavior and the way I was acting. I think Principal E. J. Oliver was probably the best educator in the state of Alabama since Booker T. Washington. Of course, there were a number of people during that time that could hold a candle to him. I think the thing that made Mr. Oliver such a great educator was that he adopted the principles of Booker T. Washington—that you've got to learn how to do something with your hands as well as your head. When you finished Fairfield Industrial High School, you could go on to college and compete.[3]

You could also go into the job market and get a job. Mr. Oliver challenged us to reach for the top. One of his sayings was "There's room at the top." "You know why?" [he'd ask]. "Just talk with everybody on the bottom. That's why you've got to reach for the top. You've got to reach for the stars." And he pushed it. He pushed it and he preached it. Then he put you in the Hall of Fame. Long before anybody had a Hall of Fame, Mr. Oliver had the hall where he was showing who had gone to Fairfield Industrial High School, what they had achieved, and how they were making their name and presence felt in the community. Also, he did something that a number of other principals were doing. Mr. Oliver made sure that we knew something about ourselves as a people. Before you finished Fairfield Industrial High School, you had to read Booker T. Washington's *Up from Slavery*. You had to outline it. That meant that if you went out on a job, you did it like Booker T. Washington did it. You did it to perfection, and then when you wiped the white handkerchief across it, you picked up no dust.

We also had Carter G. Woodson's book, *Negro History*, there.[4] That was a requirement. Later on, after I had gotten out of law school and was walking through the alley one day, Mr. Oliver was coming toward me. He said, "Boy, wait a minute." He stopped me. He said, "I'm proud of you. I always knew you had it in you. I just didn't know how to get it out of you." I said, "I've got one question to ask you. How did you get *Negro History* taught in the school?" He said, "When I took the job at Fairfield, I made a deal with the superintendent of schools, Mr. [B. B.] Baker. I told him if I don't teach *Negro History* and I don't give these people the opportunity to know something about themselves, we're lost." He said that the man told him, "Go ahead and teach it. If they catch you, I'll swear I didn't tell you to do it." It paid off.

After high school, in 1952, I got a job at Vulcan Furniture Manufacturing spot-welding chairs for dinette sets. I was drafted from Vulcan Furniture

Manufacturing in 1953 in June. That was during the Korean War. I went to Fort Jackson [South Carolina]. From Fort Jackson I went back to Camp Rucker [Alabama]. By the time I got to Camp Rucker, they had called a truce and pulled back to the Thirty-eighth Parallel. I guess Mama prayed real hard that we didn't have to go and fight over there. I stayed in the army for two years and was discharged and came back home.

I had saved eighteen war bonds, one for every month. Mama had saved a little bit, and the army paid me. Naeree [Nathaniel Reed] got me a job up at Lloyd Noland [Hospital]. He was a cook. He said, "Come on, Joe. I'm going to make you a pot washer. You washed pots in the army. You'll be a good pot washer." So I went up there and worked in the kitchen at Lloyd Noland Hospital. All the while I was up there, my mama would ask me what I was going to do. I said, "I'm working." It was getting close to September and time to start at Miles College. She asked me again, "Boy, you going to school?" I said, "Mama, I've got a job." I had already argued with her and told her that I didn't need her to keep my money. I was grown. I had been in the army. She went to the fifth grade, maybe. She said, "You're going to school, Boy. You finished high school. I couldn't go to school. You need to go." The time was getting closer and closer.

You know what the problem was? The problem was that I had spent the money I had saved and didn't have money to go to school with. I'll never forget it as long as I'm black. She said, "They tell me that if you've been in the army, Uncle Sam will pay your way to school." She also said, "If you don't go to school when somebody will pay your way, Boy, you ain't got as much sense as I thought you had." That killed me. I came out here, out to Miles.[5]

It cost fifty-eight dollars a quarter. My mama gave me two fifty-dollar bills that she had tied up in a stocking. I came out and paid to get in school at Miles. Then she gave me the money to buy my first books. That was an agonizing thing for me to have to be pushed to go to school. Once I came to Miles, I was a leader in the class. I became president of the largest freshman class they ever had. I became very active. We did fashion shows. We did a number of things to raise money to help the school. There was tremendous school spirit at that time. This was the time when the veterans were coming back from the Korean War. More women were coming to school. Our people were really into it because this was right after *Brown v. Board of Education* [the 1954 U.S. Supreme Court decision that overturned state laws segregating public schools by race].

Dean Pearson and some Alpha [Phi Alpha] men on campus decided that we were going to get people to register to vote. We were attempting to get all the fraternities and sororities onto campus, so we brought in Cecil B. King as a teacher. He was a Kappa [Alpha Psi] and brought Kappa in. I had pledged with the Alphas, but they allowed me to leave the Alphas and go to the Kappas when it was determined that we were going to bring the Kappas onto the campus. That's real strange, but we put it together.[6]

We started going down to the courthouse to get people to register to vote, and we were met with all kinds of opposition. The obstacles that they put in front of us were just superficial. You had to be able to read and interpret different things and tell who was the president, who were the congressmen, and who was this, and who was that. It was very subjective, and a lot of our people were disillusioned by some of the things they were requiring of us. Nonetheless, we did manage to become successful in our efforts to get blacks registered to vote. I had to do the same thing everybody else did. I had to answer the questions about who were the senators, how many [members] of the House of Representatives did [Alabama] have, and all that. I did it. At that time, I wasn't quite as mean as I am now or grew to be in dealing with people. We had good civics teachers at Fairfield Industrial High School. Mrs. [Ruth B.] Cook and those folks had drilled it into you. They made you read the newspapers so you would know what was going on. As a consequence, we could answer the questions fairly easily. But some of our people that went down with us, the registrars just wouldn't let pass. It was very subjective. In 1955, I registered to vote.

At Miles, we also served as role models to get other kids to want to come to college. When I got to my junior year, I became vice president of the Student Council. Jesse Walker was the president. This meant that the next year I was going to be president of the Student Council, which in my estimation was higher than being president of the class. We started protesting the situation here in Birmingham. We started complaining about the fact that they had these double standards and all the segregation was going on. Jesse Walker was the leader in this effort, and Jesse has never been given any credit for what he did. Jesse and myself and the rest of us would go up to Kelly Ingram Park. We couldn't go in it, but we would march around there protesting what was going on—no hiring of black people, the police officers, and strict segregation here in Birmingham. This was in 1955 and '56.

Kelly Ingram was a white folks' park. You weren't supposed to go in that park. One day it appears that we were going to be out there, so a white detective came to us and told us, "Look, I want y'all out of this park."[7] He said, "We got word that some Klan people are going to come through here and they're going to be shooting and doing some of everything. We don't want you in the park tonight. Don't be out here." He pleaded with us, so we went in the A. G. Gaston Motel and met in there. Word got back to the campus what was going on, and Dr. [George C.] Bell [president of Miles] called an assembly. He told us, "Young men and young women, you cannot lead demonstrations from out here on this campus because I'm in the business of educating young black people to face the world." He said, "I have to go and raise the money from whites, and whites are not in keeping with what you're doing. You will not lead demonstrations from on this campus." That was one of the reasons we [had gone] downtown. He went on to say, "You have to be sure that this is what you want to do. You have to understand that if you're going to fight, then you're going to have to take responsibility. You're going to have to be prepared to educate your young, take care of your school. You're going to have to be prepared to take care of all these things. You're not going to be able to ask the white man to do this for you because, young men and young women, you cannot fight and beg, too." The demonstrations got Jesse Walker suspended from school.[8] We finally got him back in school, and he graduated, but in the meantime, Fred Shuttlesworth was doing what he was doing over at [Bethel Baptist Church]. I started attending the meetings over at Fred's church in North Birmingham. Fred told us this was big. He said, "You students need to join with us in this fight that we have." We continued. We didn't stop.

When I graduated from Miles, I was the salutatorian of the class. In one of those slivers of time after school, I left and went to New York. When I went to New York, I saw Howard K. Smith on television with *Who Speaks for Birmingham?*[9] When that came on, then I realized that it was all out. I came back to Birmingham and went to work for Gaston at Booker T. Washington Insurance Company selling insurance. That gave me the opportunity and freedom to participate more in what was going on.

The movement was an effort that came from outside Alabama as well as inside Alabama. Things like the bombing of Rev. Shuttlesworth's church, the beating of the [Freedom Riders] at the bus station, the Klan meetings, and the beating of Mr. [James] Reeb—the white minister they beat so badly—all put the spotlight on Alabama. All this stuff was happening kind of simultaneously.[10]

But what really started the situation in Birmingham was the 1962 selective-buying campaign.[11] The president of Miles, Dr. Bell, died, and Dr. Lucious Pitts became president. Lucious understood. Lucious had been in Atlanta and working with the YMCA. He organized the selective-buying campaign, and I think it was the most effective buying campaign I had ever seen. Nobody was anywhere putting up signs. Nobody was screaming from anywhere about it. It was a method. God had to have been in it. It had to be the work of the Lord, because we managed to pull all those people out of the stores, and they didn't go downtown to buy. At that time, my brother, Luther, was a student out here. He was very active in the campaign. Frank Dukes was an excellent friend of mine, and he was one of the true leaders in the struggle.[12] We got everybody out of town, not buying. We were asking folks why, if we were spending our money, can't our women try on the hats or clothes? Why did they have two signs for the water fountain? You had to walk all the way back down to Fourth Avenue from downtown to use the bathroom. We just wanted to know why. Dr. Pitts said, "What we have to do is take away the money. We don't have any other weapons to fight with but our money." Finally, they agreed to take the signs down. The white folks took the signs down, and we let our people go back downtown to shop.[13]

After we got back downtown to shop, they put the signs back up. We had to go back at it again, and this is when we had to go into strict surveillance. We had to tell people, "If you go downtown and buy something, you're going to have to answer to us." We put up a watch to see who was having stuff delivered to them. We fronted them out: "You can't buy downtown! We're at war with this man. It's a nonviolent war." I went to GES Drugstore one day. We had people patrolling to see who was buying. My buddy came out of the store at the same time I did, and he said, "Hey." He eased up to me, and I said, "We aren't buying in these stores." He said, "I thought you were in here trying to slip [in] and buy something, but we're together." I thought he was trying to buy, and he thought I was trying to buy. We were on patrol. That was the way we did it.

Before the demonstrations and all of this other stuff, we met with white folks to try to get them to see that we weren't asking for much, that we just wanted a little dignity. We met with the white power structure. They said that nobody was dissatisfied but us niggers and that if we were so dissatisfied with Birmingham, they would give us fare to any city—New York, Chicago, or anywhere we wanted to go—and some money and help us get a job when we got there. That was cold. Dr. Pitts called meetings and began the selective-buying campaign.

Later, the demonstrations came. Before Dr. [Martin Luther] King came to Birmingham, he was in Albany, Georgia. A lot of people really don't understand the role that Ralph Abernathy played in getting us ready for Dr. King.[14] Abernathy could hold you there and keep you, make you want to wait until Dr. King came to speak. You could really feel the spirit moving through. We did not do this alone. It was a work of God, the more I think about it, the more I think about those meetings and how King showed real leadership. One night, I think we were at Sixteenth Street [Baptist] Church, and I was standing in the back. There was this guy there from the *New York Times,* writing.[15] This guy was looking at Dr. King, and he said, "Just look at him. Just listen at him. He shows superb leadership skills." Dr. King was speaking extemporaneously, and everybody referred everything to Dr. King. We waited until Dr. King got there. He was our leader. I hear black people tell you now that black folks don't need a leader, but every group of people I know that exist have leaders. Every animal that I know of, they have leaders. Fred Shuttlesworth was the leader here, and the [ACMHR] was the organization here.

A typical mass meeting was something that you probably would need to have witnessed yourself. There was singing. There was praying. They sang in the manner like the slaves sang, then they moved it on up to where we are today in singing and praying, speaking, and teaching. There was a feeling that would go through you. At the mass meetings, they would make the call for volunteers to go to jail the next day.

In my first demonstration, Fred Shuttlesworth led us to the federal courthouse steps on Fifth Avenue. We left from A. G. Gaston Motel. Rev. Shuttlesworth said, "Now, when you get down there on those steps, these white folks are going to offer you everything. Try your best to keep from leaving because we have to be arrested." When we reached the courthouse, the policemen kept saying, "Y'all go back. Y'all go back down there." When Bull Connor came, he had one of the captains tell us that if we went back, nobody would be arrested, and we'd just go on and forget about it. One or two people got up and left, but the rest of us stayed. Rev. Shuttlesworth led us in prayer. We stayed there and started singing. Bull said, "I'm asking you to leave. We're going to give you three minutes to leave, and then I'm going to arrest every one of you." We stayed, so Bull said, "Arrest them niggers." At that point, I wasn't thinking about being afraid that somebody was going to kill me. We had picked the federal courthouse steps because we didn't think they would arrest us on federal property. However, they did arrest us on federal property. This was in 1962.

I don't blame everything that happened in Birmingham on Connor. I blame it on the power structure. The power structure here was determined to keep things as they were. We were determined not to. White mobs had beaten Rev. [J. S.] Phifer and Rev. [Charles] Billups and Mr. [James] Armstrong and Fred with chains at Phillips High School and Graymont Elementary.[16] The Freedom Riders were coming in. By the time of the demonstrations, the situation was getting hot.

I think I was arrested three different times. I don't know how people kept going to jail. At the first arrest, Mr. Gaston must have known I was there, because I was the first man they let go. They said, "Joe Dickson, all the way."

I didn't know what they were talking about, but that meant that you could come out of the jail and walk out. They had key boys in there that would tell you what to do. They would get you up at three o'clock in the morning. Then they would get you up at four o'clock. Everybody would eat at one time. The key boy would tell you when to sit down and when to get up. While we, that first group, were in there—and this is very interesting—they were so nice. Fred said, "They're too nice. Something is wrong with these Birmingham police." We looked around, and Fred said, "We got to do something to make them show who they really are." There was a big fan up at the top of the jail. It wasn't putting out cool air, but it was making a lot of noise. A guy by the name of Smith who did transmissions looked up and saw a loose brick and was going to take the brick and put it in the fan to break the fan. I said, "No, Brother. You've got to realize that we don't do this. We are in here for civil disobedience." Fred said, "That's right. We aren't going to be arrested for tearing up property." So we let that slide. Finally, we got out of there.

Gaston was in complete understanding of what we were trying to do.[17] He also understood that when you got integrated with the white man, you were going to have to have some money. He told me, "You're one of our best men. We want you selling insurance. We don't want you marching, going to jail." So the next time I went to jail, Mr. [Clarence] Pegues, the agency director, came out there and told me, "Joe, the old man put his money in. He's with us, but we have to have men who are working. We don't want you to go to jail anymore." But then came that Saturday, when A. D. King and Rev. John Porter and Rev. [Nelson H.] Smith and all of them were going to jail. It was Easter Sunday [1963]. That was a time when I really understood what this movement was about and what the real deal was. I was sitting right next to Rev. Porter. They kept bringing folks into the jail. They had all the priests with their robes and things on. I said to Rev. Porter, "We're losing this one. They're mad with Dr. King, saying he broke the injunction because he told us to march. They put him in jail. You're in here. Rev. Smith is in here. A. D. is in here. We've lost this one." You know what Porter told me? He said, "No, no. We are not losing this one, and we are not going to lose this one. Martin is working from on high. He's not working from down here." I was out of jail that Monday morning on my way to Tuskegee, Alabama. They got me out of town so that I could do some work. A lady down there said that she could give me somewhere to stay. Mr. Pegues told me to go down there, ride around. I was not to do anything or say anything to anybody but just ride around all that week. They said, "We need you down there; we don't need you up here."

As I reflect on the struggle, I think about [May 7, 1963,] when we went up-town to get some kids out of [J. J. Newberry and Company]. Everybody was tearing up Newberry's and Kress's. They had gotten out of hand. Somebody called Sixteenth Street [Baptist] Church and said, "Come and get these children." We went up to get them. Fred had a white flag. He led the children back toward Sixteenth Street. When he got to the Carver Theater, the Birmingham Fire Department put a water hose on him and knocked him up against the theater. He went down. He got up with the white flag. They put the water on him again. Some of the brothers who weren't participating said, "Hey, don't put more water on him!" They didn't put any more water on him. He got on down to Sixteenth Street Baptist Church and got all the children inside the church. When he was going down the church stairs, the firemen put the water hose on again and knocked him down. We thought they had killed him.

I think that having known Emory Jackson and listened to him affected my development.[18] Emory was a Morehouse man. Martin King was a Morehouse man. They were about the struggle. I never shall forget Emory saying, "A Morehouse man won't pay to be segregated." That came from when they were in Atlanta, and they would go upstairs to the movie. I think about how we fought so hard to change things, but in 1988, I was down there with the [Alabama governor Guy] Hunt administration, and the *Birmingham World* came up for sale.[19] My wife and I didn't say anything. We certainly didn't need the paper, but I thought about Emory and all of the institutions—how we as a people always have to start over. We never keep going. We never move up. We move over. I thought about all this stuff we went through.

I'm a firm believer now. I know that when you're at war, if you win the victory, you have to occupy the land. When we won that victory in the 1960s, we didn't occupy the land. As a consequence, it's still a strong fight. What I learned from the struggle was that when whites told us that nobody was interested in this but a few Negroes and that when other blacks told us that it was a white man's world and we couldn't change it, they only charged the battery. That only makes me want to continue to fight because I firmly believe that this land is God's land. This land is our land, and we have to be respectful of each other. We should treat each other as we want to be treated.

On the day that we brought those children back to the church from uptown at Newberry's, some black guys who had not been in the march attempted to get in the line like they were marching back with us. A policeman—a white policeman—told them, "Don't you get in this line. Get back. You're not worthy." I knew then, and after I talked to Rev. Porter, that this isn't anything that we did. Trust me. When I reflect back, I think God had to have been in this.

NOTES

BCRI OHP, vol. 14, sec. 1 (April 15, 1996). Edited, annotated, and abridged by A. Michelle Craig and John McKerley.

1. Many black families were extended families during this period. See Andrew Billingsley, *Black Families in White America* (Englewood Cliffs, N.J.: Prentice-Hall, 1966), 19–21.

2. Just as students were often placed in a lower grade when they came from rural Alabama to Birmingham, the children of southern migrants in the North often found themselves held back. At least in part, this practice reflected the relatively poor state of most rural schools in the South, especially those for black children. See Horace Mann Bond, *Negro Education in Alabama: A Study in Cotton and Steel* (New York: Atheneum, 1969).

3. Booker T. Washington was born "a slave among slaves" in Franklin County, Virginia, in or around 1856. After attending Hampton Institute in Virginia, he founded the Tuskegee Normal and Industrial Institute in Alabama in 1881. Building on his training at Hampton, Washington designed the Tuskegee curriculum to inculcate the habits of "respectability" and "industry" that he believed were necessary to transform former slaves into prosperous farmers and mechanics in the South. At the same time, however, he deemphasized the importance of social integration with whites and black participation in electoral politics. This dual approach—which he articulated during a speech at the Atlanta Cotton Exposition in 1895 and later popularized in his widely read autobiography, *Up from Slavery*—catapulted him into the role of premier race spokesman until his death in 1915. See Booker T. Washington, *Up from Slavery* (New York: Penguin, 1986), vii–xliii, 1.

4. Dickson is likely referring to Woodson's *The Negro in Our History*, first published in 1922.

5. On the opportunities and limits of the Selective Service Readjustment Act (or GI Bill of Rights) for African Americans during this period, see Ira Katznelson, *When Affirmative Action Was White: An Untold History of Racial Inequality in Twentieth-Century America* (New York: Norton, 2005), 113–41.

6. Alpha Phi Alpha (founded in 1906) and Kappa Alpha Psi (founded in 1911) are intercollegiate black fraternities. Created as vehicles for race pride and professional development, the organizations also became venues for student protest. See Lester C. Lamon, "The Black Community in Nashville and the Fisk University Student Strike of 1924–25," *Journal of Southern History* 40, 2 (May 1974): 236.

7. See also Colonel Stone Johnson, BCRI OHP, vol. 1, sec. 3 (January 6, 1995).

8. See Diane McWhorter, *Carry Me Home: Birmingham, Alabama: The Climactic Battle of the Civil Rights Revolution* (New York: Simon and Schuster, 2001), 151–53.

9. CBS News sent reporter Howard K. Smith to cover the situation in Birmingham in response to the uproar created by Harrison E. Salisbury's articles in the *New York Times* (see n. 16). The resulting documentary, *Who Speaks for Birmingham?*, helped to place both the determination of ACMHR activists and the violence and intransigence (and, at times, incompetence) of the city's segregationist majority before a national audience. See Andrew M. Manis, *A Fire You Can't Put Out: The Civil Rights Life of Birmingham's Reverend Fred Shuttlesworth* (Tuscaloosa: University of Alabama Press, 1999), 255; McWhorter, *Carry Me Home*, 183–87, 190, 199, 200–210, 214, 223–26, 243–49, 373.

10. All of these events occurred during the period described except the Reeb murder. Rev. James Reeb was a white Unitarian minister and civil rights worker from Boston who was beaten to death by white attackers in Selma, Alabama, in March 1965 ("Gift by Spellman Honors Slain Cleric," *New York Times*, March 13, 1965).

11. See Manis, *Fire*, 307–9.

12. Frank Dukes, BCRI OHP, vol. 6, sec. 1 (May 11, 1995).

13. On the selective-buying campaign, see Glenn T. Eskew, *But for Birmingham: The Local and National Movements in the Civil Rights Struggle* (Chapel Hill: University of North Carolina Press, 1997), 198–205, 248–49. See Elizabeth Fitts, BCRI OHP, vol. 9, sec. 2 (July 19, 1995). On Lucious Pitts's cautious relationship to Shuttlesworth and direct action, see Manis, *Fire*, 305–6.

14. In December 1962, Martin Luther King had gone to Albany, Georgia, to help reinvigorate a civil rights campaign started by local activists and members of the Student Nonviolent Coordinating Committee. Abernathy, who had connections in Albany, had helped to arrange King's participation (Taylor Branch, *Parting the Waters: America in the King Years, 1954–63* [New York: Simon and Schuster, 1988], 540–41).

15. Dickson may be describing an encounter with Harrison E. Salisbury, a reporter who wrote two articles on racial and religious tensions in Birmingham for the *New York Times* in April 1960. The articles prompted members of the Birmingham city government to sue the paper for libel. See "Fear and Hatred Grip Birmingham," *New York Times*, April 12, 1960; "Race Issue Shakes Alabama Structure," *New York Times*, April 13, 1960; "3 In Birmingham Ask a Retraction," *New York Times*, April 27, 1960; "High Court Gets Times Libel Case," *New York Times*, January 8, 1963.

16. Shuttlesworth was the only minister beaten at Phillips High School. No one was beaten at Graymont, but the home of Arthur Shores, a black attorney, was bombed (Manis, *Fire*, 148–52, 401–3). On Graymont, see also James Armstrong, BCRI OHP, vol. 4, sec. 5 (April 10, 1995).

17. Although Gaston sympathized with most of the overall goals of the ACMHR and SCLC campaigns, he was a staunch critic of mass protest. As a leader

of the city's black professional class, he was also suspicious of Shuttlesworth's working-class demeanor and King's lack of any long-term stake in local conditions (Eskew, *But for Birmingham*, 234–35).

18. Emory O. Jackson was the editor of the *Birmingham World* and secretary of the Birmingham branch of the NAACP. Like Gaston, he was very critical of the tactics of the ACMHR and SCLC, and he disparaged Shuttlesworth and King as "upside-downers" for their focus on mass protest and immediate integration (Eskew, *But for Birmingham*, 260–61).

19. Dickson bought the *Birmingham World* from the Scott Newspaper Syndicate in 1988 (*Los Angeles Sentinel*, September 22, 1988).

JOHNNIE McKINSTRY SUMMERVILLE

BORN ON APRIL 20, 1933, Johnnie McKinstry Summerville grew up in Aliceville, Alabama. Summerville first came to Birmingham to attend Miles College. Following a stint teaching in Greene County, she returned to the city with her new husband, James, who had found work at ACIPCO. A participant at many mass meetings, she described how organizers used local issues to galvanize community support for the movement: "The mass meetings were really necessary because it was something that really made you think about what was going on. They discussed all the things that you knew and that were really close to you and your family. . . . They taught us that if you come in and help, then we all as a group can get more done than just a single person. This is what really interested us: people working together to cause these things to happen."

PEOPLE WORKING TOGETHER

My parents were from Aliceville, Alabama. That's in Pickens County. That's where I grew up until I finished high school and came to Birmingham to go to Miles College. I was the only child, and later on, when I came to Birmingham, my parents adopted a little baby boy.

In my hometown, there was a small school in the neighborhood, and our home [was] where the teachers lived. I never went to first grade because they would work with me at home. When it was time for me to go to first grade, I knew all of the first-grade material. It was just a happy, lucky thing for me that the teachers lived at our house. After we went to the fifth grade, I went to Summerville Industrial High School. It was very interesting because it was a high school and an elementary school combined. We were there with the larger children, but we were on a separate acreage.

We had the type of school where I did not stay at home during the week. I would go and board at the Summerville Industrial High School. They had a dormitory at the school. As a teenager, I would board the whole week and then come home for the weekends. We got buses. My parents didn't want me to walk to school. They would take me back on Sunday afternoon. This was the only school [in the] area that they had for blacks. The people over in Greene County would come over to our high school because their high school was so far away. After so many years, they finally got bus transportation to bring them all the way from Greene County to Pickens County just to go to school. Eventually they built a high school in Greene County. That was the first school that I taught in.

I was living in Pickens County and going across the bridge to Greene County to teach. I taught there for two years. Then I met my husband, James Summerville, and we got married. After we married, we came back to Birmingham for a while. We had our first daughter, who was born in Pickens. We lived in Birmingham, and my husband was working at ACIPCO, so I decided to give that teaching job up. I was tired of traveling back and forth from Pickens County to Birmingham for the weekend. My husband told me I needed to come home, and we established our home here.

When we first came to Birmingham, we lived in a community called Washington Park in North Birmingham on Sixteenth Street. I began to do substitute work at Hayes High School. Then I got a regular job in Montevallo at Prentice High School. I worked there for about three or four months, and then I was transferred to Shelby County at Alabaster High School. That's where I remained until I retired. It has been renamed to Thompson Middle today. It was the black high school then. After integration, the schools were in a cluster. We had only three schools, regardless of what color you were. That's where you had to go to school. It was really interesting because we didn't have the situations that you hear about [now]. We had been busing a long time before all the confusion became known. Busing was not the issue [for whites] prior to desegregation.[1]

By this time, we were living in the community of Titusville. The Klan had already started with the bombings. There was a bombing down on Center Street and Sixth Avenue. It was just a bombing out in the street at first, and then the second bomb went off right after that one. The first bomb was to get people out, and the second bomb was the one that had all these nails in it. That second bomb was meant to hurt people. It just so happened that no one went out for the first one, so when the second one went off, no one got hurt because they didn't go out. When they came with the bombing, we found that we were almost afraid to go to our house until we took a look around to see if there was a bomb on our porch or in our shrubbery. In all, we decided we needed to get involved because it was frightening.

We attended the mass meeting just about every Monday night to hear the speakers. We heard Dr. [Martin Luther] King and [Ralph] Abernathy and [Fred] Shuttlesworth. The mass meetings were really necessary because it was something that really made you think about what was going on. They discussed all the things that you knew and that were really close to you and your family. They discussed how we were living and the situations which would cause the people to become poverty stricken and in need of help. We got the impression that somebody was willing to help. Why can't we learn to help ourselves? This is what they were preaching to us: to do for ourselves. They taught us that if you come in and help, then we all as a group can get more done than just a single person. This is what really interested us: people working together to cause these things to happen. This was what the movement was about, and it really made a statement for us.

[Some people] were really afraid because a lot of times their livelihood and their support for their families depended on them keeping their jobs. Therefore, I felt like they said, "I have to keep my job and maybe let somebody else do it." That didn't frighten us. We still continued to go to the meetings and do whatever we could do. Whatever we needed to do to help the cause, we did. When we saw those little children, that is what really inspired us. People staying at home, staying out of it—that wasn't helping. Therefore, you needed to get involved in order to help others and to help yourself, too, because things were really frightening.

Our neighbors were some of the biggest supporters of the movement. Due to the bombings that took place in Titusville, the men cooperated with the security watch in our neighborhood. This had an impact in all the neighborhoods. As women, we didn't stay out to watch, but we would take the men doughnuts and coffee and whatever we could do to help and give them encouragement to let them know we were with them.[2]

When I was pregnant with my third child, they bombed the Gaston Motel [on May 12, 1963]. I was in the hospital, [and] my husband came over there to see me. I said, "What are you doing out? You should have just called." I [told him to] go back home because it was really disturbing that night. I said, "As soon as you get home, you call me and let me know that you made it home all right." I was at South Highland [Hospital], and that was not very far from our home. I wanted him at home; even the doctor had a pistol in his briefcase, because it was just strange. There was so much stuff just going on, and it was frightening.

I describe marching as being really rejuvenating. I was doing something that would maybe help the race and myself. We learned to work together. This is what it took then. There were other teachers that I knew that were out participating in the marches. We had to get out there and march and demonstrate. We really didn't think that we were going to get hurt or something was going to happen to us. We were out there trying to help. We were really putting ourselves on the line, and we never thought about it. We never thought about being killed, being hurt, or being fired. We knew that it was necessary, so we didn't think of it in that sense. We were just out there trying to help to see what we could do. One of my coworkers was Carlton Reese, and he was responsible for setting up the choir for the march.[3]

One of the main impacts of segregation was the shopping. Now shopping may be very simple, but before it was not. When we went to the store to buy something, and a black would be standing in line waiting to purchase their item, a white person would walk up to the counter and the cashier, who was also white, would stop and turn to wait on them. That had always irritated me. A lot of times I would call their attention to it by saying, "I think I was here first," to let them know I was not going to put up with it. It was my money, and I could spend it someplace else; I don't have to spend it in their store.

We were members of Southside [Christian Methodist Episcopal] Church. It was located on the south side at Seventh Avenue South. The church had to be moved to Martin Luther King Drive because the UAB Medical Center took over the space where our church was located. Our minister was active in the movement. He was marching and standing out so he could be seen. What really bothered me during this time was the threat of a bomb at our church. They had to get involved because sometimes during the service, someone would call to say there was a bomb there. The men would run around to see if there was one. That was the most nerve-racking thing that anyone could experience. It was frightening, and everyone would go home to see if there was a bomb in their shrubbery. It was really nerve-racking for me because my children and I had to sit in the car and wait for my husband to check to see if there was a bomb outside our home before we went inside. My children were too small to really know what was going on.

I remember one time we were downtown, and [the children] wanted something to eat. I told them, "We can't eat up here. We have to go back down on Fourth Avenue to eat." They asked me, "Why can't we go in here and eat?" They wanted to go up on Twentieth Street to eat. I told them, "Oh, we just don't want to go in there and eat. We'll go down here and eat." You tried to smooth it over the best that you could so they wouldn't be so hurt. Then they would run up to the fountain and drink water, ignoring the sign saying "Whites only." They would ask, "Why can't I drink here?" Unless you really lived that life, you really don't understand the difficulty, especially when you had your children with you, and they wanted to do these things. It was difficult trying to explain to them why they couldn't do whatever it is they wanted to do.

NOTES

BCRI OHP, vol. 21, sec. 2 (September 13, 1996). Edited, annotated, and abridged by A. Michelle Craig and John McKerley.

1. Busing became an issue for whites only when it was used as a tool for the integration of schools starting in the 1960s. In many states and localities with segregated schools, black children were routinely bused past white schools on a daily basis to maintain segregated educational institutions. On busing, see also Patricia Powell Berry, BCRI OHP, vol. 30, sec. 2 (August 13, 1997).

2. Some women did serve as guards. See LaVerne Revis Martin, BCRI OHP, vol. 19, sec. 3 (July 11, 1996).

3. Carlton Reese, BCRI OHP, vol. 15, sec. 3 (May 16, 1996).

JONATHAN McPHERSON

THE CHILD OF RECENT migrants from Coy, Alabama, in rural Wilcox County, McPherson was born in Fairfield (originally known as Corey and founded by TCI in 1910) on January 27, 1934. Inspired by his science instructors at Fairfield Industrial High School, he studied chemistry at Miles College and later completed a master's degree at Purdue University. Returning to Miles as a faculty member, McPherson quickly became embroiled in civil rights activism at the college and in the community. One of the earliest members of the ACMHR, he recalled the importance of a small cadre of dedicated movement activists in keeping the organization alive during the late 1950s. "There were a faithful few," McPherson recalled, but "there were so many who didn't participate." He was particularly involved with the growth of the movement at Miles, where he served as the faculty adviser to student activists. His participation, however, went far beyond simply dispensing advice and mediating between students and administrators. Describing the tactics that he and other activists deployed to enforce solidarity during the 1962 selective-buying campaign, McPherson recalled, "I remember one lady. We had to break the windowpanes out of her car when we heard that she was going downtown to shop. We couldn't do it all, but [Frank] Dukes and I put on some gloves and went to her house one night and broke all of her windows." For McPherson, as for Joe Dickson and many other student activists at Miles, "As far as we were concerned, it was war." After the 1963 demonstrations, community activists worked to maintain momentum in the movement, continuing "to have weekly meetings where we taught people how to pass civil service and voter registration tests." "I would guess that I was responsible for about five hundred people registering to vote. I had an old [1955] Plymouth car, and we had to pick the people up and take them down to the registrar. That was necessary because [we] had to help dispel the fear."

IT WAS WAR

There were seven of us in all—two girls and five boys. My parents didn't have very much education, coming up in rural and poor Wilcox County.

I lived in a section of Fairfield that is no longer there because of the freeway. It was known as Inglewood. It was destroyed by the freeway system. I went to Inglewood Elementary School. My first-grade teacher was Mrs. [Amanda] Rogers. My third-grade teacher [was] Mrs. [Betty] Buchanan, [who] still lives in Fairfield in a nursing home.

My daddy for most of his life worked at U.S. Steel. When the steel mills went on strike, he did odd jobs around the homes of whites, as most blacks [did] during that time. Mama just basically stayed in the house to take care of home.

Fairfield was a segregated society. Coming up was rough for a black person. Like most boys during that time, we would walk up and down the white community and knock on doors asking if we could cut their grass or any type of work. When I became a little older, I worked at the American Legion with my dad. They paid us twenty-five dollars a month. Basically, that was for cleaning up for them. There was a white lady that I worked for when I was in elementary school. Her name was Mrs. Sara Lee Howell, and her husband was named Jerry Howell. They had a son. I would do most anything around their house.

As a child in Fairfield, I remember one white policeman. His name was Dean. I never will forget Walter Dean. He was supposed to have been tough and rough when it came to blacks. Some black boys were walking through the white community. Dean came out and [said], "Y'all go back up in the nigger section." They started running. We were just fearful of the police during that time.

I went to Inglewood Elementary School from first through eighth grade. After that, I went to Fairfield Industrial High School. The principal was Dr. E. J. Oliver, and I am proud to refer to him because he was a disciplinarian par excellence. He always encouraged his students. If you were to check the records of Fairfield Industrial, you would find that many have gone on to achieve higher degrees in various areas. That is because of the kind of principal Dr. Oliver was. I was a member of the Socratic Debating Society and the Science Club. Mrs. Ruth B. Cook really motivated us in the Debating Club. In the eleventh grade, Mr. Henry Lewis Dobbins taught us physics. I was challenged by the various sciences, and Mr. Dobbins inspired me to go into chemistry as a profession.

After high school, I enrolled at Miles College. I went summer and winter, so I was able to finish in three years. I finished Miles in 1955. I then went to Purdue University for two years and completed my master's degree in 1957. In September 1957, I came back to Miles, and I started teaching. I taught at Miles until about 1965.

I was at the initial meetings that formed the [ACMHR]. My mother, father, and my uncle loved to attend the mass meetings. They admired Rev. [Fred] Shuttlesworth. He was a man who instilled courage into those who followed him. He was fearless, and through all of that, he kept a good sense of humor. The meetings were a result of people being oppressed—all people, regardless of how much money they had, regardless as to the extent of their education. You were just a black person. You were just a Negro. So we all felt the pain, and it was not difficult to get our people to come out to the meetings. There were a faithful few, [but] there were so many who didn't participate. There were many who now claim that they participated, and they didn't. Over the years, people claim they did things, they were involved, but those who were really there know who those are that were not there. There were some churches that even Rev. Shuttlesworth could not go to. I remember one meeting when Rev. Shuttlesworth and Dr. [A. G.] Gaston almost fought. Dr. Gaston admitted that he was afraid. They almost got into blows over a difference in philosophy. Shuttlesworth wanted to move, and Gaston was a little slower. Dr. Gaston did put his money out and supported the movement that way.[1]

Later on, we participated in the [December 1956] meeting when Rev. Shuttlesworth wanted to test segregation on buses in Birmingham. I remember [that] we all signed pledges or agreements that we would not participate in any violence and that we would not strike back if we were struck. We had our designated points where we would board the bus in downtown Birmingham and ride. I sat in the front of the bus and made sure that whites were behind me as well as in front of me. The only persons who started mumbling were coming from the back of the bus, black folk. So the driver stopped when he got to the car barn on Third Avenue and about Fourteenth Street. I heard him say, "We got a smart nigger on the bus." He got off and headed to the office. I guess he thought I was going to get up and move. I stayed there, and finally he came back. I was the only one who was in front in an integrated fashion. We had been instructed what to do: take a name, [and] a number, if we saw the badge, whatever, and, of course, I did that. He said, "Oh, I see you can write." But when he came back, he didn't say anything. So I rode the bus. I got off in Fairfield. I was not arrested.[2]

In [1957] or '58, we took civil service examinations. A law was on the book that a black person could not even take the civil service examination, but Rev. Shuttlesworth had gone to court and wore them out, so finally they had to remove that restriction. Every time blacks would go down, they couldn't pass, couldn't pass, couldn't pass. So I went down and I took several examinations—police, deputy sheriff, clerk II. I passed all of them, but the only one they mentioned was the policeman examination. They removed my name from the others. I saw it in the paper. They say I failed to come to the interview, but I never did receive a notice.

After being removed, I went down a second time to take the test. I passed it again. So they called me down for an interview, and I went. I remember Bull Connor. He asked me would I arrest a white man if I were hired as a policeman. I told him, "Sir, I would think if you hire me as a policeman in the city of Birmingham, you would want me to see that the laws of Birmingham are enforced. If a white man violated that law, my job would be to arrest him." And the next thing I knew, they took my name off the list and said I had moved to Hueytown.[3]

Although I was a professor at Miles College, if I had been offered a job as policeman, I would have taken it because we were trying to break down barriers. I didn't have a Ph.D. at that time. But I would have taken the job. Just like these schoolkids when [they] first [went] into the schools, we wanted to break barriers down. I would have accepted the job so that I would have paved the way for others and [helped] break the barriers down. But they never did offer me the job.

I was involved [in the movement] as a faculty member at Miles. With [Miles president] Dr. [Lucious] Pitts's blessings and encouragement, I was the faculty adviser to the students. Frank Dukes was the president of the Student Government Association.⁴ The word *boycott* you could not use because they had outlawed boycotting. So we just called [the student-led boycott] a "selective-buying campaign."⁵ We had an old mimeographing machine down in the printing room where we would print out leaflets to encourage our people not to shop downtown. [The leaflets asked,] "Why spend thirty-five dollars in this section of the store, and you can't spend thirty-five cents for a hot dog in this section?"

Sometimes we started rumors that were not true. I would say an elderly lady was beat [up] when she got off the bus. It was effective in keeping some [people away] from the stores. I remember one lady. We had to break the windowpanes out of her car when we heard that she was going downtown to shop. We couldn't do it all, but Dukes and I put on some gloves and went to her house one night and broke all of her windows. We wanted to let her know to stay out of the stores. As far as we were concerned, it was war. We wanted the people to stay out of the stores.

That effort really hurt the merchants. However, the business community refused to acknowledge the presence of the movement and Fred Shuttlesworth at first. At that time, we didn't even have a black attorney who would file these cases for Fred Shuttlesworth. I remember they had to get a black attorney out of Jacksonville, Florida. And so many preachers and churches would not allow Dr. [Martin Luther] King to hold meetings. There were just a few churches around the city [that welcomed King].

When we participated in that Good Friday march in [April] 1963, we met at [St. Paul United Methodist Church] down below Sixteenth Street. Andrew Young and Dorothy Cotton were there. They were keeping the audience inspired. We were just in anticipation. We wanted to put on our marching shoes. Dr. King was in conversation with the Kennedys—President [John F.] Kennedy and Attorney General [Robert F.] Kennedy—and they were trying to get him to call off the march. We had been there all that morning. About one o'clock, Dr. King came out and gave the word that we were going to march. We started and went up past Kelly Ingram Park and [turned] right at Fifth Avenue North and Eighteenth Street. A white policeman wheeled his motorcycle in front of Dr. King and said, "Halt! Halt!" We all fell down on our knees. They got the paddy wagon there and started loading us up. We went to jail. And that was my first time being in jail. But the unusual thing about it, when I got there, there was an elderly gentleman. His name was Mr. [William] Meadows. He was always at the movement, and he was there in jail. I said, "Brother Meadows, what are you doing here? You are too old." [He said,] "I am going all the way. I want to see what the end will be like."

Now we were in jail. You could hear how the people would converse with each other. They wanted to see how Dr. King was doing. But they had a way that they were singing, and you could hear the singing coming from those cell blocks. We were in one part, and they had put Dr. King in isolation. That's when we later found out that he wrote that "Letter from the Birmingham Jail." I stayed in jail overnight, and the next morning someone made bond for me. There were two other professors from Miles College who participated in that march. One was a white minister. His name was Rev. [Ralph] Galt. There was [also] a Christian Methodist Episcopal minister, Rev. Nathaniel Lindsey.

Even after the demonstrations of 1963, we continued to have weekly meetings where we taught people how to pass civil service and voter registration tests. I would guess that I was responsible for about five hundred people registering to vote. I had an old [1955] Plymouth car, and we had to pick the people up and take them down to the registrar. That was necessary because [we] had to help dispel the fear.

NOTES

BCRI OHP, vol. 46, sec. 4 (June 2, 1999). Edited, annotated, and abridged by A. Michelle Craig, Horace Huntley, and John McKerley.

1. Diane McWhorter also refers to the "rumor" of this confrontation between Shuttlesworth and Gaston in *Carry Me Home: Birmingham, Alabama: The Climactic Battle of the Civil Rights Revolution* (New York: Simon and Schuster, 2001), 335–36. On Gaston, see also Joe N. Dickson, BCRI OHP, vol. 14, sec. 1 (April 15, 1996).

2. See also Andrew M. Manis, *A Fire You Can't Put Out: The Civil Rights Life of Birmingham's Reverend Fred Shuttlesworth* (Tuscaloosa: University of Alabama Press, 1999), 115–16.

3. According to McWhorter, *Carry Me Home*, 286–87, this confrontation between McPherson and Connor took place at a city commission meeting on August 28, 1961. When Connor dismissed Frank Dukes and other Miles students who had presented the commission with a petition calling for the repeal of the city's remaining segregation ordinances, McPherson spoke in the students' defense.

4. See Frank Dukes, BCRI OHP, vol. 6, sec. 1 (May 11, 1995).

5. See Joe N. Dickson, BCRI OHP, vol. 14, sec. 1 (April 15, 1996).

LaVERNE REVIS MARTIN

LaVERNE REVIS MARTIN was born in Birmingham's Collegeville neighborhood on June 18, 1937. Martin grew up next door to Fred Shuttlesworth's family, and both her parents were community activists. Her
mother, like many other women activists, supported the movement by
giving her time and labor. While the division of some tasks conformed
to conventional gender roles—women acting as babysitters, for example—men and women also worked side by side, sometimes in unex-
pected ways. For example, Martin recalled that she and Minnie Eden
took shifts keeping guard over the Shuttlesworth home, and Martin
claimed to have once discovered a bomb. Although she did not men-
tion whether the women were armed during their shifts, she did suggest that like black men, black women struggled at times with the philosophy of nonviolence in the face of white supremacy. When a white
man spat in the face of a fellow activist during a sit-in at Woolworth's
Department Store, Martin recalled, he "smiled and didn't retaliate." "He
was nonviolent and did what we were supposed to do. I was real glad it
wasn't me, because I knew I wasn't nonviolent."

I'D SIT RIGHT OUT THERE WITH THEM

My father was from Meridian, Mississippi. He moved to Sumter County and
from Sumter County to Birmingham. My mother was from Birmingham,
Alabama. My mother finished Parker Industrial High School, and my father
stopped school at the fourth grade to help take care of his family. I was born
and raised in Birmingham, in Collegeville. I have six sisters and one brother.
I'm the baby girl, and there's one boy, who's the baby of all.

I went to Hudson Elementary School. It was fun. It was a neighborhood
school. Collegeville was a nice community. It was very quiet. A lot of schoolteachers and nurses lived in the community. There were mostly single-family
homes. That was before the times of the government housing projects. There
were homes everywhere until the government tore them down and built the
projects.[1]

My mother owned a cleaner's—Social Cleaners. My father worked at U.S.
Pipe and Foundry. He was also president of the Collegeville Park and Rec-
reation Board, so we were all raised in the park, the one park that we had in
Collegeville.[2] Everybody out there knew him. He was known as an activist,

even when he retired and went into the cleaning business. He helped my mother pick up clothes all over the neighborhood. My mother ran the cleaners, so there was always something for us children to do. We grew up working with the public. I grew up surrounded by entrepreneurs. My grandmother had a business too. It was a little café.

I went to ninth grade at the Annex and then to Parker High School. The Annex was a group of little houses where we had school. I was in the choir. I took business, sewing, dressmaking, and designing. That was something I loved to do. I did a lot of sewing in the neighborhood, and sometimes I did a little repair. After high school, I went to [the Alabama] State Vocational Trade School [now Lawson State Community College]. My daddy told me I had to go to school or get a job, so I decided to go out to vocational trade school and further my education in dressmaking and designing. After school, I got married. I have four children. There are two boys and two girls. I have twelve grandchildren.

My father was totally involved in the movement.[3] He was on the executive board of the [ACMHR]. He was there for all the planning committees and all the programs that were set up. We attended mass meetings. They were just something that you'll never forget. We would always sing "We Shall Overcome," and ministers would come from different churches. There were times when we would go from church to church to the meetings. There was always somebody guarding the churches, trying to keep us alive, but the meetings were fun. I went every Monday. My sister, Robbie Revis Smith; my brother, James Revis; and my sister, Alfreda, all went to the meetings. My mother didn't attend the meetings. My mother was like a support person. She was always there with the babies and lending a helping hand with her business, but she did not attend the meetings. She was supportive of the meetings. There were a lot of people in our neighborhood that went to the meetings and to jail—Frances Foster White, Virginia Clark, and different ones like that. A lot of people in Collegeville were faithful until they died.

My parents' house in Collegeville was on the corner right across the street from Bethel Baptist Church. The Shuttlesworth family lived next door to the church. My parents had a little room at their house that they enclosed on the front of the porch so that people who were guarding the Shuttlesworth home and the church would be able to keep watch. My daddy sat out there and guarded during a shift. I took turns and guarded my shift, too. I'd sit right out there with them. Dexter Brooks used to come out there and guard, and Miss Minnie Eden—different ones like that would come out there and sit.

At the time of the first bombing of Bethel Baptist Church [December 25, 1956], I was living in Chicago. At the time of the second bombing [on June

29, 1958], I discovered the bomb before it went off. I was working for a little restaurant, a small café, in Collegeville. I was the manager. My boss, Mr. Lomax, brought me home from work. As he went to put me out, I saw all this smoke up in the corner on the side of the church. I alerted the guards and went around to the back of the house. It was at night. It was like before day, in the morning. Nobody was sitting on the front in that little room that my dad had built for them. They were around back. That's why they missed it, so I went around there and told them there was a bomb out there.[4]

I don't know exactly who was out there, but John L. Lewis, whose real name was Will Hall, and Colonel Stone Johnson came out, and they walked toward the bomb. I was standing on the porch, and John L. Lewis lifted that bomb up and put it in the street. Colonel Johnson was right behind him, but John L. picked it up by himself and put it in the street. It went off and it made a big hole in the middle of the street. I saw it. My parents and my children were inside the house. My daughter, Kimberly, was a baby at the time. She was lying on the bed, and glass was just all around her. She has a scar on her forehead that resulted from that. When I looked around and tried to find her, I couldn't find her. One of the neighbors had carried her to the hospital. I went from hospital to hospital trying to find my baby. They stitched her up, and she has that scar today.[5]

After I discovered the bomb, and it went off, I was just horrified. The police came and they wanted to insist that I go down and take a lie detector test. They said that I must have planted the bomb, put the bomb out there. That's when my daddy was very outspoken, very firm. When he spoke, you listened. He told them that I was not going down there that night. He said, "You see the shape she's in! She's upset." He said, "We'll think about it, and if I decide she can, she'll come down tomorrow." I went down to the police station and took the lie detector test the next day. They put me through an ordeal. They asked me a lot of questions. They were really trying to say that Mr. Lomax and I planted the bomb. He had brought me home that night, so he had to take it, too. They were saying that we must have put the bomb out there ourselves. It was in a five-gallon can, and the bomb was down in there. But I passed the test. There were all kinds of questions. They wanted to know our background, and then they asked over and over whether we put the bomb out there. They wanted to know what we did afterwards—exactly, word for word. I told them for sure I didn't put the bomb out there.[6]

If we saw someone doing something, we would try to alert the police. That's basically all we could do. The police were not there to protect and serve, but we were supposed to be nonviolent. After one of the bombings, my sister, Alfreda, was trying to come to the house to see if my parents were hurt—to see how they were doing. She and her husband tried to get up to the house, and they almost went to jail for trying to get up there to see what was going on. The police would not allow them to go that way, even though the family was still up at the house. I was at the house. The police were very rude, acting like we were the enemy.

Actually, if you saw a policeman at that particular time, and you could outrun them, your best bet was to do that. They were putting your hands on top of the cars and doing all sorts of things to people at the time. They weren't there to protect and serve. I was stopped once, and they had me put my hands over the car. I never drank anything, so they couldn't get me with alcohol or anything like that, but they searched me right out there in the street. I didn't have any weapons. They talked nasty to me, saying some vulgar things to me, but they did turn me loose. Another time, I was coming down by A. G. Gaston Business College, and a police car got behind me. I put my foot on the gas and ran and circled some little corners that I knew he wouldn't be familiar with and lost him. That was at night.[7]

I was always in the movement marches. It was an experience. I grew up next door to Rev. Shuttlesworth. With my father and Rev. Shuttlesworth, I just knew I had to do what I had to do. I knew what was right to do and what I believed in. I had no problem participating in the movement, because I knew there would be a change. We had to make the difference. It was what I needed to do. There were a lot of people who were scared. [Some] parents were afraid, and they didn't even allow their children who wanted to participate to go. But I was fortunate that my parents were involved, so I didn't have that problem.

One Sunday morning, we were going to the eleven o'clock service at a white church. When we got up the steps of the church, there was a well-dressed white gentleman who came to the door. We were well dressed, too. He said, "We're segregated here." He couldn't even pronounce the word. He wouldn't let us in, so we didn't do anything. We just turned around and left. That's the way we were instructed to do. There were approximately twenty of us, male and female, that went to that particular church. We were assigned to that one church for that day. It was on Twenty-sixth Street, right next to Carraway Hospital. It was that big church on the corner.

I also sat-in at Newberry's, but there was no incident. Woolworth's was the only one where I was involved with an incident. I went to Woolworth's and sat at the lunch counters, when a white gentleman coughed and spat in the face of the man next to me. The man next to me smiled and didn't retaliate. He was nonviolent and did what we were supposed to do. I was real glad it wasn't me, because I knew I wasn't nonviolent. I would have hoped that

I could have been, but he did the right thing. They served us. They didn't want to serve us, but that time they did. The white man just didn't want to be sitting beside us. There were no arrests made.

I was at Sixteenth Street Baptist Church [on May 2, 1963,] when everybody went to jail. My father went, and my sister, Robbie Smith, went. I was there, but it just so happened that I didn't get arrested. It wasn't that I was not in the way, but I didn't get arrested that particular day.

I would describe Fred Shuttlesworth as the bravest person I know in all walks of life. I would say that he had courage to do anything and everything. If he made up his mind that he was going to do it, he did just that. As a pastor, he was very good. He was a good minister and preacher. I remember the experience when he and his wife were beaten up at Phillips High School.[8] That's the school my children later attended. I worked hard at that PTA and Band Booster Club and stuff like that.

I think those are all experiences that I'll never forget. We made a difference. It makes a difference to me when I see someone in a great position. I've been in management a lot. When I had my office, I felt good when both black and white employees worked under me in different capacities at different times. Had we not marched, had we not done all those things, we would never have gotten to be in the positions we are in. Doctors and lawyers and everything came out of Collegeville. Knowing that we had to make it gave us a sense of responsibility. The movement made a big impact.

NOTES

BCRI OHP, vol. 19, sec. 3 (July 11, 1996). Edited, annotated, and abridged by A. Michelle Craig, Horace Huntley, and John McKerley.

1. The growth of black, single-family homeownership reflected a fairly recent trend in Birmingham. Between 1926 and 1951, Birmingham's racial segregation ordinance severely limited the number of single-family districts available to black residents. See Jimmie Lucille Hooks, BCRI OHP, vol. 36, sec. 2 (May 27, 1998).

2. Segregation ordinances banned black residents from using most of the city's parks during the early part of the century. Although an ACMHR legal challenge succeeded in overturning this restriction in 1962, city officials closed the parks rather than integrate them. See Glenn T. Eskew, *But for Birmingham: The Local and National Movements in the Civil Rights Struggle* (Chapel Hill: University of North Carolina Press, 1997), 147; Diane McWhorter, *Carry Me Home: Birmingham, Alabama: The Climactic Battle of the Civil Rights Revolution* (New York: Simon and Schuster, 2001), 247.

3. On James Revis, see Eskew, *But for Birmingham*, 297; Andrew M. Manis, *A Fire You Can't Put Out: The Civil Rights Life of Birmingham's Reverend Fred*

Shuttlesworth (Tuscaloosa: University of Alabama Press, 1999), 109–10, 118, 169, 283, 329.

4. This story is related from Colonel Stone Johnson's perspective in Horace Huntley and David Montgomery, eds., *Black Workers' Struggle for Equality in Birmingham* (Urbana: University of Illinois Press, 2004), 43–44. In Johnson's version, Martin is identified as "Lavonne McWilliams." On these two bombings, see also Manis, *Fire*, 108–13, 162–73.

5. Johnson also remembered the shrapnel and breaking glass, but he emphasized the experience of the men in the street: Elijah Dawson "was about ten feet from [the bomb], and he was the only one who got a scratch. A little shrapnel of steel hit him on the check. The bomb blew all the glass out of the church, and for five to six blocks around, dishes broke on the folks in the pantries and windows broke out of houses as much as seven or eight blocks, but the church still stood" (Huntley and Montgomery, *Black Workers' Struggle*, 43–44).

6. Martin's story of her interrogation fits into a well-established pattern of accusations made by Birmingham's white officials during this period. To distract attention from the Ku Klux Klan and other white vigilantes, officials spread rumors that blacks were responsible for the bombings and other acts of violence. See McWhorter, *Carry Me Home*, 535.

7. The everyday reality of police brutality is a recurring theme in the interviews. See Colonel Stone Johnson, BCRI OHP, vol. 1, sec. 3 (January 6, 1995); Joe Hendricks, BCRI OHP, vol. 8, sec. 1 (June 23, 1995); Jessie Champion Sr., BCRI OHP, vol. 10, sec. 6 (November 1, 1995).

8. See James Armstrong, BCRI OHP, vol. 4, sec. 5 (April 10, 1995).

PAUL LITTLEJOHN

PAUL LITTLEJOHN was born in Birmingham on September 28, 1937. Littlejohn recalled how many African Americans, including his parents and siblings, resisted movement activism. "I knew if we said something [about the movement], the first thing my mother and father would say [was], 'Boy, you ain't got no business getting involved with that because it don't concern you." Though he participated in the 1963 bus boycott, other blacks were afraid of losing their jobs: "They would say, 'We got to go. We got to get where we're going. We can't go nowhere else. This is the only way we've got to go.'" The 1963 demonstrations resulted in new opportunities for municipal employment for black men and women, but

Littlejohn hesitated to take a city job because of his lingering distrust of Birmingham's white officials. As Littlejohn's description of the interview process reveals, white officials continued to use more subtle methods to target black applicants and especially activists: "[The interviewer] said, 'I've got to check your references and send a letter to the church you go to, to see if you're trustworthy, honest.' He asked me if I had been in jail. I didn't tell him I had been in there for the movement because they didn't want to hire you if you had been in jail any kind of way."

YOU'VE GOT TO STRUGGLE

I have six sisters and two brothers living. I was number four. Mostly, all of us were born at home except the last two. Dr. Ward used to always come to the house when one of us was born.

At the time I was born, we lived at Twelfth Street and Fourth Avenue. It was Avenue D at the time—Twelfth Street and Avenue D. We lived in two rooms. There was a front room and a kitchen. We had something like a little back porch. There were eight of us living there, including my mother and father. We had a big bed, and we made a pallet on the floor. We mostly just slept on the floor. At the time, it was fun because we were kids coming up. We just didn't realize what was happening. We just had whatever our parents had, and that's what we had to deal with. At that time, my mother did not work except at home. My dad worked for the railroad. He was a common laborer.

I first went to Cameron School on Eighth Avenue and Fourteenth Street South. I attended Cameron until I got in the fifth grade, and then we moved to Lane School. That was on Thirteenth Street and Avenue D. When I got home from school, we had to get coal and cut wood. We had to make sure that my younger brothers' and sisters' clothes were cleaned and washed. We couldn't question our mother. Whatever she said do, you did it. We used to beg her, "Don't tell him," talking about our father, because she would take care of you first and then when he got home he would do the same. She didn't spank us. She whipped us. She had something like a razor strap. Whatever she could get her hands on was what she would hit us with. She would tell you, "I love you, and I'm doing this because I love you." I couldn't understand until I was older why, if she loved me, she was doing this to me.

We had a close-knit community. Whenever and however we needed to help each other, we just helped each other. Whatever they had, you were welcomed to it, and whatever we had you could have. We had a neighbor that we called Miss Nosey Jolly. She knew everybody's business in the neighborhood and always told on the children. We didn't have a park. We mostly played in the streets. She used to tell us to stay out of the streets, and we didn't want to do like she said. Then she would tell on us.

We were active in church. We attended New Pilgrim [Baptist Church]. At the time, Rev. Howard Perry was the pastor and would come twice a month. Rev. Nelson Smith came to that church in 1953.[1] When he first came, he got involved with young people. We didn't have anything to do, so we hung around on the corner, and he got involved with us. He encouraged us to come to the church, sit down, and have rap sessions.

When Rev. Smith got here, he had been involved with the movement. He always encouraged us to be involved. He also convinced us that we could be anything we wanted to be. So when he got involved, all the young people just wanted to follow him. I was out of high school, and sometimes we would go down [to church] just to act up. He would come around and talk with us. He would tell us we were getting to be young men, and we needed to make a change. It was kind of hard at first to make a change, because when you are living in an environment where you didn't have anything, you would just go from day to day. You didn't know half the time whether you were going to eat. Sometimes the neighbors would help you, but we still didn't have anything. We didn't have any money. He just kind of got us involved, and a lot of times he used to take us down to the church and get one of the cooks to feed us. We would go out there and play softball and football, and he would come right along and play with us. He was a young fellow and something like a big brother. Sometimes he was closer to some of us than our father. We could go to him and talk with him when we had problems. When he came to New Pilgrim, he got a chance to talk and give us some kind of uplift. It looked like we had just met somebody that made us want to be all that we could be. Yes, he had that much influence on us.

I started with the [ACMHR]. A lot of times I used to attend meetings with [Rev. Smith]. Sometimes we would just get together and ask some of the fellows to attend the meetings with us. At that time, our mother always told us, "Don't go and get in no trouble. Stay out of [the movement], because it ain't nothing but some junk." I knew if we said something, the first thing my mother and father would say [was], "Boy, you ain't got no business getting involved with that because it don't concern you." At that time, I thought it didn't. But as the movement went on, then I just got more involved.

At the time we were boycotting the buses, it was kind of hard because you couldn't stop the people from riding on the buses. They would say, "We got to go. We got to get where we're going. We can't go nowhere else. This is the only way we've got to go." We used to tell them, "Let's walk." A lot of the older people were kind of afraid they were going to lose their job. At the time, we young people didn't have anything to lose, but the adults had jobs. After I got older, I understood what they meant, but sometimes I wanted to stand up and say something. But I also knew, if I went home, what my mother and father would say. And I had to go home. My brothers and sisters didn't get involved. My two brothers that were older than me moved away from Birmingham. They said they didn't want to be around the environment. They went to Cleveland.

The city had gotten where they said they wanted some black bus drivers, policemen, and firemen.[2] So we went and took the test for policeman, and we said we didn't want to be a policeman. And then we took the bus driver test. [The interviewer] said, "I've got to check your references and send a letter to the church you go to, to see if you're trustworthy, honest." He asked me if I had been in jail. I didn't tell him I had been in there for the movement because they didn't want to hire you if you had been in jail any kind of way. So I didn't go [to work for the city] in 1964, and I wouldn't go in '65. So, finally, I made my mind up in '66, and I went on down there. I've been there ever since.

There have been a lot of changes. When we first went to the bus company, whites outnumbered us ten to one. And when we were hired, the man told us, "Whatever [the white drivers] say, don't say anything back to them." He said that whatever a white lady says in line, we're supposed to say, "All right," and go ahead. But we didn't accept that. We had the movement, so we just made up our mind that we weren't going to take it. If anything came up, we were going to go to the movement and tell them what had happened. But it just so happened they didn't bother us too much. One of the first blacks they had hired, Wylie James, told us what to expect, and we used to always say we couldn't be an Uncle Tom. And he would say, "You ain't got to be Uncle Tom. Just do what you're supposed to do. Once you do it, you'll get along." He said, "It ain't no Uncle Tom doing what you're supposed to do."

People died for what we're about to lose—some of it—because our young people have just gotten so they don't want to put any hard effort in doing what they are supposed to do. I tell them, "It was a hard struggle." I tell them, "Don't take it for granted that everything's all right." We still have some things that we fought for. Nothing comes easy. You've got to struggle.

NOTES

BCRI OHP, vol. 18, sec. 3 (June 24, 1996). Edited, annotated, and abridged by A. Michelle Craig, Horace Huntley, and John McKerley.

1. Rev. Nelson H. Smith Jr. was an early supporter of Shuttlesworth and a founding member (and longtime secretary) of the ACMHR. In 1963, he was part

of the ACMHR-SCLC team that drafted the Birmingham Manifesto, which out-
lined the black community's grievances and reasons for turning to mass protest
(Glenn T. Eskew, *But for Birmingham: The Local and National Movements in the
Civil Rights Struggle* [Chapel Hill: University of North Carolina Press, 1997], 7,
125–26, 221–22). See also Andrew M. Manis, *A Fire You Can't Put Out: The Civil
Rights Life of Birmingham's Reverend Fred Shuttlesworth* (Tuscaloosa: University
of Alabama Press, 1999), 72–73, 95–99.

2. Continued pressure on city officials produced some gains for black residents
in municipal employment during the mid- and late 1960s. For example, as Glenn
Eskew notes, "After street demonstrations in 1966, the city finally hired four
Negro policemen, nearly two decades after Atlanta had made a similar move"
(*But for Birmingham*, 326).

CARLTON REESE

CARLTON REESE was born in Westfield, Alabama, outside Birmingham,
on February 7, 1942. A musician and student at Miles College during
the early 1960s, Reese participated in numerous demonstrations and
served the movement as a director of the ACMHR Choir during its
later years. The composer of many now-famous songs, he emphasized
the role of music in inspiring activism and sacrifice on behalf of the
cause. "The choir kept up morale for the people," Reese remembered.
"People would really sing in the movement—leave the church singing
and move on out into the streets and just march, march, march." As a
student and aspiring teacher, he noted the impact of economic intimidation on black educators. "In order to keep their jobs," Reese recalled,
"some people didn't want their names called even though they were
with it." Although he had been somewhat insulated from these pres-
sures while at Miles, Reese had to battle job discrimination after his
graduation in 1964. Unable to find work in Birmingham, he first taught
in Mississippi and later in Shelby County, Alabama, where he continued
to encounter racism in the school system. For Reese, these experiences
demonstrated the need for continued vigilance despite the successes of
the civil rights movement. As he noted, "There's always a need to write
freedom music." Reese died on July 9, 2002.

FREEDOM MUSIC

My father was from Plattersville, Alabama [in Chilton County]. My mother was from Birmingham. Both of them are deceased. My father's name was Theodore Roosevelt Reese Sr., and my mother's name was Cornelia Gayles Reese. My father's education only went to the sixth grade. My mother finished Fairfield [Industrial] High School. I was born in Birmingham in a little steel plant community called Westfield, Alabama.

I was the fourth of eight children. My [oldest] brother, Theodore Roosevelt Reese Jr., was a student here at Miles College. The second brother was Lloyd Gayles Reese. He resides in Paterson, New Jersey, and is a graduate of Miles College. My sister, Catherine Reese Williams, resides in Clarksville, Tennessee. And I graduated from Miles College in the field of sociology and history. I have another brother, Joseph, who played football at Miles. And there's Mary, John, and Cornelia, the baby, who died about six months after her birth.

Westfield was a regular little country community. U.S. Steel was the owner of the town.[1] We were surrounded by the steel plant. My father worked in the steel plant for over forty-six years in the construction mill. The plant was about six or seven blocks from our house. My mother was a housewife. We lived near the commissary. Everybody lived closely together. If you needed some sugar, you would go next door and borrow the sugar. We were just [those] kind of neighbors—certainly different from what we are now, because so many times we don't even know our neighbors. It was closely knitted. We started out early with our mothers and fathers being sure that we entered Sunday school and stayed involved in religious activities. Basically, church was all we had to be involved in other than our schoolwork.

I was a student in Westfield No. 2 School from the first grade to the fourth grade. Then I went to Westfield No. 1 for the fifth through the eighth grade. I went to Westfield High School from the ninth through twelfth grades and graduated in 1960. I was involved in a lot of extracurricular activities. I was in the High Y and choir. I organized programs to raise money for the school. I was involved with the academic program and just about everything. In fact, when I finished high school, I was awarded the All-Around Boy medal. I remember Mr. C. L. Reeves being principal of that school and being a very efficient administrator. After he left, Mr. Paul Ware was there, and he followed in being very, very efficient in his work. He carried out a strong line as far as discipline was concerned. We were taught by some of the better teachers. In fact, those Jefferson County teachers were labeled as some of the best teachers that could have ever been in any system because we were really taught well.

They would go off during the summer and come back with new innovations to teach us. We learned a lot in high school. I had a very good experience.

Even before learning anything about the technicalities or mechanical parts of music, my family was musically inclined. We were all playing from memory. They used to say, "They play by ear," but it was just a God-given gift. In the beginning, my mother played, my father played, and it was just through the family. We started early. I played little Sunday school songs for church when I was four years old. Then I started playing for the junior choir. Upon finishing high school in 1960, I entered Miles College. My brothers and myself played for the chapel programs and other extracurricular activities at Miles.

My brothers and sisters were not involved in the civil rights movement. Theodore Jr. died after a certain period of time. Lloyd went off to the army and moved away. My other sisters and brothers were not actively involved, but my father was altogether for my being a part of the movement. He knew the importance of us becoming free. He would hear people say, "Don't say 'Yes, sir' to them white folk." My daddy said, "You can 'Yes, sir' them, if they deserve it. If he's your boss, or if there's something you want out of him, say 'Yes, sir' and get it. It's not being an Uncle Tom when it's done appropriately." He taught me to fight for whatever I thought was right as far as my human dignity is concerned.

Eventually, I was known as the musician, songwriter, and director of the movement choir. I was active in the movement during the 1950s. I used to play and sing in the [ACMHR] Choir here in Birmingham and carry other talents in to make music for the movement. The [ACMHR] was a religious organization. They had preaching and singing. Different leaders all over the community would get people involved in the movement so they could see what it was to make a sacrifice for the cause of freedom, justice, and equality. Rev. [Fred] Shuttlesworth and some more members, along with Dr. [Martin Luther] King and the rest who came to Birmingham to help, requested that I become real active in the movement just before the 1960s by taking over that choir and making it be an active part of the movement.

Music was very important in the movement. People begin to respond when they hear music. Without a song, the day will never end. We realized that, so when they asked me if I would take on the responsibility, I told them I would. I began to write songs and teach many of my original numbers and a lot of gospel numbers and songs that other people were doing so that we could get people involved in the movement. There were many songs, such as "I Want to Be Free," "Old Freedom," "Ain't Going to Let Nobody Turn Me Around." These songs were done here in Birmingham, and they moved all over the United States of America. People began to sing them everywhere.

We had "I'm on My Way to Freedom Land," and just a number of them. There are so many, I can't name them all.

The activists inspired me to do a lot of songwriting. Fred Shuttlesworth would come in. Dr. King would come in. Wyatt Tee Walker, James Bevel, and all the other activists would come in, and they would talk about the issues and the sacrifices and what we needed to do. It becomes very easy to write when you are actually involved in the situation where there's a need for it. As they talked, I thought of lyrics and put the tune to them. Many of them were original. Some of them were arranged songs that were similar to gospel tunes. We just took them all and put them together.[2] The music reached a lot of people. We wrote songs like

> I've got a job; you've got a job
> All of God's children surely have a job.
> We've got a job to do.
> We can't get freedom until we get through.
> Carrying the cross for our rights.

In the songs, we talked about people like Bull Connor—how mean Bull Connor was. At that time [Albert] Boutwell was [mayor]. We also sang about Governor [George] Wallace.[3] We made the people aware of a whole lot through the songs. The white people could not stand this kind of thing. That's why they would be rebellious in putting up with us. Doing these songs would really provoke their thinking.

The songs affected people all over the nation at these movement meetings. While we were writing and singing these songs, a lot of them were copyrighted. We received no credit for it, but we know that we did them, even some of the songs in our hymnbooks today are just listed as American folk songs. I've never tried to really fight about it. I feel like I'll get my just reward, and the Lord has been good to me. I did copyright some of the songs, but when I was invited to the Smithsonian Institution to do a workshop, I found that there were many numbers copyrighted by people who sat in the movement—brought their tapes and recorded the numbers and carried them away. Those people were writing stories. You would be surprised that while we had our minds on becoming free and this kind of thing, people were taking this material to make a living. They knew it was going to be history. We weren't really thinking about it that way. We were thinking about making a way for people to become free in Birmingham, Alabama, and abroad.

"We Shall Overcome" was written from the old gospel song "I'll Overcome (Someday)": "I'll overcome, I'll overcome someday. If in my heart I believe, I'll overcome someday." It became the theme song really of the whole movement. "We Shall Overcome" became the unity song where you would fold your arms together and sing. The words mean that all of the obstacles we're encountering, one day we will overcome. One day we are going to sit down and worship together and walk the streets together. Little white girls and little black boys will be able to pray together, sing together, and go to school together. Everywhere you go, whether in the United States of America or outside the country, you hear people singing "We Shall Overcome." The song became a national song—a song of peace, understanding, and hope that one day we will overcome things that keep us from being together.

We must remember that music tames the wildest beast. Everybody loves music. When a person is sad, he wants to find a song that makes him glad. When he gets weary, he finds a song that makes him cheer up. When you are riding along in your car, and you flip on that radio and hear a song that relates to your feelings or to some kind of story or experience that you have encountered, it brings joy to your soul. People just relate to music. Even in our churches today, we know that the truth is about the Word of God, but some people come to church just to hear some good music.

I distinctly remember one of the first demonstrations, when I led the students from Miles College. I guess there were about 150 or 175 of us. We went out through Five Points West and were arrested down in that area. A lot of students got involved, not only from Miles College. When other students heard about the marches and demonstrations, they came out of other schools and got involved. I also sat in at Kress's lunch counter. The waiters didn't want to wait on us. They called us "niggers." They spat on us. They did everything to try to keep us from sitting there, but we sat. We were instructed from Day 1 that nonviolence was the way, and it still is the way. We sat. We sat there until many of them began to physically push us out. I didn't get arrested on that charge, but many others got arrested for sitting in, not only at Kress's but also at the bus station and other places.

Another time, I was in a demonstration down at Kelly Ingram Park when the dogs were out. I was bitten by a dog, but didn't get set upon by the water hoses that were out there. If I had not moved out of the way, I would have been attacked, but I didn't care because Dr. King and Dr. Shuttlesworth and the other activists had reminded us that we were not to fight back. We were to endure all of these experiences. There were numbers of people who got bit by the dogs, a number who encountered being beaten by the police and other brutalities. It was an experience we'll never forget.

Every time I got in jail, they would get me out, and I would go back into the movement. I'm still dedicated to the movement. I'm in SCLC now and the Birmingham [branch of the National] Alliance [against Racist and Political

Repression]. At the time, though, I was so dedicated to the movement that I was anxious to get out of jail to get back and play and keep things going. The choir kept up morale for the people. When the activists were late coming in on an airplane, we kept it going. We did a lot of things with our music that caused people to make a sacrifice, to get up and go out into the streets and march. People would really sing in the movement—leave the church singing and move on out into the streets and just march, march, march.

When I was first arrested, the police paddy wagons came to get us, and a lot of folks ran. At one time, I tried [to run], but they got me because they knew I was active in leading other people to come in the demonstrations. It was just one of those things. They put us in jail. We were all crowded together. We didn't have anywhere to sleep, but we weren't worried about sleeping. We carried on a lot of singing and praying in the jails. The guards and people in charge of all the prisoners would get highly upset, because when white people heard this kind of singing, it got to them. They really couldn't stand that kind of thing. There's something about the kind of singing that black folk do that stirs the hearts of people. I'm not saying that other ethnic groups cannot sing. I'm saying that our music represents trials and tribulations. We are used to anthems and hymns, and we're used to much folk music, but the down-home gospel and old Dr. Watts's songs represent trials and tribulations and those kinds of experiences.[4] When people mistreat you, they can't stand to hear that kind of thing.

Another time I went to jail was on Good Friday 1963. On Good Friday, when we all marched, the circumstances were just like the other circumstances. We were fighting for freedom, justice, and equality, and it was about bringing us all together. The police were set to throw us all in jail when this kind of thing happened. Many of us got beat on, but we kept going. We were instructed to keep going and not fight back because fighting back would only make the police retaliate. You had to know how to get out of the way. There were many who got blasted by the water hoses—knocked to the ground. But these experiences made us more determined to fight for our brothers. It was not only just for black folk, it was for white folk and [other] minority groups. The movement was for anybody who needed to fight for their civil rights.

There were no whites participating in the marches on a day-to-day basis. Some whites were involved, but not from Birmingham. There were whites from other areas who had experienced being involved in movement activities and they came to be a part of it—people like Guy Carawan and a lot of other folk. Guy Carawan was writing songs, too. I won't make any negative comment about it. He has written a lot of songs. If I'm not mistaken, they're from Tennessee.[5]

Whites have become more lenient now than they were back then because of the rules that have been passed. I imagine many of them wanted to be a little more cordial towards blacks, but they weren't because of trouble they knew they would get into with their class of people. Because of this, a lot of people didn't know black people. The only black people they knew were the people who worked out of their kitchens and raised their children. They never thought that blacks had any kind of ability, but there are some smart black folk, and people have to realize that. After many years of being involved in the movement, people got a chance to learn that black people have brains just like everybody else.

I was never afraid to get involved in the movement. A few members of my family were afraid. I never shall forget a member of my family who was working as an instructor in the Jefferson County school system. She was afraid for me and for herself and her job. That was one of the things that caused a lot of people to become afraid; they knew they were going to lose their jobs. Many of us who did not have those jobs could do more than those who were employed. In order to keep their jobs, some people didn't want their names called even though they were with [the movement]. At Miles, there were some teachers who did not go along with the struggle because they were not ready for change. A lot of the teachers were not complimentary but never showed me any negative side of being involved in the movement either. Then there were people like Lucinda B. Robey who didn't give a rip. Lucinda B. Robey was a school principal, and she knew her rights. She was there at the movement, day in and day out. She was not afraid to speak out, and she will always be remembered for that. If anybody said anything negative about me being in the movement, I didn't want to hear it. My mind was on one thing—to get involved so that our people could be free.

Whatever their contributions, we appreciated everything that everybody did. We know that the sacrifices we made opened the doors for many people in Birmingham, the state of Alabama, and the world. It was because of the Birmingham situation that the [1964] Civil Rights [Act] was passed. It was a hard struggle. It was a struggle for me, period, I'll tell you. When I finished Miles College in 1964, I couldn't get a job in Birmingham because I had been involved in that movement and had gone to jail. I had to go to Mississippi and teach school for a couple of years.

After teaching school in Mississippi, I came back to the outskirts of Birmingham, in the Shelby County school system, and got hired there. I worked there for over twenty-four years. I went through a lot of mental stress there, still being nonviolent as I was taught to be. After some in that system found out that I was a part of the movement, I encountered a lot of experiences. Let me just say this: It's stressful when you find out that people are still carrying on segregation, having in their minds that they still don't want to mingle with blacks. They figured out means and ways by which to get rid of blacks. Every time a black moves, he's replaced with a white. Sometimes people would pretend they are going to give you a position and never give you this position. It causes stress. I hope, as Dr. King and Dr. Shuttlesworth and all the other civil rights activists said, that "one day all of us will become free." We've got to remember that as long as this world exists, there are still going to be prejudices. There's going to be prejudice with white and black and white and other minority groups. There's going to be prejudice among our own culture groups.

The only thing that black people have had to depend on is the church. The mass meetings were similar to a good, down-home church meeting—a good old Holy Ghost church meeting. Instructions were given in the meetings as to what to do about certain issues, but we always remembered that in order to receive anything, we must keep God on our mind and be guided by the Holy Spirit. As I said before, when I mentioned Dr. Watts's hymns, the meetings consisted of good gospel singing and good, old-time praying. I talk now about how it was so that we can take those things we used to do, make some changes, and make things better.

We have a lot to be thankful for. We've accomplished so much. However, we must not keep our eyes closed now, because we are not free. If we don't watch it, we'll be going back into slavery. Sometimes marching may not be the answer to the problem. There may be meetings behind closed doors or talking together. There might be other means or ways to solve problems, but if the time comes that we need to march again, fine.

Even though I didn't get credit for some of it, I'm proud that my music has spread all over the world. In reality, with God, I got credit for what I did. I know that music caused a lot of people to make sacrifices for the causes of freedom and change. We made a new light in the world. A lot of people don't realize how important it was to be involved in the movement. A lot of people don't realize why they have jobs now. They don't realize that the sacrifices were meant for the good of all people. Everybody who is working a white-collar job now ought to be proud that the movement existed, and they should never forget from whence we've come. We've come a long way, but yet we still have a long way to go.

I thank the Lord for my music. I am writing some secular music now. I'm getting ready to write some more gospel music and record a new album. Any person who is in music will be inspired. If movement meetings come up again, and they have them like they used to, musicians will get involved again. There's always a need to write freedom music.

NOTES

BCRI OHP, vol. 15, sec. 3 (May 16, 1996). Edited, annotated, and abridged by A. Michelle Craig, Horace Huntley, and John McKerley.

1. See Diane McWhorter, *Carry Me Home: Birmingham, Alabama: The Climactic Battle of the Civil Rights Revolution* (New York: Simon and Schuster, 2001), 42–47.

2. The "freedom songs" of the 1960s have diverse roots. They freely mixed contemporary figures and themes with older structures and lyrics from African American gospel, blues, Euro-American folk tunes, and labor protest songs. As early as 1961, the Labor Education Division of Roosevelt University in Chicago published a collection, *Songs of Work and Freedom*. In her 1963 review, critic Dena J. Epstein noted, "The songs are drawn from varied scenes of industrial America—picket lines, mines, mills, farms, the high seas, the hobo camps—with the addition of some traditional folk songs from other lands, freedom songs, and songs of a better tomorrow. As might be expected, most of the songs date from the period 1900–1945, but the earliest is 'The Cutty Wren,' which the editors attribute to the Peasants' Revolt in 1381, and the most recent is 'The Song of the Guaranteed Wage,' 1955" (*Notes*, 20, 3 [Summer 1963]: 409).

3. The African American musical tradition contains many examples in which black people used song to criticize antagonists rather than risking open (and potentially violent) confrontation. This tradition was particularly evident in work songs, which allowed black slaves (and later wage workers) to protest their living and working conditions without appearing directly to challenge white authority. See Lawrence W. Levine, *Black Culture and Black Consciousness: Afro-American Folk Thought from Slavery to Freedom* (Oxford: Oxford University Press, 1977), 239–70.

4. Dr. Isaac Watts was an English preacher and composer during the early eighteenth century. Many of his "long meter" hymns entered the African American musical tradition through a hymnal compiled by Richard Allen in 1801. See V. de S. Pinto, "Isaac Watts and William Blake," *Review of English Studies* 20, 79 (July 1944): 214; Horace Clarence Boyer, "Gospel Music," *Music Educators Journal* 64, 9 (May 1978): 35.

5. Guy Carawan and his wife, Candie Carawan, were from Tennessee's Highlander Folk School, founded in the 1930s to encourage and provide training in organizing for members of the labor movement. By the mid-1950s, some leaders of the emerging civil rights movement visited Highlander. See John M. Glen, *Highlander: No Ordinary School, 1932–1962* (Lexington: University Press of Kentucky, 1988).

ELIZABETH FITTS

ELIZABETH FITTS was born on January 9, 1943, and grew up in Titusville. She attended Miles College, where she first came into contact with formal civil rights protest organizations during a presentation by Andrew Young and James Bevel. Although she recalled considerable apathy among many of her fellow students, Fitts was inspired by this call to action. She took part in the antisegregation campaigns in Birmingham during 1962 and 1963, and she later used this experience as she traveled around the country as a SCLC staff member. After returning to Alabama to complete her education at the Tuskegee Institute, Fitts continued her activism as a member of the Tuskegee Institute Advancement League.

WE WERE CALLED RABBLE-ROUSERS

My mother was born in a small place called Hope Hull near Montgomery, Alabama, and my stepfather was born in Ohio. They met and married in Birmingham and decided to raise their family here. I was born the oldest of three children, with two younger brothers.

We lived in Honeysuckle Circle, which was a community in Titusville composed of working-class black families. It was a safe place to live, and the neighbors were just like your parents. They would spank [you] if they saw you doing something you wasn't supposed to do and tell your folks. My mother was a domestic worker, and eventually she monogrammed shirts for the Coca-Cola Company because she was an excellent seamstress. My stepfather was a freight worker for Ryder Trucking Company. My mother never finished high school because she had to help work on the family's farm. My stepfather, however, did finish high school, and both of my parents were very smart individuals.

As a teenager, I attended Ullman High School, where George C. Bell was the principal. He was very strict. I enjoyed school and I never missed a day, even when I was sick. Every day at school, Mr. Bell would ask me to recite my presentations, such as the Creation,[1] before him, and with his guidance I won several oratorical contests. Although a lot of my fellow classmates did not like Mr. Bell, I have many fond memories of him. At Ullman High, we loved football, and our biggest rival was Parker High, which was on the north side of town. Several fights often broke out between the two schools at the football game.

After high school, I entered Miles College and majored in English. I commuted to school with several of my former classmates, Hazel Loretta Brown and Cleopatra Gibson, and I eventually joined the band. It's actually funny that I was a part of the band because I couldn't play a note on my trumpet. One day, we had an assembly at school my freshman year, and Andrew Young and James Bevel came to speak at Miles, trying to recruit students to become involved in the civil rights movement. My classmates appeared to be apathetic to the situation in Birmingham, and I became so upset that I jumped to the microphone to scorn them for not taking a stand. Although my fellow students showed little interest in what the activists had to say, I was inspired by their message and immediately decided to join the demonstrations.

I immediately began my participation in the selective-buying campaign in 1962.[2] Stores that were not favorable to any of our goals were targeted for boycott, and those stores that were friendly to the cause, we shopped at. It's a little amazing that I became involved in the selective-buying campaign because I was not a part of any student organization on campus at that time except for band. But the message I heard touched me. I attended my first mass meeting at the Sixth Avenue Baptist Church, and I remember wanting to be a part of the movement. I can still remember us singing "We Shall Overcome" and listening to Andrew Young and James Bevel giving uplifting speeches. Some of the professors from Miles College attended the mass meetings, but most stayed behind the scenes. They told us that as long as we kept up with our studies, they did not care if we participated in the movement.

I finished my first year at Miles College and became completely involved in the movement. In Birmingham during Easter week in 1963, I was arrested for demonstrating and placed in jail with older women who participated in the movement. There were no mattresses on our cots, so we used our coats to make pads for the older women to sleep on. When the coats ran out, we asked the warden for Kotex pads to line the mattress. I spent four days in that jail, and the food was horrible. The grits were brown, the eggs were powdered, and the biscuits were hard. I was very happy when I was allowed to go home. My mother was afraid for my safety, and she often stayed up until I came home.

The leaders began to map out the successful D-Day plan and explain to us the different strategies they developed.[3] I participated in many demonstrations, but the D-Day protests in [May] 1963 [were] my first real involvement in the movement. I remember the plan was for one group to get arrested, and then the next group would continue where they left off. The strategy was to fill the jails with children, and throughout the streets there was nothing but paddy wagons filled with children. I remember one police officer asking me when would the protest end, and I responded that we would continue to fight until we got our freedom. Luckily, I was not injured during the protest, and I continued to assist the SCLC with its various projects around the United States.[4]

I traveled to various cities across the South, helping to register black people to vote. We were called rabble-rousers and were harassed in every city where we conducted protest. While in Danville, Virginia, a young man and I were arrested in an elevator, and the police beat him. Later that night, they made that young man run on broken glass along the railroad tracks to torture him. I eventually left Birmingham and went to Atlanta, where the national headquarters for the SCLC was located. I became very good friends with Dorothy Cotton and Dr. [Martin Luther] King, who always called me Liz Taylor. I traveled a lot of places with Andrew Young and James Bevel, but me and a few other guys were called the SCLC's "crackpot voter registration team." Dr. King would have retreats where the SCLC tried to regroup and strategize. We were required to have reading materials that would motivate us to stay focused on our mission. After one of the retreats, I became a full-time worker for the SCLC and was on their crackpot team.

My mother was not happy with my decision to leave school, but I felt that other things were more important at that time. I wrote her constantly to assure her that I was fine, because I didn't have the money to call long distance. The SCLC decided to buy us a van to travel in and do different projects. The first place we went was Orange, Texas, and our contact person was a powerful attorney named Barbara Jordan.[5] She smoked a tiny little pipe and was intimidating at first, but she gave us connections with local members for food and shelter. Texas was a very interesting place because we had to boycott businesses that were owned by blacks. The black owners refused to serve black people in their establishments, so we picketed them to convince the owners to desegregate. My experience in Birmingham was very useful in Texas, and local members helped to make signs and poster boards to use during our demonstrations.

When we finished in Orange, Texas, the owners agreed to desegregate their facilities. My worst experience was in Plaquemines Parish, Louisiana, where blacks were forced to live on plantations.[6] One white man owned the plantations, and blacks lived in little huts with dirt floors, and they cooked outside in big pots using the same pot for cooking and washing clothes. Dr. King used a rented helicopter to drop handbills over the plantation so that the people on the plantations could read them. Believe it or not, only one black man could read on the whole plantation, and he told the others what the handbill said. It was almost like a concentration camp. People began to come to the local meetings being held at the Baptist church. Police officers covered up their badges and rode through the church, breaking up the mass meetings. A thirteen-year-old girl was killed at one of the meetings when a police horse kicked her in the middle of her chest.

I eventually returned to school in 1964 and enrolled at Tuskegee Institute. At first, the transition was difficult, having to adjust to studying all the time, but I did meet new classmates dedicated to the cause and we founded the Tuskegee Institute Advancement League.[7] Several people came and spoke at our school, such as Stokely Carmichael and Jim Farmer. When a good friend of mine, Sammy Younge, was murdered, we learned that the local whites had a hit list with Sammy's name, Betty Gamble, Wendell Paris, and my name, Liz Fitts.[8] Sammy was a member of the Student Nonviolent Coordinating Committee and had become a little too outspoken for the local whites that saw him as a threat. I was never a part of the Student Nonviolent Coordinating Committee, but [the league and the committee] did work close together on campus issues.

I participated in the voter registration march [in 1965] from Selma to Montgomery on what became known as Bloody Sunday. I remember it rained, and it was frightening because state troopers were there and they showed no mercy towards marchers. Students from Tuskegee who protested after Sammy was killed also came together to join the march from Selma to Montgomery. We were able to transport students to Selma with buses that we were able to obtain. At the time, Dr. [Luther] Foster, who was the president of Tuskegee, arranged a meeting with [league] members to talk to us about our activities on campus. He didn't approve of ladies wearing jeans or acting "unladylike," and our group broke a lot of the restrictive rules at Tuskegee. Although Dr. Foster did not approve of what we were doing, he did not stop us. I remember A. G. Gaston sending a telegram telling us that we needed to be in the classrooms, not outside protesting, but we still continued.[9] During one demonstration, we took over the Dorothy Hall building when the trustees were on campus. Often we sat in the street to protest activities we did not agree with. Every demonstration we had, I was a part, but by 1968 I graduated and calmed down.

Being in the movement made me a better person. [Since I've been] teaching at Alabama State University, several of my old friends are upset that I am not the same radical person I used to be. I believe things have changed, and now you can handle situations differently, without resorting to protests.

Now [when] I look at the movement, I see that integration has hurt us in many ways. When I was younger, school was a place for learning, and teachers taught us. But now, many students I see coming into college do not have the proper skills. In integrated situations, teachers do not care about the students' education. I believe the movement is not over, and we need strong leaders to guide us to the future. Too many of our leaders are [so] concerned with putting themselves in the political arena that they lose sight of what is important. Dr. King got the Nobel Peace Prize, but his main focus was the people. To me, many of our leaders are not doing their job for the people. I think we need a new leader like Dr. King to lead us. I have my master's [degree] in speech pathology and my doctorate in special education. I teach students who do not know what the SCLC was or barely know who Dr. King is. My belief is that those who do not know history are doomed to repeat it. As an English teacher, I want black students to articulate themselves better. I wish our colleges and churches would do more in our community concerning education. Affirmative action is being taken away, and we must educate our children to continue the fight. Our fight is more for the youth, and their fight must continue for our survival.

NOTES

BCRI OHP, vol. 9, sec. 2 (July 19, 1995). Edited, annotated, and abridged by Desiree Fisher and John McKerley.

1. James Weldon Johnson, "The Creation," http://www.poetry-archive.com/j/the_creation.html (accessed April 7, 2009).
2. On the selective-buying campaign, see Joe N. Dickson, BCRI OHP, vol. 14, sec. 1 (April 15, 1996).
3. "D-Day" was the name given by SCLC organizers to the mass youth protests on May 2, 1963.
4. On the continued activism of Birmingham's D-Day generation, see Gwendolyn Gamble, BCRI OHP, vol. 12, sec. 1 (January 24, 1996).
5. Barbara Jordan later became the first African American woman from the South elected to Congress.
6. See Adam Fairclough, *Race and Democracy: The Civil Rights Struggle in Louisiana, 1915–1972* (Athens: University of Georgia Press, 1999), 327–28.
7. See Robert J. Norrell, *Reaping the Whirlwind: The Civil Rights Movement in Tuskegee* (New York: Knopf, 1985), 172–77.
8. On Younge's death and the demonstrations that followed, see ibid., 174–84.
9. On Gaston's conservative approach to racial politics, see Joe N. Dickson, BCRI OHP, vol. 14, sec. 1 (April 15, 1996).

JAMES ROBERSON

JAMES ROBERSON was born in Jefferson County, Alabama, on June 14, 1943. Like LaVerne Revis Martin, Roberson grew up in Collegeville, the child of movement activists and a neighbor of the Shuttlesworth family. He credited much of the movement's early success to Fred Shuttlesworth's leadership and the activism of the neighborhood's black workers. According to Roberson, while the members of the city's black middle class often found reasons for accommodating a system within which they had prospered, "the poor people . . . wanted something better and didn't have anything to lose," and they gravitated toward the ACMHR and movement activism. Moreover, whereas Shuttlesworth was comfortable being "confrontational," he recalled, "some ministers . . . did not partake of any of this, so their churches were never available for the mass meeting. [It] was a radical move to go against segregation and take a stand."

THE POOR PEOPLE WANTED SOMETHING BETTER

I lived in Collegeville, directly across from Bethel Baptist Church. You would leave my house, and [in] ten seconds you would be at the church. Rev. Shuttlesworth lived next to the church before the bombing.

I was always involved. My dad used to write plays about the struggle of the black man, and we would have plays at church as entertainment. Rev. Shuttlesworth was my minister, and the NAACP was strong until they outlawed it.

Martin Luther King gets the majority of the credit, but in reality Fred Shuttlesworth started the movement [in Birmingham]. He called Dr. King in from Montgomery to assist. King had profound [patience], more so than Fred. Rev. Shuttlesworth would be hot tempered. Sometimes he wasn't the coolest thing around. [Shuttlesworth] would say, "Lord, forgive me," and go along with it. He was a little different than Dr. King. At that time, Dr. King did not have the same notoriety. We knew he was a beautiful speaker. I've seen Dr. King stand up and do a profound delivery without a piece of paper. He was just profound. He had a way of expressing himself that would make you want to move, make you want to make a commitment. [But] every Monday for years, [Shuttlesworth and] the Alabama Christian Movement for Human Rights [held mass meetings]. When they outlawed [the NAACP] in '56, Rev. [Shuttlesworth] said, "That's not going to stop us." He organized the [ACMHR]. Reverend had a vision. He was divinely appointed. Because everybody knew things were not right. Everybody knew that we were second-class citizens. Everybody knew that whites looked down on us.

Sixteenth Street [Baptist] is [noted] as the church of the civil rights movement, but really Sixteenth Street was thrust into national prominence when the girls were killed [on September 15, 1963]. But the grassroots of the civil rights struggle was not at Sixteenth Street—it was at Bethel Baptist Church in Collegeville. And in reality—and this is not negative on Sixteenth Street—but it was [the] church of the bourgeoisie blacks.[1] They were the educators and the doctors, and they had arrived. In our finite thinking, they didn't want any part [of the movement]. They were comfortable. Now, you had some that were there, but it was the poor people who wanted something better and didn't have anything to lose. I would say that if Rev. Shuttlesworth was the pastor of Sixteenth Street, I don't know he would have gotten the same following as he did in Collegeville, where there was only hope that we could do better than what we were doing.

In December of '56, they bombed [Bethel Baptist Church]. There are certain things in your life that you'll never forget. Some of them are like marriages and death and commencement, things like that. But, in '56, I was a teenager. Where my house was built, I lived in the back section of it, and my mom and dad lived on the other side. It was not a big house. I'm less than one hundred yards from the church. So when the impact hit, it felt as if the earth had just erupted. You could feel the thrust of it and the smell of it. It was so powerful. You can think of a shotgun shell and how loud it is and multiply that maybe by two thousand. It was a powerful impact with thrust behind it, and when you looked out and you could see the electrical wires popping and you could smell the odor. Those things you can't erase. And then my dad ran and checked on us. He said the church had been bombed. My dad and Mr. [James] Revis were the first two people to go in and see about Rev. Shuttlesworth. Glass was everywhere. My mom collected little ceramic pieces. The impact of the bomb had knocked all the glass out of the windows. The odor was there. Things were still falling in, and I just knew Reverend was hurt. I was in love with Rickie, the second daughter of Rev. Shuttlesworth, and she was in the house. Fred and Junior were in there, [too]. The entire family was in the house. It was not empty, [but] no one was injured.[2]

When that first bomb went off, the parsonage was right next to Bethel Baptist Church, and there was a walkway or crawl space about thirty inches [wide]. You could walk between it. That bomb was put between the walls of the church and the house, and Rev. Shuttlesworth's bed was in that same room. When that bomb went off—they said sixteen, eighteen, or twenty sticks [of dynamite]—the impact of that bomb ripped out the left side of the house, and the house caved in. Reverend was in that side. When Daddy and Mr. Revis went in to check on the Reverend, there was a rafter or joist that had come from the ceiling that had gone through the bed. To show you how God works, the impact of the bomb threw Reverend out of the bed. When it threw him out of the bed, that wood went through there. He got up, put on his preacher coat, and came out on the porch. By that time, the community was there with guns and shotguns. Everybody was there because we had been involved in a lot of things, trying to desegregate the train stations and the buses and all that. Reverend came [out] on the good side of the porch without a scratch, without a scar, without a drop of blood, without no loss of sight, no loss of hearing, and preached goodwill and love and giving direction. The Reverend never showed any fear. That gave me inner strength to believe that he was chosen. Now, he was a little man. He's not a gigantic guy. Sometimes I thought he was crazy, some of the things that he would do. He would confront Bull Connor.

There were some angry black people because [whites] had bombed this [church] and tried to kill Reverend. Mr. [James] "Puny" Bell had his gun and was not ashamed to show [it]. He was waiting on the police to come because we figured the police had something to do with it. [Shuttlesworth] said, "Take Puny Bell home. He's not ready for this. Y'all take him home. When they get here, we don't want any violence, no confrontation at all."

Most people don't realize [what] the police department in Birmingham was like. I go to some African countries, and democracy is not everywhere, but the military is sometimes more powerful than anything that you have [here]. The Birmingham Police Department was like an armed military. They did what they wanted to do. In [Collegeville], they had one car. I'll never forget it. Car No. 13 used to have a black cat [emblem] on the rear bumper. They had one policeman nicknamed Kid Glove. He would get out of his car, put on his gloves, and fight you. Things were a little different. Shooting a black was not a big thing. So Reverend would have confrontations with the police department. He would go down to the terminal station [and stage a sit-in].[3] He was always confrontational.

The police was always at the mass meetings. In every mass meeting, there would be at least two white policemen sitting down, detectives sitting in the meeting.[4] And then you would have four or five cars outside. There were blacks within the movement who were informants. And through the intelligence underground, we knew some of them who were working for the policemen to find out things that were going on.

A mass meeting was like a pep rally. It was a pep rally with religious overtones, with a sense of direction. We would meet at this church on the north side one Monday, and the next mass meeting would be at East Birmingham. There were some ministers that did not partake of any of this, so their churches were never available for the mass meeting. [It] was a radical move to go against segregation and take a stand. Some of us became prisoners within our own mentality—that this is the way it's supposed to be. There were others who had hope.

At the mass meeting, we had good singing. Carlton Reese, who is still in Birmingham, was the organist. He could make that organ talk, and we had good, upbeat singing. Then we would have the announcements, and Reverend would talk about where we're going and what we were going to do and where we are in this lawsuit and where we are in another one. And then we would have a sermon and go out fired up. That was every Monday. My daddy never missed a mass meeting until he had his first stroke in '94. He had been to every one. In those days, it was important that if you were in the fight, if you were in the struggle, you attended a mass meeting. They were always packed. Being the way we were, you had to be a part. If you had the kind of parents I had, you had to be a part.

We had our own security. The police were watching us, and we were watching the police. We had young guys, [and] a lot of old guys. [Stone Johnson and I] spent many nights together talking, and John Lewis and Mr. [Merritt] Stoves and Reuben Davis and Clifford Davis and the guys my age, the teenagers. They had their own security system. We would watch and let them know what was going on. If we saw strange cars, we would take a tag number down, and things like this. I was a part of that, and I sat on [the] Revises' porch. We built a room with glass all the way around it, and you could see the south side of the church, the front of the church, and you could see the left side. So from that position, we had the front of the church covered, we had the sides of the church covered. We set up a little space heater, drank coffee, and had shotguns. When we really thought something hot was going on, we had somebody on the third floor of the church looking out, covering the back end of it. These were volunteers. There was no money exchanged. It was just a commitment to protect the property and to protect Rev. Shuttlesworth.[5]

They used [the youth] in bus segregation, [too]. We would ride the buses and sit up front. I wish I could find one of those green boards [used to segregate the buses]. I hope somebody took one. But we would ride the buses, and [the police] used to have a black car. If there was any problem on the bus, they would call this particular security guy, and he would come and arrest you or whatever. When the guy would get off to call the security people, we would get off the bus and catch another bus and do the same thing and come back and report what we did. I was never arrested. The first time I defied the segregation of the bus, there was fear. The only way I could describe it [is] if I had a brown bag and had something in it that was alive and told you it was a rattlesnake and sat it on your lap. You didn't know if it was going to strike or what was in it. That's the kind of fear that gripped me when I first violated the rules and sat up front. Now, that fear was self-induced because of my upbringing, but then the whites had the power to kill, to shoot, and to maim.

NOTES

BCRI OHP, vol. 18, sec. 2 (June 25, 1996). Edited, annotated, and abridged by Horace Huntley and John McKerley.

1. See Lynne B. Feldman, *A Sense of Place: Birmingham's Black Middle-Class Community, 1890–1930* (Tuscaloosa: University of Alabama Press, 1999), 140–43.

2. According to Shuttlesworth, Deacon Charlie Robinson and his wife, Blanche, were also in the house at the time of the bombing (Fred Shuttlesworth, BCRI OHP, vol. 23 A, sec. 3 [December 11, 1997], 16). See also Andrew M. Manis, *A Fire You Can't Put Out: The Civil Rights Life of Reverend Fred Shuttlesworth* (Tuscaloosa: University of Alabama Press, 1999), 108, 110.

3. On March 6, 1957, Shuttlesworth defied segregation ordinances and sat in the "white" section of Birmingham's Terminal (Train) Station (Manis, *Fire*, 126–29). See also Rev. Lamar Weaver, BCRI OHP, vol. 3, sec. 4 (March 16, 1995).

4. See Joe Hendricks, BCRI OHP, vol. 8, sec. 1 (June 23, 1995).

5. On the movement's security guards, see Colonel Stone Johnson, BCRI OHP, vol. 1, sec. 3 (January 6, 1995); James Armstrong, BCRI OHP, vol. 4, sec. 5 (April 10, 1995); Reuben Davis, BCRI OHP, vol. 13, sec. 4–5 (March 20, April 3, 1996).

ANNETTA STREETER GARY

ANNETTA STREETER GARY was born in Birmingham on December 26, 1946. The light-skinned Gary at times struggled to find her place in a world divided between white and black. Although her skin tone often conferred certain privileges, it could also be a liability in the increasingly polarized context of the 1960s. "It was not an issue with our friends unless someone got angry," she recalled. "Then they would call me half white or something like that." Gary was a member of an all-girls club, the Peace Ponies, that became a vehicle for supporting the movement. Moreover, whereas Gwendolyn Gamble and others stressed the role that black parents played in bringing their children into the movement, Gary's testimony suggests the ways in which young people's participation could energize their parents' activism: "[My mother and father] began to attend the mass meetings after the first time I was arrested."

I WANT MY FREEDOM

My parents were born in Birmingham, and so was I. The majority of my youth was spent in Titusville. I have two sisters. I'm the [oldest] of three. My mother was a graduate of Tuskegee Institute, and my father completed two years at Miles College. My mother was a youth director for the black YWCA. My father was a barber, self-employed. I went to Catholic school in the first grade [at] St. Mary's in Fairfield. In fourth grade, I was allowed to transfer to public education. I went to Washington Elementary School, where W. C. Madison was my principal. [He was] a very fine man. I have several teachers that I remember during that time: Mrs. [Louise] Towns, who was my eighth-grade teacher; Mrs. Baldwin, who was my seventh-grade teacher; [and] Mrs. Beans, my sixth-grade teacher. Those are just some of the ones that come to mind. I don't remember any of the nuns at St. Mary's by name, but I remember the experience. At that time, Catholic schools were very, very strict, and at one time I thought I wanted to be a nun. I knew at a very, very early age that I wanted to be a teacher. When I was in Catholic school, none of my teachers were black. All of them were white nuns. When I went to the public school, it was completely different. Washington was larger. Even at that time, the classrooms were larger, [and so was] the number of children in the classroom. We were treated with love at Washington. We were like a family. I guess the same thing was true for St. Mary's. I do remember that at St. Mary's, we had more equipment than we did at Washington. My instructions, I don't feel, were any less.

After Washington, I went to Ullman High School. George Bell was my principal. I have one teacher that really stands out in my mind. That's Miss Odessa Woolfolk. She was my eleventh-grade American history teacher and my twelfth-grade world history teacher. She was a little woman that made a big impact on my life. She is a very, very intelligent woman. Her classes were—she made them so lifelike, like you were there. She was just a good instructor. I remember that was during the civil rights movement. A lot of teachers, after they found out that I had gone to jail, did not look too highly on that. Miss Woolfolk made a big to-do about it. She made me feel like a hero. It was just her demeanor, the way she treated us. It was like we were a part of her. I know a lot of things she could not say and not do because her job was at stake. She would just casually turn her head and pretend she didn't know what was going on.

In the [1950s], I can often remember going to movies with my father on Sundays. No one would be on the bus but us, but yet we had to go to the back of the bus. We were very inquisitive girls, and we wanted to know why. I never will forget—I guess I had to have been about eleven or twelve years old, maybe not quite that old. We got up on the bus on Sixth Avenue, going to the movie. My daddy decided that we weren't going to sit on the back of the bus that day. He got us, and he sat us up in the front. He sat there with us. The bus driver pulled over right there. He pulled over, and he told my father that either [we were] going to move back, or he was going to call the police. I remember there were several older women on the bus, and they told my daddy that you don't do anything like that when you have children with you. They kind of chastised him because we were crying. We were kind of upset. All we knew was that the bus driver was going to call the police on our daddy. It was very, very devastating to us. So he got us, and he moved us back to the back of the bus. The bus driver went on. He never did call the police. My daddy often told us, "We could have made history if y'all wouldn't have cried."

We were so young, and we did not understand. You can look at the color of my skin and see that unless you just knew that I was black, you would not be able to tell. It was not an issue with our friends unless someone got angry. Then they would call me half white or something like that. It really, really bothered me as a child. We had parents that were able to sit me down and explain that we don't control our color. That's just like the white man holding us down because we are black. We are not in control of our color. Like I said, my mother and my father were both light-skinned. [With] my genes, I had no choice but to [have a light complexion]. Yes, it was always as a child, and even now I have people to question me about my race.[1]

I was in a social and savings club at the time, the Peace Ponies. I don't remember how we came up with that name. I do remember there were eight of us, just girls. We were tenth- and eleventh-graders. They were all from Titusville. The way we got involved [was] we came to a couple rallies over at Sixteenth Street Baptist Church. Then we got so we were following the movement around. I really don't remember exactly why we went to that first meeting. I know [that] after we went to that first meeting, we decided that this was something that we were going to do as a project, our club. We would go to the meetings, to the rallies. On Saturdays, they would have training. We would come to the training.

Like I said, we were going to the training. Mrs. [Lucinda B.] Roby would take us down on Saturdays to the meetings if we didn't have a way. Hosea Williams was one of the ones that were training us. They would talk to us about nonviolence. How, regardless of what someone did to you then, you were not to resist them. We made signs. They talked to us about what we were to say when we were arrested, if we were arrested. At that time, a lot of parents lost their jobs because children were participating. In the mass meetings, they would have different ones that had already been arrested come up and tell their stories and tell what had happened to them.

I remember the first time I heard Dr. [Martin Luther] King speak. It was as if he was hypnotizing you. When we would leave out of the meeting, it was just like we needed to do something right then. We were sitting back, and we could hardly wait until they started the demonstrations. I cannot count the number of times that I've seen Dr. King. I tell my children that at school a lot of times. People who were not involved in the movement, after everything was over with, then of course, Dr. King became a hero to them. But he was a hero to me even before this. It was just something about him. I knew that he was God-sent. That meant a whole lot.

The first demonstration I was involved in, I was not arrested. It was during a time when Dr. King was in the county jail. We went down along with some preachers. I guess it was a group about twenty-five to thirty. We went down, and we kneeled on the steps, and the preachers prayed, and we sang. I never will forget that the fire chief came up, but for whatever reason they did not do anything. They just stood by the side. They did not do anything on that particular day. It was on a Sunday. They didn't do anything. After we prayed, we disbanded. I think it was maybe the next Saturday that I was arrested for the first time. We were dropped on Third Avenue, right there by Loveman's [Department Store], and we marched from that corner up to the alley that was in between Loveman's and [J. J. Newberry and Co.]. What we were trying to do was to keep people from going in. We were marching because that was after they refused to let blacks eat at the lunch counter in Newberry's. What we were doing was picketing so that blacks would not go into Newberry's. That is where we were picked up. We were taken to Jefferson County [Jail].

I remember when we were taken to the county jail. We were fingerprinted. They took our pictures, and then they began to question us. They asked our name. The first thing that was asked of me when I got up there, the matron, the police matron or whatever she was called, looked at me and said, "What are you doing in here?" I said, "I want my freedom." She just laughed, that was so funny to her. When I said I was black, she called several other people in to see me. At that time, I was a little girl with long pigtails. She just had no idea that I was black. They separated us. [They] took the ones with my complexion, [and] they put us in a separate group from the rest of them. They put us in a dayroom that had no facilities for sleeping or anything like that. It just had a big iron table and iron benches. They said that's where the prisoners would come during the day. They put the others back in the cells. Yes, they did. This was at Jefferson County Jail. Not many children went to Jefferson County. This was before D-Day, before May 3, [1963]. It was in the later part of April, maybe about the middle of April. I was arrested on Saturday morning, and I stayed until Monday night.

It was an experience that just can't be explained. I remember the closing of the doors. We had one matron that came on in the evening shift [who] was not so bad as those other jailers or whatever they were called. They were white. They were tough. The food, [you] could not eat the food, period. There was no way to eat the food. They had us scrubbing, gave us rags to scrub along the front of the cells. If you were too loud or whatever, you were given extra duties, extra things to do. It was a large dayroom. It wasn't but about the eight of us, my club members also. All of us went. At night, when the night matron came on—remember that I said she was nicer to us—she allowed us to bunk up with the ones that were in the back. So what we did was kind of double up so that everybody could have somewhere to sleep.

[Movement supporters] came up to get us. The civil rights movement had gotten people to put their houses up [for our bail]. They came up and called our name. I had on a new sweater. I was so glad to get out of there that I ran off and left that sweater. Never looked back. I was glad to hear my name called. We went to a [mass] meeting the next night because it was so late that night we went home. Then we reported to the meeting, and this time we went to Bethel Baptist Church over in Collegeville, Fred Shuttlesworth's church. We gave an account of what had happened to us at that time.

At school, they were real interested about what had happened. You been to jail—we were fifteen, sixteen years old, and it was impressive to them. We had several kids that were beginning to become involved in the movement. This was, like I said, before D-Day. In my class it was not as many because I was in an accelerated class, and for whatever reason, the kids in that class did not participate like other students at Ullman High School.

The night before the demonstrations, they told us that they were going to come around to various schools. They encouraged us to go to school because a lot of kids were talking about just not going to school. That was not the effect that they wanted. They wanted you to go to school so we could really help to turn the children out of school. I remember, as the day wore on, no one showed up from the movement. We [were] thinking, "What's going on?" Finally they got over to Ullman. Hosea Williams was the movement person to come. I think it was about one thousand and something children that came out of Ullman High School on that day. I can remember now the feeling. It was just like, "It's here! It's about to happen!" And the joy of seeing all of these children coming out to participate in the movement. It's a feeling that you just can't describe. Mr. Bell was running around like a chicken with his head cut off. Mr. Bell did not want us to leave that school. One teacher, like I said, Miss Woolfolk, turned like she did not see. Mrs. [Cleopatra] Goree was another teacher that acted as if she did not see. Now, we had a number of teachers that told us we were wrong, that we were breaking laws and we were putting our parents' jobs in jeopardy, that we would be penalized. That did not stop us.

We went down to Sixteenth Street Baptist Church. We went out in groups. As soon as one group cleared, then another group would go. The idea was that they were not going to be able to handle all of us. They did not have enough police to stop us. Kelly Ingram Park, as far as you could see, was just people, people everywhere, which was a difference because, like I said, when we first started, the first couple of demonstrations that I took part in, there were fifteen to twenty people. This time, as we came out and we had our signs and all, I remember that I started crying when I looked up and saw all of the people. I guess it was just the idea of what was about to take place, the things that we had heard about, that Dr. King had talked about, how the movement was just moving forward. It was just overwhelming.

My club members were there, but we were separated. I think it was two, three, or four of us together in one group, and three or four in another. We went around the corner, and I guess that must have been Seventeenth Street. We got right around the corner from Seventeenth Street; that was when the water hose met us. By me being small, I was one of the first ones in line along with one of my club members, Jackie. We had been taught that if they put the water hose on you, to sit down and cover your face so that the pressure of the water would not hurt your eyes. We were taught to sit down, and if we balled up into balls, then the water would not hurt as much. But that was not so. I can remember us balling up, hugging together, and the water just washing us down the street. Sitting and balled up, and the water just washed us down the street. Forceful. It was like pins maybe, sticking you in your arms and legs and things. [The] water was very, very forceful.

Afterwards, we went back to the church. What I did was to leave the church and go home and change clothes. One of my club members did not leave, and she was arrested on that day. She was arrested again on that day. She got arrested again prior to getting back to the church. I looked up and saw my parents. My parents had come down and, like I said, I went home to change clothes because I was soaked. I changed clothes and came back down. My parents brought me back. They were apprehensive, but yet they knew that this was something that I truly believed in. I guess they felt like, "Well, she's been to jail before."

They began to attend the mass meetings after the first time I was arrested. They began to attend the meetings because the day that the water was put on me, they did not even know that I had come down. They just happened to be standing out around. I did not tell them that I was going that day. They took me home, and I changed clothes, and they brought me back downtown. I was never arrested again. I tried, especially when all my other club members were in jail, because all of the others managed to get arrested on D-Day for the second time.

My father and several other men in the neighborhood set up night patrols. They had someone posted right there on the corner of Greensprings and Goldwire. They had someone posted right at the entrance on Fifteenth Avenue, off of Greensprings, down the hill, because that's the area. Some were round by Center Street School, just all over the neighborhood. Anywhere where a car could come in, they had someone posted. My daddy did not believe in weapons. I know that he was not armed, but I know that some were, because everyone did not believe in nonviolence.

[On] September 15, 1963, Sixteenth Street Baptist Church [was] bombed. We were home that Sunday. When the church was bombed, it was like a dark cast on that day. Just looked like a gray day. It happened that Cynthia Wesley was in my sister's class. Denise McNair's father and my mother finished Tuskegee together. Carole Robertson's father was a music teacher at Washington Elementary School. The only one that we were not connected to in some kind of way was Addie Collins. My grandmother was a member of Sixteenth Street Baptist Church before her death, so I was familiar with the church and everything. It was a sad day. I attended the funerals along with my club members. We attended the funerals. We did not attend Carole Robertson's funeral. We went to the three funerals that were held together at Sixth Avenue Baptist Church.[2]

NOTES

BCRI OHP, vol. 36, sec. 4 (June 4, 1998). Edited, annotated, and abridged by Horace Huntley and John McKerley.

1. For a discussion of color in the black community, see Angela Davis in Jay David, ed., *Growing Up Black* (New York: Morrow, 1992), 216–17. For more recent commentary, see "Study Finds That African American College Students Prefer Light Skinned Blacks as Dating or Marriage Partners," *Journal of Blacks in Higher Education*, May 24, 2007, http://www.jbhe.com/latest/index052407_p .html (accessed July 28, 2008).

2. Martin Luther King Jr. convinced the families of Cynthia Wesley, Denise McNair, and Addie Mae Collins to take part in a joint funeral at Sixth Avenue Baptist Church on September 18, 1963.

JAMES WARE AND MELVIN WARE

THE WARE BROTHERS were born in Birmingham, James on March 17, 1947, and Melvin on December 6, 1948. They discussed the murder of their brother, Virgil Ware, at the hands of two young white men, Michael Lee Farley and Larry Joe Sims, on September 15, 1963, the same day that Klan members bombed the Sixteenth Street Baptist Church. Both the bombing and the shooting illustrated some whites' willingness to use violence in the wake of the movement's organized challenge to white supremacy and racial segregation. "I was really shocked [that] they caught" the murderers, James Ware recalled. "I never thought they would."

I'M SHOT

James: I grew up out in Pratt City, what they call Blount Crossings. My mother and father were both originally from Birmingham, born here. I had five brothers and one sister. I was the oldest. I sort of stayed with my grandmother for the longest time. She lived in Pratt City, too. When I got about thirteen or fourteen, I went back and stayed with my mama [because] my grandmama died.

I always had a big deal about wanting my own car. My brother [Virgil] and me were going to get a paper route, and we were going to start throwing the paper. That particular Sunday, another one of my uncles came from Docena, and he said, "Y'all come out there, and I'll give you a bike." My brother was going to get the papers in Pratt City, and [each day] after I got out of school, we were going to wrap them up and throw them. So we rode out to Docena to see about a bike. The guy out there didn't have it ready, [but he] said when he finished putting it together, he would bring it to us. That particular Sunday, we were on our way back, and [Virgil] was on the handlebars, riding along. I was pulling him. I was bigger than all the rest of [my siblings]. They were little compared to me. I looked like my daddy.

We saw a bike coming from the other direction [with two white boys on it]. We just kept on pedaling. They got so close [that] they just overcame us. When [Virgil] got shot, he said, "Wow, I'm shot." He just fell off the handles and fell to the ground. I stood over him, and I guess five or six minutes later a car came by, and I told them what happened, and I told them where we stayed. So they turned around and went back to Blount, and we were about a mile [or] a mile and a half from home. They turned around and brought my mom and dad and people down there. He was dead by that time. He didn't say anything after that, after he said, "I'm shot." He was fourteen and I was sixteen.

Melvin: That day, I was watching a football game. James and Virgil had gone to Docena to purchase a bicycle from my uncle. They flashed on the news about the bombing of the Sixteenth Street Baptist Church. I just shook. I was just about twelve, and my mind just dawned on them. I thought about their safety during that time. [When they weren't back] after about two o'clock, I just walked and was tossing and turning. My mother had gone to the usher board, and when she had gotten back, a lady asked her if all of her children were there. She said no, two of them were not there, and [the woman] said, "You better come with me." That's when she went and found my two brothers. [Virgil] had got killed, and James was out there. The whole experience affected me very deeply [because] it was like a piece of pie. You bake a pie, and then you take a piece out, you have a piece missing. That's really how it affected me. I thought about what Virgil would be doing now if he were still living. I would've liked to see him grown like us and have a family.

It was real sad when I had to go back to school. My teachers and classmates had taken up some money to buy flowers at the funeral, and everybody [gave] their condolences [and told] you how sorry they were. It was sad. I don't think my teacher tried to protect me; she treated me just like any other kid. I lost my brother over nothing. At the time, I thought it was all for nothing. [But] as time [goes] by, I believe it was for a reason. I believe there's a reason for everything. No question about it: that [day] launched the civil rights movement with the bombing of the four girls and Virgil's death. I think they had another boy that got shot on that same day.[1] I think President Kennedy declared that a day of mourning to let the flags fly at half-mast. Then he was assassinated about a month later.

James: When Virgil got shot, I really didn't know that [Sixteenth Street Baptist Church] had been bombed. I don't guess I knew anything until the next day. We left early that morning and went to church, and I don't think we told anybody we were going to go pick up the bike. We left early, and we stayed out there all day riding around. It was something like a junkyard more or less, just riding around on the bike. I didn't know anything about the church until the next day.

I remember the day my brother was shot 'cause I stayed there with Virgil so much. I don't even remember who stopped and went and got my mama and daddy. I believe [those people] were white. Anyway, they went and got [my parents]. When I went home, I didn't come out of the house no more. I told the police what happened. That's all I did. I told them it was two guys on a little red scooter. The one on the back did the shooting. I had to testify at the trial.

That was the first time I had seen [Farley and Sims] was at the trial. They had said at the time that they thought we had rocks. We didn't have anything. [Virgil] had both his hands on the handlebars, and it took all I could for pedaling, so we didn't have anything. At the trial, that was never brought up. If it was, I don't remember. They asked me to point him out, and I pointed to the two guys. I never know how the police found them that quick, I tell you the truth. When they came to my house, I remember Detective Woods saying, "I think we got a lead on who they were." Next thing I know, we were at the grand jury, and they went on with the trial.

The verdict wasn't right. I figured they would have gotten way more than what they did for what they did.[2] To tell you the truth, I didn't even expect them to catch them. Thank God that they did. I was shocked when that guy called me and wanted to apologize. One of them did call to apologize. He said, "I want to apologize for what happened," and he said, "I know how it feels, I lost a nine-year-old son." We didn't go into any details about it, though. I went on and accepted the apology [because] you can't go around hating the world. Let the Lord take care of that. I was really shocked [that] they caught them. I never thought they would.

I guess Virgil and I were closer. Virgil was the type of person you could get along [with]. You tell him you want to do something, and he liked it. All of [my siblings] were good, but he liked to work like I did [because] he would go all the way into Pratt City to get the paper from the paper house. He said he would have them ready for me to throw them. We were going to split the car, I guess. I didn't give up on the car. Melvin and me, we went and got a job at a service station on Sixth Avenue, that Shell Oil station. We worked for them, and we cut grass over the mountain. I still ended up getting a car. It was a '54 Ford, I believe.

Before that happened to my brother, I had joined the basketball team at Jackson-Olin [High School]. I stopped that and didn't do much after that. [I] went to school and went to gym, stuff like that. I shot basketball at school, but I had to be in before dark. My mama was kind of scared for a while, but she got better after some years. She said she lost one, and if she lost another, you would have to bury her, too. So I didn't try to holler with her too much. I just tried to do like she said. But we were already grown then. She wouldn't even let me walk to school on the track with the other kids after that happened. She would pay a guy a dollar and a quarter. He took a lot of children to school. When it started, I didn't want to ride with him. I wanted to go ahead and walk with the other guys and things. After that happened, they made us ride to school.

School was pretty good. I liked it about like anybody else. I always had a big dream about getting bigger and going to work and buying what I wanted to buy. At [Jackson-Olin], I took up carpentry when I was in the eleventh grade, I worked at a service station, and in between that I was working over the mountain cutting grass. My daddy had a job over there, and he got me a job cutting grass over there. I remember one time I was in high school, and they gave a little test. They called everybody in there and asked everybody what they wanted to do after high school, what they wanted to be. I told [the teacher] at that time I wanted to work at big steel, TCI, because at that time it was where you could make a lot of money. I just wanted to work at that job out there. I met some guy out at Blount that worked out there, and he said he was going to help me get on. They finally called me out there, but I had just started that Monday at Alabama Byproducts. The guy at Alabama Byproducts said, "Don't go out there [because] they always lay off out there, and you won't hardly get laid off at ABP." I never did. I was fortunate. I've been out there twenty years, and I've been pretty fortunate so far. Never laid off yet.

NOTES

BCRI OHP, vol. 30, sec. 4 (September 17, 1997). Edited, annotated, and abridged by A. Michelle Craig and John McKerley.

1. Johnny Robinson was shot by a police officer the same afternoon. In October 1963, a grand jury refused to indict the officer, Jack Parker, in connection with Robinson's death (*Birmingham World,* September 18, 1963, October 16, 1963).

2. Both Sims and Farley were convicted of second-degree manslaughter and sentenced to seven months in jail, but a judge later reduced the sentence to probation because, in his words, "they came from 'good families'" (*Chicago Daily Defender*, January 21, 1964, July 3, 1967).

WILLIE A. CASEY

WILLIE A. CASEY was born in Birmingham on October 23, 1947. Casey first found his politics on the playground while he was a student at Carver High School: "One day, there was much discussion about Martin King, the demonstrations, and the boycotts," recalled Casey. "I knew about King, but that day I didn't know the demonstrations were going on. I knew we had a test." Following his friends out of school (with his teacher's covert blessing), Casey joined dozens of other students on their way to a mass meeting at the Sixteenth Street Baptist Church. After some impromptu training in nonviolence, Casey and his friends joined the demonstrations and were promptly arrested. While fun and excitement remained his primary motivations, Casey also came to see the experience in a broader light. "I [knew] there were a lot of black folks together, and we were doing something that was real. It was kind of exciting to be a part of something that big. Just being in a crowd of people, it is easy to get caught up in the moment." Furthermore, his description of his experiences in Cincinnati, Ohio, where he went to live with his sister and her family after his brief stint at Carver High, suggests the influence of the larger civil rights movement on how young people understood race in the North as well. Although he was shocked and inspired by the educational environment of his new, integrated high school, Casey noted that race remained an important factor in students' interactions. "Every Friday we had 'civil rights fights'—black kids against white kids."

YOUNG AND DUMB AND NOT AFRAID

Both of my parents were from Hale County. As far as I know, my grandfather was George Casey. They said he came from Mexico or somewhere, but he was an Indian. I was born in Birmingham. I'm not sure if I was born at home or at the hospital. It was known then as Norwood Hospital; now it is called Carraway. Dr. Molden was the doctor.

My grandfather lived to be about one hundred. He was in real estate. He had a few houses, a church, and a store. We also owned a part of two farms. My father was a railroad man, a fireman. During that time, they used to give him passes, and we would ride the train all the time for free. My father had maids come in and clean the house. He was a real first-class person. He had clogged arteries. Today they have the ability to do a heart bypass; then, the pain was very excruciating. My father could not get rid of the pain, so he committed suicide. I saw it. I saw him do it. He didn't know I was looking at him. He was on the front porch, and I was looking through the side window. I saw him pull the trigger and then the gun went off. Our house address was [at] 2501 Twenty-fourth Street North. I was about five years old when the suicide happened.

That was the dreariest Sunday of my life because he was a very unique gentleman. He was always talking about how to own stuff, how to be somebody, and about his heritage. He wanted to build a store near the house and work there to make money, so his kids could go to college. In fact, it's strange that kids are a lot tougher than adults give them credit to be. We all dealt with it in different ways. For me, it was something that didn't happen.

I was actually seven when I started school. Mrs. Audrey Washington was my first-grade teacher. I was pretty bright. Our principal was a hard taskmaster. He made all the kids wear a tie. If you didn't wear a tie, the principal would spank you with a big razor strap that he called K. I think you got one lick for not having on a tie. The teachers knew that if you came to class without a tie to send you down to the office. That was probably the most outstanding memory of my school era. There was no tolerance, only strict discipline. For a kid like myself, the discipline was positive because school was a big play period to me. I was the big clown of the class. Pain didn't bother me. The principal would spank me, and it was nothing. I got punished for what I did, and he would tell me not to do it again, and I would do it again. I can see how it kept other kids in line. A lot of kids would shout at me for getting them in trouble.

I went to Carver High School for one year. School wasn't interesting here in Birmingham. I remember we had a library, and the books were copyrighted in 1938, '42, '45, '46, all before I was born. All the books I read were history books with a little geography, math, English, and whatever, but they were all outdated.[1] I didn't get interested in learning until I left here and went to Ohio. I was shocked that in Ohio, the schoolbooks had current features and articles. Most books in the Birmingham schools were about [Harry] Truman and Teddy Roosevelt. It was all history, but I couldn't relate to it. When I got to Ohio, it amazed me to see books that had [John F.] Kennedy and [Nelson] Rockefeller in it or current events such as the Cuban [Missile] Crisis. It got me interested in going back to school.

Back in Birmingham, I was not interested in school that much, except going to play period. One day, there was much discussion about Martin [Luther] King, the demonstrations, and the boycotts. I knew about King, but that day I didn't know the demonstrations were going on. I knew we had a test. The test was going to be at the three o'clock class, but we were talking about walking out of school and going to the demonstration. I was all for that. The teacher sort of encouraged us, in a roundabout way. He told us, "This is something I can't tell you not to do, but I think it is something you should do. If I were you, I would probably do it, but I can't. I have a job and a family to feed. However, I'm not going to stand in the doorway because there are too many of y'all in here." We were outside the school, so if we wanted to stay there, we could stay, and if we wanted to leave we could leave. He was encouraging us to leave. Like I said, I knew I had a test coming up, and I knew I hadn't studied, so I was out of there.

We left Carver High School [and] headed for the Sixteenth Street Baptist Church. Before this point, I had never seen the church. We walked down the railroad tracks, which caused us to be late. The program had already started. There had to have been fifty to eighty of us. When we arrived at the church, I witnessed a large crowd of people outside and a lot of people inside the church. [A man] told me to go inside and hear what they were saying. Since we got to the church late, we sat in the last pew in the balcony. The church was full of people, wall to wall. I don't know who the gentlemen were, but they were talking. I got there at the end and heard that we were going to march out of the church. We were told, "If you have any knives, guns, or weapons, put them in these buckets with your name and address." If you were violent or potentially violent, you couldn't be in a march. This was a nonviolent march, and they didn't want anything to excite or provoke the police. When they started lining us up, I was about the twentieth person on the front row.

We started walking for about two or three blocks, singing "We Shall Overcome." Then the cops stopped us, let the dogs out, and put us in a paddy wagon. I was in the center of the paddy wagon. They crammed us in there like sardines. It must have been thirty of us in there. I don't know how long we sat there, but we sat there an hour or so in the heat of the day. Being young, it was no big deal to me. It was still fun at that point. They finally took us over to the city jail on Sixth Avenue and put us in cells. We must have been three hours or so in the cell. About three hours later, they came and got us and put us on a bus and carried us to Juvenile Court. It was dark then, must have been eight or nine o'clock. It was cold, and all we had were light coats. We stayed in Juvenile Court for two or three hours. It must have been one or two o'clock in the morning, and they put us on another bus. The Juvenile Court was full, so they didn't know where to put us.

I was young and dumb and not afraid. I didn't care. I [knew] there were a lot of black folks together, and we were doing something that was real. It was kind of exciting to be a part of something that big. Just being in a crowd of people, it is easy to get caught up in the moment. That night, they finally put us on another bus and carried us to Bessemer and put us in jail. We stayed down there about two weeks. First we got our [bunk beds], and then we just started talking. I had a bunk, and my friend had a bunk. No big deal, just young boys talking about what had happened. It was all very exciting to us. We stayed in a big holding cell. This was a jail cell but there were no bars up. The next morning, they opened the cafeteria. There were metal tables, and we just had to find someplace to sit. It was fun for the first three or four days. The first night, we sung a few songs. The second night we sung a little bit, [but] then it was like, who are we singing to? Later, we got so bored we started smoking toilet paper as cigarettes. We started telling stories. On Sunday, we were all sad. We knew it was Sunday because it was a very sunny day, and through the bars we saw people going to church. I really missed going to church. My father owned a church building, and I am very religious. It depressed me not being able to be outside and seeing people walking to church.

I think they forgot about us. I don't think my parents—my sister was serving as my parent—knew where I was. They knew I got arrested, but my sister was in Youngstown [Ohio] at the hospital. She had two kids, and her daughter was having an operation. Her son had seen me on TV. They knew where Cliff, my brother, was, but they didn't know where I was. She thought they had strung me up somewhere.

I didn't see Cliff until Tuesday, when I got back home. Another demonstrator named [Jerome] Washington, his parents came and got him out. He lived two blocks from me on Twenty-sixth Avenue. I told him to go by the store and tell my family where I was. The cops didn't notify them. I don't know why, because I had given them my name and address. It didn't frighten me. It was just a matter of wanting out of there. A lot of kids had gotten out. There were people getting out all the time. We stayed there. There were still about thirty or so still in there.

I came home after I got out. It was a pretty, sun-shining day. I had a good meal. Everybody was glad to see me, and I was happy to be home. I learned a big lesson. James Orange lived next door to us, and he came [over] and told me he was proud of me.[2] He said, "You're a real man now." It made me feel real good. That was the first comment I really got.

I never attended any more mass meetings. I didn't know what it was about. I knew more after I left [Birmingham]. I finished high school in Cincinnati and went to college in Ohio. There was a tremendous difference in education between Ohio and Alabama. I went to school at [Cincinnati's] Central High School. It was on Central Parkway. It was so big. It was about thirty acres. It was a huge school. It must have had ten thousand students going there. They had all kinds of programs too, from A to Z. They had vocational classes there to teach plumbing, electrician, airplane mechanics, and many other skills. The school's stadium was as big as Lawson Field [the high school football field for the Birmingham Public school system]. They tested me, and I came out general. As a general student, all I had to do was my lessons. I understood what they were saying all the time, and I knew the answer to the questions. I just couldn't write it down. The teacher would say it was spelled wrong, and I would say, "What?" [At that time], they didn't have all that testing in Birmingham.

I had to repeat the ninth grade because I was so far behind the other students. I worked for a civil rights lawyer named Walter [S. Houston]. He always said what was on his mind. I used to clean his office, and we made a pact to always be honest with each other. He used to test me on this all the time. Some Saturdays when I would clean his office, he would leave thirty or forty bucks in his drawer. I would just clean around it. He always kept me in school and would help me. We had a really good relationship. I always have a tendency to draw people to me, and sometimes I would get in the wrong crowd. It was in my junior year of high school when they mailed me a letter saying I was expelled from school. I thought I had gotten through, but there were racial problems there also. The problems got bad because [Martin Luther] King was around and people were made more aware. My sister told Walter that I was expelled from school. He said, "No problem, I'll get him back in." Every Friday, we had "civil rights fights"—black kids against white kids. That summer, [H.] Rap Brown came to Cincinnati and talked about how America does so much wrong. The difference between the two was [this]: King was pushing to give us our rights, and Brown was saying we already had our rights, and we needed to exercise them.

Walter helped me get into college. I went to [Western Kentucky University]. I was there for four months and got thrown out of school. There was a shooting, a big misunderstanding, and I got thrown out. Walter said, "Go on and pack your bag. I've got somewhere else you can go." He sent me to Chicago. That was a neat experience. In Chicago, I met a gentleman by the name of Jeff Fort.[3] It was a very neat experience to say the least. We had gangs in Birmingham, and we had gangs in Cincinnati, but Chicago had the Disciples. You had to be a part of this clique if you wanted to be out front. The things they wanted you to do was shoot a windshield or go steal something out of a grocery store. I said, "No." I came from a strong family background. Most black folks will tell their kids, "You're as good as other kids are. You're not better than they are." Walter used to tell me that I was better than other kids. If I had not been told that, I would have joined a gang. I wasn't pressured to join. I just didn't do it.

It was during this time that I figured it was time for me to straighten up. I had already got kicked out of one school. The year's tuition in Kentucky was lost when I came to Chicago. I didn't want to take any of my brother's tuition, so I dropped out one quarter. I went to work. At that time, when you dropped out of school, you were placed on the listing for the draft board. I got drafted, and they talked me into joining a four-year program. I went into the military and became a drill sergeant and a boxing champ.

After the military, I went back to Cincinnati. My sister kept pushing me to go back to school. She had an application for Central State [University, a historically black school in Wilberforce, Ohio]. I applied to enter Central State and was accepted. I majored in marketing and studied at Central State for four years. I left Ohio with my wife and my little baby. We came to Birmingham with the intention to go to Alaska in the spring. We never made it. We're still here.

NOTES

BCRI OHP, vol. 19, sec. 6 (September 4, 1996). Edited, annotated, and abridged by A. Michelle Craig, Horace Huntley, and John McKerley.

1. Rather than purchasing new texts for black classrooms, segregated school systems routinely reused out-of-date texts from white schools. On this practice, see also Gwendolyn Gamble, BCRI OHP, vol. 12, sec. 1 (January 24, 1996).

2. On Orange, an SCLC youth organizer, see Glenn T. Eskew, *But for Birmingham: The Local and National Movements in the Civil Rights Struggle* (Chapel Hill: University of North Carolina Press, 1997), 254.

3. Fort was the leader of the largest youth gang in Chicago, the Blackstone Rangers.

JAMES W. STEWART

BORN IN BIRMINGHAM on October 28, 1947, James Stewart was the son of an obstetrician and an English teacher. Like Annetta Streeter Gary, he recalled tensions over skin color within the city's African American community: "[A]t that time, to even call someone *black* was a no-no. Those were fighting words." After becoming involved with the move- ment through the actions of a fellow student, Stewart attended several mass meetings, where he received training in nonviolent direct action. The first time he was at a meeting that was the subject of a bomb threat, he learned about the dangers that activism could bring: "[W]hen we were going to meetings, it was much more serious than us just getting together as teenagers and sort of hanging out and listening to different speakers talk to us." In jail, Stewart felt terror at the repressive, institu- tional arm of white supremacy in Birmingham and courage from his fellow activists' expressions of hope and solidarity. The police "did some stuff to us that I can't forget," he said. "I was shocked that these people, No. 1, were doing that; No. 2, they were in authority and doing that; and No. 3, they hated us so much and didn't even know us, but they had so much hatred for us." Yet despite the dehumanizing conditions, Stewart and his friends refused release for several days: No one "else was getting out, and we understood that we would get out as a group."

I FELT EVERYBODY SHOULD BE INVOLVED

My father is Dr. R. C. Stewart. He was from Gibson, Louisiana. He was one of four boys and seven sisters. They all worked together, and they all helped each other. My mother is from Philadelphia originally. Most of her family is now in Washington, D.C. She and my father lived in Birmingham for quite a long time. I was born here in Birmingham. I had a brother who died in 1957 who was older than I was. His name was Robert Chauncey Stewart. I have a younger brother who is Gilman Douglas Stewart, and he and his family live in Seattle. He is about ten years younger than I am.

My father was an ob/gyn. Originally, he was an internist, and he wanted to do a fellowship. He had a very tough time being an ob/gyn in his day, and he got a lot of help from Carraway Medical Center. Dr. Boulware there helped him a lot, and Dr. Ben Carraway himself. My mother has a [master's degree] in English. She taught school. She taught in Texas. She has taught quite a few places. She taught here at Daniel Payne College, and then subsequently she taught English at UAB.

I attended Washington Elementary School. It was a very good atmosphere. Washington was a strong school. Dr. Waymon Matheson was the principal. I had very good teachers. I remember when I got into the fourth grade, my teacher, Miss Henry, started doing very practical things, teaching math by looking into the newspaper and having [us] shop for various things and adding them up. She made a game of it. She would challenge us to look in the dictionary to see who could find a word first. She taught us how to use the words at the top to gauge what might be on the rest of the page. It was a very exciting time educationally for me. I thought the teachers that I had were very good.

In that day, everybody lived in the same neighborhood: doctor, lawyer, Indian chief, worker. Everyone lived in the black community if you were black. So, my father being a doctor, we lived right in the community. I played with kids from Loveman's Village, from Southtown Project. We were all in there together. We all knew each other, and we all just survived and grew up playing with one another. But the community was 100 percent black. All of the friends, all of the interactions in that community, everything was black.

[But] at that time, to even call someone *black* was a no-no. Those were fighting words. Those were just as much fighting words as the N-word. However, as a lighter-skin black, I was called "high yellow" most of the time. [It] was more acceptable for people to call me "high yellow" or to make references to my nearly being white, all these kinds of things. Those were things that we laughed at, but if I retorted with a comment about someone's skin color being darker than mine, then everything stopped. All bets were off, and I had reached beyond the limit of what was acceptable at that time.

After Washington, I went to Ullman High School, which is now a part of UAB. But at that time, we would look down the street and say surely UAB would never [expand] as far as to encompass Ullman High School. [UAB] was on Twentieth Street at that time, and we were up on Twelfth Street. Ullman for me initially was a little bit traumatic because I was younger going into high school. I was twelve turning thirteen in October. I remember encountering the guys who would ask you for "block fees." I really didn't know what a block fee was, but I learned to pay a few of those in order to survive. But I had friends around me who were showing me and telling me different things. Also, I don't remember who, but there was a challenge to me academically. A couple of my friends and I said that we were going to try to go the first two years and make straight As, because we wanted to go into the honor society. We went to an assembly once [and] looked in the auditorium and saw that there were people who were going into the honor society with a 3.89, 3.95 [grade point average]. A couple of other students and I decided we were going to try to do that. Did I do that? To be honest with you, I can't remember. But I know that the academic challenge made me really pursue and focus in on my academics. I don't know if that is the reason why I achieved academic excellence at Ullman. If I hadn't had that, there were a lot of other things that could have pulled me off.

Dr. [George C.] Bell [the principal] was a character. He would always come in, and I have seen him come in and stand up on a desk and count the people. He was not a young man, even when he was a principal, but he was a delightful man. He set a precedent for us. He was a strong man. He was in control of the school. He wanted us to do something with our lives, and he challenged us. So when I was going through high school, I had an academic goal. But I was also "among the fellows," if you will. And they seemed to accept that in me, and they knew that I could play basketball with them at nine o'clock, and when it got dark, I would go home, clean up, eat dinner, and I would do my homework. The next day we would come in, and they would [ask], "Why is it that you have your homework? I thought we were all together." But I realized that I didn't [have to] neglect my academics and have Cs and Ds just to be accepted. That part of acceptance was excluded, and people seem to [have] accepted that.

The teacher who had the most impact on me was Odessa Woolfolk. Miss Woolfolk challenged us to apply civics to everyday life. There were times when we would look at news clippings. We would look at current events. We would talk about current events. We would give our opinions on current events. No one up until that time had asked us what our opinion was. We didn't know whether we thought a Republican had a better platform than a Democrat or what we thought about a particular policy, so I think that is what really influenced me to begin to look around me and to see some of the things that were incorrect in Birmingham and some of the racism that was actually law at the time, the Jim Crow laws.

I remember riding down Sixth Avenue to town or to Ullman High School, and having to take the "Colored" sign and always keep it in front of you, so it could be three-quarters to the rear. When you got on the bus, you would have to take the sign and make sure it was in front of you. No [black person] sat on the bench seats, ever. The very first seat. No one ever sat on that. No one black ever sat on that, and no white person ever got on the bus between there and downtown, but we still had to respect that. I can remember my mother dragging me away from a water fountain because I learned that the square, taller ones had the cold water. She wanted me to drink out of the white ones that were lower, but they had warm water, and they were the "Colored" water fountains.

I can remember being chased by the Klan. I was headed towards Bessemer. Some boys pulled up behind me very close, and I saw them in my rearview mirror. This was at night. They were white boys. They began to yell, and [it looked] like they were drinking. They began to move very close and flash their lights. So I looked in my rearview mirror, and I saw that one or two had hoods on. Now, at my age, I was petrified, and I was alone. I don't know why I was alone at this time, but I was alone driving in Birmingham in that area. So I turned off [onto] a side street and began to turn into neighborhoods, and eventually I turned up into a driveway and turned my lights out and just laid down. I heard them turn the corner, so they didn't see me pull up, and they went by. When I saw that they had really gone by, then I sat up and turned around and went home. I don't know if they were Klan members—I didn't check their cards. But I saw some hoods. So these could have been white boys who were putting pillowcases over their heads to just frighten people like myself. It didn't matter whether they were card-carrying Klan or not. They chased me because I was a black male, and it was something to do.

Growing up, a lot of things happened like that. I didn't tell my parents about that incident. I didn't want my parents to keep me inside all of the time and never let me go anywhere. I guess I didn't want to be confined on that basis. That is the same drive that made me ultimately stand up to the system and say, "No, I am not going to be confined here. I can't gauge my life based on what you want me to do and you don't want me to do."

Then there was Gertrude Grant, who in high school began to talk to me about the civil rights movement. She said, "You know, they are having movements at some of the churches." Some were at St. Paul's, a church around the corner.[1] On the south side, Rev. [Nelson H. Smith Jr.] had meetings [at New Pilgrim Baptist Church], so I began to go to those meetings and get involved and listened to the things that the men and women were saying about discrimination and having to make a change.[2] Probably the most dynamic person for the young—or for me, rather—was [SCLC organizer] James Bevel. Rev. Bevel looked like he was not too much older than us. He wore blue-jean suits all the time, and he always had the buttons on them. He was bald-headed, very identifiable, and he knew how to really talk to us about taking the responsibility for the movement, carrying it on, and getting involved.

My parents were not directly involved, and initially I had some feelings about that. At that age, I felt everybody should be involved—we should all go down, the entire city. Even when we began to demonstrate, I saw a lot of the older black adults not going, and I judged them at that time. But I began to understand when I got older that they had jobs. I found out that under no uncertain terms, if you were absent, if you were arrested, if you were anywhere near the civil rights demonstrations on [D-Day] or anytime after, you would be fired. So they had families and mortgages and things like that. And I think that is why [the] youth provided a certain strength and energy to the civil rights movement.

I became a regular at the mass meetings, and every one of them was packed. Churches were filled to the brim. There was standing room only. People sat around on the floors. We heard men like Dr. [Martin Luther] King, Jesse Jackson. We heard dynamic preachers, and they were talking directly to us. And they were telling us [that] it's our responsibility, it is up to us to draw a line in the sand and say we need to do something to address the racial problem. We saw friends from other sides of town. The movement meetings were always exciting, and we felt like we were doing something. There was a time when Jesse Jackson was talking, and I [remember] a man handed him a note. He just walked right up and handed him a note in the middle of his presentation, and Jesse looked at the note and he folded the note and put it in his pocket. He continued to preach for maybe five more minutes or so, and he said, "If you are wondering what the note said, the note said there is a bomb that is going to go off in this church." Now, initially I said, "Why did he not tell us that?" He said, "If you only knew how many times people have called at every movement meeting to say there is a bomb. They want us to leave, but tonight we are not going anywhere." I can tell you I had my feet turned toward the door, as I was saying, "Yeah, yeah, we are not going anywhere." Afterwards, I realized that the purpose was to make us disband and disperse and stop what we were doing. I said, "No, we are going to look at all the ways that they are attacking us, and we are going to not be moved."

We did not move that night; we stayed. There was no bomb that went off, and the attitude at that time was, if there was a bomb that goes off, so be it. But we were not going to leave based on a threat, because that was a common practice. Something changed with that perspective, having that perspective, and I am glad he actually told us that that night. So we knew that when we were going to meetings, it was much more serious than us just getting together as teenagers and sort of hanging out and listening to different speakers talk to us. I remember seeing Rev. [Fred] Shuttlesworth at the meetings. He was around quite a bit. Dr. Shuttlesworth, [and] Dr. A. D. King was around. He spent quite a bit of time with us in jail, and Rev. Bevel and Rev. N. H. Smith. Those are the ones that I remembered being around quite frequently.

I think I was prepared when I first went to jail. As a matter of fact, I know I was. Initially, we were at the point where we said, "We have had enough.

We will go to jail. We will do what it takes to bring the racism in Birming-ham to an end." We went to a meeting at Sixteenth Street Baptist Church. Dr. King was there, and by this time, I was among the leaders who were chosen to come to a small meeting and sit there and get the game plan. Dr. King spoke very directly to us and told us that the purpose was to overcrowd the jails, to overrun them, to bring public attention to what was going on in Birmingham. Some of us would get to the courthouse. That was the goal: to go to the City Hall and pray. Some of us would get there, and some of us would not get there. Some of us would be arrested. They told us to make no comment when we got in jail. They told us to be nonviolent. They gave us a real understanding of the purpose. Now, [nonviolence] didn't get in right away. I remember sitting in the meeting, and they asked us if we had any weapons. They asked if we would please put them in the basket when it came around, and the basket went around the room and it was empty when it got back. I don't know if it was Dr. King or someone else who spoke to us more assertively, kind of like a minister who didn't get enough money the first time the basket was passed. But he said something to us about the importance of not having weapons, and the next time the basket went around, it was filled with all kinds of weapons that we had which were our personal security. We had to give that up for the greater cause, and we did.

The day of the demonstration I came directly from home. It was May [2], "D-Day," or "Demonstration Day." So we did not go to school that day. We went directly to the church, gathered up, and received our instructions. We had several groups at the church. I do remember when the door was opened. My group was selected to go out of the front door and down the steps. When the door was opened, I was shocked at the number of people outside. And I could see reporters with—at that time their microphones had blocks around them, square blocks—and they had ABC and NBC [on them]. I remember hearing a man saying, "They're coming out! They're coming out!" There were lights and people all around, and we went down the steps, turned left, and went up Sixth Avenue. We crossed Seventeenth Street and started up the hill.

When we got there, Bull Connor pulled up. He got out, and there was an-other policeman who stepped out with a huge bullhorn. He said, "Stop," and he gave us the instructions that we are parading without a permit, and [he said,] "If you don't disperse, you will be arrested." We didn't disperse. Bull Connor told them to arrest us and make sure they got the leaders and throw them in the paddy wagon. We were crammed into the paddy wagons that were meant to hold maybe eight people at the most, two in the four cubicles that they had. They crammed three and four of us into one cubicle, and they continued to press the door until they got it shut and locked. I was fifteen then.

The paddy wagon was an experience. I can't deny that. But when we got inside the jail, they did things to us that I didn't imagine they would do. And I think the most shocking part for me is that these were men in authority. These were the city officials. If the city officials were doing this to us, then what recourse did we have? That's what I remember going through my mind. If the city commissioner, if the police chief, if Bull Connor is here on their side, then what side do we have? All bets are off. And I saw that played out in jail. When we went into jail, they pushed us around. They put us in a holding facility that should have held maybe thirty people, and this was an empty room. They put [between] three and four hundred boys in the same room. There were so many people in that room that we had to sleep in shifts. We would lie down. Certain ones of us would lie down on the floor and try to sleep, and the rest of us stood around the walls or sat in the windowsills so that they could sleep. And when we couldn't stand any longer, we would kick them and arouse them and have them stand up, and then we would sleep. And this went on for the full four days that I was in there. The toilet facilities were deplorable. At the end of this room there were five toilet seats, and that's how you went to the bathroom. You went to the bathroom in front of [between] three and four hundred people. The only ventilation was a screen that ran across the ceiling, right up over the toilets, and the ceiling was very high. When it rained, it rained in on us through that same place. They turned the air-conditioning on at night. They turned the heat on during the day, and this was in May.

They did some stuff to us that I can't forget. I was shocked that these people, No. 1, were doing that; No. 2, they were in authority and doing that; and No. 3, they hated us so much and didn't even know us, but they had so much hatred for us. When we got to the initial interview after they brought us in, I saw the interviewer grab a friend of mine and jerk him. He literally pulled him over the desk. He grabbed him by the collar and pulled him over the desk and onto the floor because he said "No comment." He told him that he would lock him away where nobody would ever find him, and that went for the rest of us if we said "No comment." He jumped up with such anger that the chair just fell flat on its back as he lunged for the boy. He gets up, straightens the chair, straightens his desk, and looks at me and says, "Now, what is your name, Son?" as if nothing had happened. So I told him my name is John Davis and my mom's name was so-and-so, and my daddy's name is so-and-so, and I am twelve years old. I gave him so much erroneous information so quickly [that] he started to laugh. He said, "Slow down, Boy, slow down," and he began to write it. I think that was why they had a difficult time finding me. My mother said that they had a real difficult time finding where I was because I had given them that incorrect information. I spent four days in jail. I ate mostly candy bars. I like Three Musketeers now because I survived on candy bars for those three days. I don't know what they are called—the trusties, key boys, or some of those people would actually sell them to us. These were blacks who were already in jail for another reason, and they were trusties and in charge of us.

My mother sent attorney Oscar Adams Jr. to get me out. He found me and asked me if I wanted to come out, and at first I refused. I think he actually found me on the third day, and he went back and told my mother that I didn't want to get out. On the fourth day, he came back, and I decided to leave. Nobody else was getting out, and we understood that we would get out as a group. I did not want to take an independent action. But I think that after the fourth day, I was getting sick. A lot of people were getting sick in there, and the mood had changed. I can remember A. D. King—now, this was [Martin Luther King's] brother. He was a pastor. He sat there, and he kept our spirits up. We were separated from everybody else, but I remember him being right there among us. And he would sing, sometimes for fifteen minutes by himself. He wouldn't give up. Eventually, one or two of us would begin to sing, and some others would begin to sing, and then we would all join in, and it would lift our spirits. My mother and my dad said, "You need to come out." They provided the bail. I think it was for me and maybe three or four of my friends who had all gone in together.

They came and got me and told me that I was leaving. People put all kinds of notes on me because they knew I was going, so they wanted me to call their mother and call their brother and tell them they were okay. My parents actually found out I was in jail on the news. My dad was in St. Louis at a medical convention, and my mother was home. They reported the Birmingham arrests, and kids were arrested on D-Day, and they saw me. They saw me on television from St. Louis. My dad saw me from St. Louis. He said he was sitting there, and they said this is something about Birmingham, so all of them gathered around the news. His brother said, "Isn't that James right there?" He called my mother, and she said, "I know, I know, I am looking. I see him." They knew that I was going to the movement. I don't know if they were surprised that I went. I think they kind of knew that I would go.

When we got back to school, I remember my homeroom teacher came in crying. Her name was Mrs. Evans. She came in crying, and she called our names, and she said, "You all have been expelled." Now, I am working on a 3.9 average in my senior year, and I am told I am expelled along with the rest of us. We were just shocked. We left school, and we spent the next couple of days just walking around, sitting around, talking about what had happened: "What does it all mean? What is going to happen to us? Will we get back into school?" One night, we went to one of the movement meetings. We almost didn't go. We went in late and sat on the last row in the back. They were making a presentation. They were saying that the courts had decided that those who were expelled would be able to go back to school, and there was a huge roar in the place.[3] People were excited, and they brought out these flags. They said, "We are going to give these American flags to each one of you." They said, "We will start in the back, and you just come down and get the flags." We were sitting on the back row, and they came and said just go down and get the flags. That was an exciting time, too. That was a victorious time that we remembered. Something [had] happened on a national level that kind of restored my faith: the fact that there [was] somebody out there who [thought] that some of this just possibly could be wrong.

[My parents] were aware of my attendance at the movement meetings, and in a sense there was their approval. They probably would have wanted to talk me out of going to jail because of the danger there, but they agreed in principle with what I was doing in terms of going to the meetings, listening, and working with the movement. Strangely enough, I felt much more mature. There was a cause. There was a movement. I was involved. There was reason, and the enemy was there where you could see him. I think now, racism is so covered [that] it [has become] insidious, and we don't really see it and it is not apparent. And sometimes we have a tendency to think that it has gone away, and there are even some of us who say it's 100 percent dead and gone, and there is no more. But during those days, we sat up in the balcony of the Lyric Theater. The Alabama Theater, we did not go near. We did not have the McDonald's where we could go in, and we could not go in the Woolworth's or Kress's or any of those places and eat or anything. There was a store right across from Ullman High School, right across Sixth Avenue. The store was right on that corner, and there was an Italian man who had a small restaurant. We would have to go around to the back and get hamburgers or whatever we wanted to get from that store when school let out. So there were things that I remember that make me know that racism was out there, and it was alive, and things needed to change. My parents had to pack to drive across country without stopping. There was no Holiday Inn, Hampton Inn. [They] couldn't stop anywhere to eat or sleep. Always take your lunch. My mother cooked food [until] three and four o'clock in the morning. We piled into the car and we drove. And we were careful about where we got gas and used the restrooms.

My parents, I think they were very cautious about the messages they wanted to send. So at the same time they would tell me they were proud of me, they would talk to me about not going too far or getting myself into dangerous situations. I was a leader at that time, and I had it in here to make a change. I remember my father telling me, "You know, you may not be able to take everybody with you." He said that a couple of times, and I said, "What do you mean by that?" And he said, "You may need to at some time go in and make some changes and come back and get some people and bring them to where you are, and then you go again and come back and get some people and bring them to where you are." He said, "If you are waiting for the door to swing open and everybody is included," he said, "that may not happen." That is exactly where I was. I said the whole thing should come down, and we should all go in. As I got older, I understood what he meant by that.

Two of [the girls killed in the Sixteenth Street Baptist Church Bombing] were very close friends. I knew them: Cynthia Wesley and Carole Robertson. As a matter of fact, Carole was the cousin of my wife now, Judy. I didn't know that until after we were married, and we came to Birmingham. That had a major impact on me. That was like a real blow, a setback. To have them just die innocently like that, I will never forget. I was a pallbearer in Carole's funeral. Just to see the people coming out and to know that somebody hated us as a people—didn't know any of them, but they hated us so much that they decided the way to win is to now kill their children. That was a youth Sunday, and a lot of children were at the church that day. It raised the stakes, and it made me angrier, but it made me more determined.

NOTES

BCRI OHP, vol. 48, sec. 4 (July 15, 2003). Edited, annotated, and abridged by Horace Huntley and John McKerley.

1. On St. Paul's African Methodist Episcopal Church, see Glenn T. Eskew, *But for Birmingham: The Local and National Movements in the Civil Rights Struggle* (Chapel Hill: University of North Carolina Press, 1997), 226, 263.

2. On Smith, see Paul Littlejohn, BCRI OHP, vol. 18, sec. 3 (June 24, 1996).

3. On May 20, 1963, the Birmingham Board of Education expelled more than one thousand black students identified as youth activists. The NAACP ultimately had the decision overturned on appeal (Eskew, *But for Birmingham,* 308–9).

GWENDOLYN SANDERS GAMBLE

GWENDOLYN SANDERS GAMBLE was born in Birmingham on December 17, 1947. After growing up in Kingston, she moved to Titusville, where she attended Ullman High School. For Gamble, black people's responses to white supremacy began at home: "Talking about [racism] at home led to discussions in the schools." Although she described her father, a steelworker, as "[not] quite . . . nonviolent" enough for the movement, her mother accepted training in nonviolent direct action. Her mother also took Gamble and her sisters to mass meetings. Gamble built on this foundation as she took part in a series of actions and organizing campaigns with the SCLC in Birmingham and elsewhere across the South. "There's no better way to get to a child than through another child," Gamble recalled. Her experience as an organizer, however, also demonstrated the profound ambivalence and at times opposition that some black parents and school officials expressed toward youth activism. While some teachers directly or indirectly aided the students, other instructors regarded student activists as "troublemakers," who "were disturbing the school [and] disturbing their classrooms." Still, Gamble found that the influence of Birmingham's black adults compared favorably to what she encountered in St. Augustine, Florida, where she worked as an SCLC youth organizer. After discovering that she and the other organizers could not "get the children involved as much as [they] did here in Birmingham," Gamble concluded that the difficulties resulted largely from black parents' resistance. "Some people called us . . . 'the intruders,' outsiders coming in taking over their little town," she recalled. "These were black people."

THE VOTING, THE WATER FOUNTAIN, AND THE BOOK

My father is from Tuscaloosa and my mother from Selma. I have three sisters and one brother. My father has an associate degree, and my mother was a high school graduate, twelfth grade. My father is retired from U.S. Steel, where he was a foreman in the coke department. My mother was a housewife. She also worked in the clothing factory that was named Simon and McGilner at the time. I finished Ullman High School in 1965, and from there I went to Daniel Payne College from '65 to '66.[1] In between that time, I went to different technical schools for career training, where I took IBM keypunch and I became a keypunch operator. I have also had some pretraining in nursing that I took at Daniel Payne College. I took courses at UAB. I have an associate degree from Samford University in paralegal studies, and since Samford, I have been studying education at Birmingham-Southern [College].

I'm presently employed by the Birmingham public schools, West End and Elyton Community School, where I am a program assistant in the Community Education Department. I design programs for the people in the communities, for the children at the school, especially at my school, Elyton School. I also create other programs like GED. I have basketball teams. I supervise five after-school programs. This is a program where the students are housed at their schools. In other words, we give them activities to do until the parents are off their jobs to come and pick them up. I'm in [kindergarten through fifth grade], so we're talking about five to eleven or twelve years old.

I started school at Kingston Elementary School, and I went through the fourth grade there. From Kingston to Center Street School, I went there a short period. From Center Street to West Center Street, and from West Center Street to Ullman. When I grew up in Kingston, from 1947 through 1960, it was fairly quiet. Most of the women were housewives. They stayed at home. Most of the men would work in either U.S. Steel or they drove milk trucks, the coal trucks, and delivering ice. Most of the people were buying their homes in the Kingston area. There were, of course, at that time, no housing areas, but they had shotgun homes and double tenant homes where they rented from different sources.[2] But the majority of people at that time were buying their homes.

When we moved to Titusville, it was like a step up. [Authorities] bought our home so they could build the projects, so we moved to Titusville, and the people were on a different grade, I would say, from the people in Kingston. When we moved to Titusville, they had occupations at the post office, schoolteachers, nurses, whereas in the Kingston community, the environment wasn't that big of a variety for people having those types of jobs. I was more impressed by what I was seeing because I was used to seeing those shotgun homes in Kingston. We moved from shotgun homes to two-story homes, brick homes.

[My involvement in the civil rights movement] starts back at Kingston. I think what made a big impact on my decision [was that] I was tired of looking in my fifth- or sixth-grade books and seeing a white child that had that book in the fourth grade. I would see where they would put their teacher's name, their grade in there, and the year. That let me know that I was behind that child. Educationally, I was two years or more behind that white child. I felt that I deserved the right to be at the same level, if not above the level, of that white child. That was the first thing that triggered it. The second things were listening to my mother and father talk about having to keep their mouths shut, not saying anything because the white man take it the wrong way, call them a "smart nigger" or whatever, and they had to keep their mouths closed for something that they believed in, for speaking up for something they believed in. Another thing, I went shopping with my mother, and I wanted some water, and I went to the "White" fountain. At that time, the "Colored" sign and the fountain was much lower; it was just a little sink, and right beside it was a white cooler, nice cool water, had "White" on it. I didn't understand why I had to go to the dirty sink when I wanted some cool water. I would bring these things up because they meant a lot to me to talk about them, especially in my home. I think the bulk of conversations would come from my home. Talking about it at home led to discussions in the schools. I found out that a lot of the children felt the same way. [But] a lot of them felt there was nothing wrong with it. And then there were a lot of them that were taught not to say anything at all. I have always been told to be my own person, stand up for what I believe in, as long as I'm doing it in a mannerly way.

My mother went to register to vote. There was a poll tax that she did not have money to pay for. There was a lesson that she should have been studying to pass this test, and I said for someone who lives in this country, this is a right that you should have without paying a poll tax, without taking a test. Whether you can read or write, you should have the right to voice your opinion of whom you wanted to be elected. And when she was studying this book and still didn't pass that test, we knew then that somebody need to do something. I knew that the white man up the street didn't have to go down there and take a test. If he could read or write, he was allowed to vote. So it started, I believe, with the voting, the water fountain, and with the book.

My mother was very active in the movement. Mother was the first one to make the step. My father was not so active because he wasn't quite as nonviolent as you should be to work in the movement, but my mother was, so she went to the first meeting and she came back and told us about it. The very next night we went. I was outspoken, and my sisters and I got involved with the training process and recruiting other students.

A typical mass meeting was something that I always looked forward to. It included hearing, shouting, singing, having a hallelujah good time, meeting, greeting, loving, caring, and sharing with other people. You got to see people and meet people that you didn't know. You found more people more concerned about each other. You knew that you would get to hear some great speakers because the nights that Dr. [Martin Luther] King was not available we always heard Rev. [Fred] Shuttlesworth or Rev. [Nelson H. Smith Jr.].

It was always somebody there to give us a message that we needed to hear and that we enjoyed listening to. There were meetings for the children, but I didn't think I belonged with the children. When you say "children," I would refer more to the smaller children because I recall the teenagers my age being in the main sanctuary. I don't remember policemen actually attending the meetings. You would find them patrolling the area. Being a teenager, of course, I would be outside and inside. But I do recall seeing them patrol the area. I do not recall anyone being on the inside except perhaps a news reporter—you would see them occasionally in the building.[3]

I went to protest at least twenty times. We were never just sent out. We were always briefed: what to say, what not to say, where we were going, what information to give, and what information not to give. If we left out knowing that we were not going to jail, we knew how many times we had for the cop to ask us to disperse, to leave. So we pretty much knew exactly where we were going. We were timed to the minute. You have five minutes, eight seconds to get to your destination. There were times that we tried to not go the route that the cops thought that we were going. That was the strategy that was used to try to make it to that destination, to get that opportunity to sit at the lunch counters. There were never less than ten to the group. Mainly, I would say pretty close to fifty people. You may have fifty going to this destination, and fifty going to another. But as you left, your names were called, and you were lined up so they could know exactly where you're supposed to be and exactly if you were going to jail or if you were not going to jail.

Mostly, my destination was J. J. Newberry's downtown. Newberry's was the most prejudiced place in town. Newberry's refused to serve black people at the lunch counter, upstairs or downstairs. They didn't want you to have a seat. Now, you [could] come to the edge of the counter, place your order, and take it out, but after all of the tries, they refused. They refused to let you sit there. And at that time, that counter was pretty busy.

My first arrest, I think I had the flu. When I got there, I had to strictly scrub floors because I put my head down, and my punishment was to scrub those floors with a toothbrush. I was arrested because I refused to move after being ordered by an officer and also parading without a permit. That was in front of J. J. Newberry's.

Once they threw as many of us as they could into the paddy wagon, the dog would be the last treat, because they knew we were frightened of them. The dogs were trained to attack blacks. They took the black dummies and the black rags, trained them to attack them. It was to frighten us, and they did. So from Newberry's to the jail, the dog was in the paddy wagon with us. We were told not to say anything; we didn't communicate at all. We did exactly what we were instructed to do, so we didn't communicate. We just prayed and hoped that dog didn't turn on us. And he didn't. As long as we were still and quiet, we didn't disturb him.

The first time I went to jail, I was in there three to four days. The second time, I was in four days. I remember thinking, "Why am I in here with these people?" I felt that we were there for a different cause from the other people that were arrested for other reasons. I felt that we should have been in a different place. If I'm going to be arrested, I should be in a holding cell, somewhere away from the criminals. But they put us all in the same cell with the criminals. And of course, that made me feel like, "Are they saying that I'm a criminal?" The other inmates treated us fine. They didn't try to assault us in any way. They didn't ask too many questions, really. It was like they had already been schooled—"You have these people coming in, and they're coming in for this reason." I recall only a few questions even being asked by the inmates. It was so many of us there that they couldn't find much for us to do. We would sleep at night on a bunk in a cell. In the day, they would take us and put us in a day cell. That's where fifty or one hundred children might be in that day cell. And all you do is sit around. That's all we did, except the one time I put my head down, and I had to scrub. You were supposed to sit or stand. They couldn't feel that you were lounging in any way.

I had two sisters that demonstrated. I have cousins that demonstrated but were not arrested. My sisters were arrested. As a matter of fact, one sister, Dorothy, went more than I did because she was the type that couldn't really stay in there long and she made it understood: "I'll go, but I can't stay." So they would go and get her, but before we looked up, she was back in there. My mother and father did not participate, but they supported us. Our father never told us not to go. He just knew it wasn't for him, so he stayed away. We had some children who had been dared by their parents not to move, so they didn't. But I believe overall it was quite effective. We had the majority of the children to leave the classrooms or to leave the schools and to join us in the march. That's how we got those thousands of children out there.

Meatball and Tommy Wrenn, aides of Dr. King, asked us if we would attend various workshops.[4] My two sisters and I did attend. We got special training so we could go out and recruit other students involved in the movement. They knew that the adults had to work. They had to provide for their families. And also, more harm would probably come to the adults than to the children. So that's how we were chosen. My sisters and I always had a persuasive way about us. The children did listen. I guess setting examples and being a good role model is what really got it started. We tried to get more of them to the movement so they could actually see what's going on and let them realize that we are in this for the betterment of all of us and not just a few. But we needed their help. Even two thousand couldn't have done it. It took all of us. Probably some things were said that no one else had ever said to them. There's no better way to get to a child than through another child.

We had different assigned classrooms to go to. We never entered into the classroom. We passed by the door, gave a cue, and the next thing you knew, they were following us because the word was already out that we were going to turn the school out that day. They had already heard it. At the meeting, they had told us, "We're going to leave. Gwen, you have this area; you have this floor. Deborah, you have this floor." They had a map of the building. They knew which door to take. We knew which door to take them out of, which route to take to the destination. So all we had to do was give them a cue after they got the word, and those who wanted to follow followed.

We had some teachers that were afraid. Then we had some teachers that believed in it and wanted to do more than what they were actually doing. I know a few teachers who actually knew why I was coming because they attended the mass meetings. They would actually turn their heads and look out the window [as if to say], "If you walk out, I didn't give you permission. I didn't see, so go while my head is turned." Then we had some that said we were troublemakers. We were disturbing the school, disturbing their class-rooms, but the children went anyway.

I was told in the eleventh grade that I would be expelled. My sister was entering the twelfth grade, and she was told that she would not graduate be-cause of the days that were missed out of school. But being expelled, I was not, because there was a hearing about that, and it was all thrown out of court. The principal told us that we would be expelled. They had gotten notices from the [Birmingham Board of Education], but first they pulled our records from the family court and also from the city jail. If your name appeared on that list, then your parents were sent notices, and the principals were sent notices that you would be either expelled if you were below the twelfth grade, and if you were getting ready to graduate, you would not graduate.[5]

Because of my experience in recruiting here in Birmingham and being pretty successful in doing so, my sisters and I, along with some other recruiters, were asked to go to St. Augustine, Florida.[6] They were having a problem get-ting the people out to register to vote. They were still having a problem at the lunch counters. They were having a problem going to the beach to swim.

We rode a chartered Trailways bus. On our way to St. Augustine, the state troopers were trailing us. This was the Florida state troopers. Apparently they had got word that this busload of black children were coming, and they stopped us on the side of the road and wanted to know where we were going. They [said that they had] heard that the Klansmen had got word of our being in the state. They [said they] just stopped us for our own protection and to escort us into St. Augustine.

Some people called us the intruders, outsiders coming in, taking over their little town. These were black people. It was harder to recruit them than it was to recruit the people in Birmingham. They didn't want to even listen to what we had to say. I think what they wanted us to do was to go to jail for them and let them stay at home. But we couldn't get them to come out to mass meetings as we did here in Birmingham. We couldn't get the children involved as much as we did here in Birmingham. And it could be because of the way the adults took their approach, as far as receiving us in St. Augustine. Our contacts were the churches. That was just as hard as contacting the people in the communities. We had just a few people that were willing to learn so they could go out and teach the other children in the community. They were so laid back that when the Klansmen wanted to march, the black people were on the sidewalks. The Klansmen would march between them in the black communities.

For the demonstration, Dr. King was supposed to lead the march, and I saw him when he came in. But for some reason he didn't go. Rev. Shuttlesworth and [Ralph] Abernathy, Tommy Wrenn, Meatball, and a few others led the march that night. And I was like midway in the line. There were maybe three hundred people protesting through the square. We were marching, and suddenly people came from bushes. I'm talking about white people. Some had on their [hoods], and some were just plainly dressed. They started fighting everybody that they could come in contact with. And at that time, of course, by them jumping from bushes, it was really scary.

I do remember being picked up and taken away from the square, back to the headquarters. And Dr. King was standing outside when we drove up. The driver of the car that I was in told him that [a] riot had broken out. I was still dizzy. They took me to the hospital in St. Augustine. They wouldn't see me; they wouldn't let a doctor look at me. So I had to be placed back in the car and they had to drive me all the way to Jacksonville. Jacksonville is about [forty] miles from St. Augustine. That's where I was hospitalized. I had a slight concussion, and I was hospitalized for six or seven days.

Believe it or not, St. Augustine's officers were much nicer than in Birmingham. They were more passionate, more concerned. I do recall one particular warden. When we were there, we were served strained baby food for breakfast, lunch, and dinner. This one particular warden was quite concerned, and he asked us if we had any money. For those of us who had money, he took the money, went across the street, and bought us sodas, chips, crackers, and other items. He knew we were hungry and weren't being treated fairly, so he did that for us, and we shared everything that we were able to buy with everyone in there. That was quite different from the arrest in Birmingham.

After St. Augustine, I was active until the last actual meeting that we had. We would attend the meetings in Atlanta and Gadsden and Anniston.

NOTES

BCRI OHP, vol. 12, sec. 1 (January 24, 1996). Edited, annotated, and abridged by Horace Huntley and John McKerley.

1. On the role of students at Daniel Payne College (a school associated with the African Methodist Episcopal Church that closed in 1977) in the movement, see Andrew M. Manis, *A Fire You Can't Put Out: The Civil Rights Life of Birmingham's Reverend Fred Shuttlesworth* (Tuscaloosa: University of Alabama Press, 1999), 231.

2. There were several housing projects in Birmingham. See James Armstrong, BCRI OHP, vol. 4, sec. 5 (April 10, 1995); Washington Booker III, BCRI OHP, vol. 1, sec. 2 (January 5, 1995).

3. Police and plainclothes informants were often present at mass meetings. See Joe Hendricks, BCRI OHP, vol. 8, sec. 1 (June 23, 1995).

4. William "Meatball" Dothard and Tommy Wrenn were two of the many local activists recruited by SCLC organizers James Bevel, Dorothy Cotton, Bernard Lee, Ike Reynolds, and Andrew Young in April 1963. These local activists then worked to organize young people, creating a chain of youth activists that mobilized many smaller groups of young people. For a top-down perspective on this process, see Glenn T. Eskew, *But for Birmingham: The Local and National Movements in the Civil Rights Struggle* (Chapel Hill: University of North Carolina Press, 1997), 254, 261–62; on Dothard, see 263, 385 n. 10.

5. On May 20, 1963, the Birmingham Board of Education expelled more than one thousand black students identified as youth activists. The NAACP ultimately had the decision overturned on appeal (Eskew, *But for Birmingham*, 308–9).

6. The Birmingham campaign acted as a training ground for further activism across the country. For a useful but largely top-down study of the St. Augustine campaign, see David Colburn, *Racial Change and Community Crisis: St. Augustine, Florida, 1877–1980* (New York: Columbia University Press, 1985).

CAROLYN MAULL McKINSTRY

CAROLYN MAULL McKINSTRY was born in Clanton, Alabama, in Chilton County, on January 13, 1948. At age two, she moved with her parents, both of whom were teachers, to Birmingham's Ellsbury neighborhood. Insulated from segregation's outward expressions by her parents, McKinstry remembered first becoming aware of its meaning through the televised images of civil rights activists. Determined to strike a blow against the system, she staged a brief, six-block protest on an empty city bus. Recalling the fear and exhilaration of the act of defiance, McKinstry noted, "[W]hen I got on the bus, probably fortunately, there wasn't enough people riding the bus that day for it to be an issue where I was sitting." "Actually, the bus driver seemed somewhat tolerant of us, because I think I probably got on the bus with a little bit of a chip on my shoulder and a look at him that sort of dared him to say anything about where I sat." Energized by the mass meetings, McKinstry took part in a mass demonstration in which firemen used high-powered hoses against the demonstrators. Although the experience transformed her, it also brought with it a new realization of the dangers of resistance to white supremacy and the potential costs of activism. When she saw her mother for the first time after the demonstration, McKinstry "was actually proud, but . . . had some question marks there about the tactics that [the SCLC was] using." "I felt that you could actually be hurt. Serious things could happen with what they were doing."

THE WATER HOSES HURT A LOT

I have four brothers and one sister. I'm in the middle, two boys older, two boys younger, and then my sister is the baby. We moved to the Ellsbury community in ACIPCO.

Both my parents taught school. My dad taught physics and chemistry. He had a master's degree. He waited tables at night but taught school during the day. My mom had a degree in elementary education. My father retired from Huffman High School. However, he was part of Parker when it still had the name Industrial High School. He taught there for many years under that name and then under the Parker name. Then [he taught at] Carver High School and was subsequently moved to Huffman when the integration order came. My mom retired from Pratt Elementary School. Some of the schools where she taught when she first came to Birmingham [were] Hooper City Elementary School, Northside, Lewis Elementary, but she retired from Pratt.

Our neighborhood was a fairly middle-class neighborhood. We had quite a few professional people there. There was any number of teachers that lived on our street. In fact, my eighth-grade teacher lived on my street, and my seventh-grade teacher lived two streets behind me. So it was quite common to have your teachers or principal living close by. We had two black CPAs in the city of Birmingham, and one of those lived directly across the street, Maurice Rouse, one of our bondsmen during that time. We knew him because he owned the vending company, too, and we could sometime get old records from him. In fact, one of my brothers worked with him for a long time, traveling to the different little cities stocking the record machines. So we knew all these people quite well, and they took quite an interest in what you did, particularly if you were doing well in things.

Some of these people were active in the movement. Dr. Jessie Lewis lived directly behind me. Mr. Shortridge, who had a funeral home at that time, was right on the corner.[1] Most of the people in that immediate three- or four-block area were in fairly professional jobs. Now, probably about three blocks down Finley, toward the farmers' market, was where my elementary school was and where a lot of my classmates and friends lived. A lot of those children's parents worked at places like ACIPCO or TCI and Stockham. I went to A. H. Parker High School. I loved it. It was a great source of inspiration to be there. When I came in the ninth grade, one of the first things I remember, within the first two months they had this honor society induction. I remember I was so moved by it because we were in the auditorium, and they had darkened the lights and it was very quiet. Then there was this very nice light procession, and students marched in holding a candle. It was a very humble, spiritual-type ceremony. They went up on the stage and stood holding the candles. Then at some point, somebody came out and read this announcement about how one can qualify to be in the honor society. So I decided that next year I would be one of those students being led up to the stage. There were a lot of things to aspire to. We had a lot of extracurricular activities: business club, teachers' club, and science club. I think I may have been among one of the first female students to take the mechanical drawing class from Mr. [Cornell] Hawkins. At that time, girls couldn't go over to the building where the men were, but I convinced Mr. Hawkins that I needed to be in that class. He went to bat on my behalf. Our principal, R. C. Johnson, who we all called Big Red, looked big and mean. He would see you in the hall: "Little Maull"—that was my maiden name—"what are you doing in this hall, and do you have a pass?" I can remember a couple of times when I didn't have a pass but was allowed to escape.

• • •

My parents had never really allowed us to ride the bus. There were a lot of things my parents didn't tell us. Rather than saying "You can't," they conveniently dropped us off or picked us up rather than have us get on a bus and have someone tell us that we could not sit up front. So this particular day, I was watching something on TV, and it was when some of these people had first come to town. That's when I became aware of the signs designating where you could sit on the bus.

I said, "I'm going to ride this bus. I'm going to find out and see. I'm not moving that sign. If I sit down, I'm going to stay there." I just started thinking these things in my head. So I had to have an excuse to go downtown—I had to have permission. I told my mom one day, I said, "I need to learn how to start taking care of bills and taking care of things. Don't you need me to pay this bill for you?" She had an account at Parisian's [Department Store]. So I said, "Let me go by and pay it." I made it appear to be an educational experience. So she said, "Okay, but you come right home." I said, "I'm just going to pay the bill, and then I'll come right home." I did pay the bill, but when I got on the bus, probably fortunately, there wasn't enough people riding the bus that day for it to be an issue where I was sitting. Actually, the bus driver seemed somewhat tolerant of us, because I think I probably got on the bus with a little bit of a chip on my shoulder and a look at him that sort of dared him to say anything about where I sat. The boards were there. In fact, there were people when I was sitting there that came up to the front of the bus and paid their money and then went around to the second door to board the bus. I was trying to figure that out, too. That was one of those things where my parents didn't sit down and say, "This is the way it is." So that was something that was a little bit surprising to me—that they would pay their money in the front and then walk around to the back door to get on the bus.

No one reacted when I sat in the front. The bus driver had a look. That's why I think he was somewhat tolerant. I think he suspected what was going on in my mind. I probably had a look. He did not say anything. Where I lived from downtown, the number of bus stops between there and my home was probably about six. So we're not talking about a lot of time—maybe about ten minutes. Actually, I was a little nervous, a little frightened, when I first boarded the bus. As I sat there, I was trying to understand. I didn't have a good understanding of why it was this way. The only other bus I really had ridden was a school bus that picked us up every morning to go to Parker High School, but it was called a Special. It was ten cents to ride. I was in the ninth grade.

I didn't give my father an opportunity to tell me "No" for any of this. They found out about most of what I had done after the fact. My mother pretty much let my dad take the lead with the "Yes" or the "Nos." Both of them taught school, and they had four boys that they wanted to live to be male adults, so a lot of what they did was done with the idea of protecting us. My dad was very stern, very strict. I would make my own decision. If I decided to do it, it didn't matter if I was the only one doing it.

I was a sophomore and pretty much a straight-A student. When I graduated from Parker High School, there were 437 children in my graduating class, and I was number 7 out of 437. I loved school, loved to study, loved to read. I was just a person who responded to unkindness. Anytime I saw things that I didn't think were right or were unkind, I would say something. I think my grandfather was one of the first people who convinced me that I always needed to speak up if I didn't agree with something. They gave me freedom to do that. My parents actually gave us the freedom if we didn't agree with what they said. I personally felt very, very inspired and motivated when I listened to the speeches at the church. I wanted to be part of that. It just felt exciting, it felt good, it felt right, and I wanted to be part of it. So I felt if I had discussed it at home, they were going to tell me "No," so I didn't.

We've been [members of] Sixteenth Street [Baptist Church] since I was two. We moved to Birmingham, and my mom joined that church immediately. I attended as many mass meetings as I could. I just loved the atmosphere. I was constantly at the church, and I was aware of things that were going on. Plus I worked there in the summer. When school was out, I would go there and stay all day in the summer, answer the phones and do different things. So I became aware of people coming in and out of our church. I became aware of things that were being planned: the meetings, the speeches. It was commonplace to see some of these people come through. So I became very accustomed and very comfortable talking with these people. I just found it inspiring. I really liked being around them.

Maybe it was because of what we could feel when we went to the [mass] meetings. They sang the songs, and they gave the speeches and even gave you the opportunity to stand and say or ask questions if you needed to. It made you feel part of it. The singing was just motivational. It just made you ready to do something. The mass meetings were always very crowded. I remember quite a few students, but I don't remember numbers. I remember that they would start with a song. Then we would get a prayer. I had occasions to hear Dr. [Martin Luther] King speak many times. I had occasions to hear Jessie Jackson; James Bevel, out of Nashville, I think; and a couple of other people that I can't put a name with their face right now. Rev. [Ralph] Abernathy, I remember him being present. Dr. King was usually saved for last. The younger speakers, Bevel and Jackson, sort of helped get people in and grouped. The singing would get people revved up and ready to receive whatever they had to say.

Prior to the marches, there was always a request for the surrender of any weapons or potential weapons such as pencils, fingernail files, etc. They would even come back a second time and say, "Now we have to trust you, but now make sure that you've given us anything that you have in your pocket." At that time, it was common for the high school boys to have a little pocketknife. So usually on the second go-round, you would still pick up a few more things in that big wastebasket.

I remember my first demonstration. We walked from Parker High School, and we didn't get very far. We got to Eighth Avenue, where Atlantic Mills's Thrift Center was. We were stopped at that point and told that we could not go any further. We were ordered to disperse, and we scattered and ended up at the church. The goal was City Hall. There were a couple of times when the goal was for everybody to end up at City Hall to have a mass rally. I don't ever remember getting there. They even brought out the little white tanks to control our movement.[2]

We were told that someone would come to the school when it was time for the students to leave. They gave us an approximate time, roughly 11:00 to 11:30. Parker had a gate entrance to the street, and the gate had a chain, but it was enough of a gap in between that gate that you could squeeze through with no problem. So when we got the signal that it was time to go, most of us just squeezed through the gate. However, there were a lot of students that walked out the front doors, and many teachers just did not see them. I don't know if Mr. Johnson saw them, but he didn't indicate that he had seen them. So we were ready. We were waiting for a sign or a person to let us know when it was time, and we got the signal.

They had mapped out a route for us. They had not told us about water hoses, but they had told us about dogs: "If the policeman attempts to do this with the dogs, what are you going to do?" They would even have little role-plays where you could see what to do and what not to do. They said if a policeman spits on you or if he slaps you, this is how you respond to that. They didn't talk about the tanks. They didn't talk about the water hoses. I suspect those things were a surprise on the day that we marched. That's what I was thinking later: "They didn't tell us about this. Maybe they didn't know."

The water hoses hurt a lot. I was hit with the water hose on this side running from the water. I had a navy blue sweater on. The water tore a big hole in my sweater and swiped part of my hair off on that side. I just remember the sting and the pain on my face. It was very painful, and you couldn't escape. There were a few points where we were trying to stand up and hold onto a wall. It was just a terrific pain from the force, which I later learned was something like one hundred pounds of force per inch. That was the point at which I started rethinking, "Do I really want to be a part of this, or do I have what it takes to continue on this level?" I think I made the decision then that I would offer my contributions in another way, that I would assist in some other ways. I honestly was afraid of the dogs, did not like being wet up. I felt very disrespected when I was wet up with the water and my hair. We were just marching.

I was not arrested. I went back to the church briefly. I remember going in the ladies' room to just try to dry off a little bit. I ended up getting a ride with someone to get home. When my mom walked in the door, she knew something was different, but she didn't know what I had done. I explained to her where I had been and what I had done. At that point I was actually proud, but I had some question marks there about the tactics that they were using. I felt that you could actually be hurt. Serious things could happen with what they were doing.

When my daddy was made aware of what had happened, he was very angry that I had done this. He was angry with me. He instructed me not to go back. He just talked about these people were crazy. You might expect anything to happen. They would stop at nothing to keep things the way they were. [He] just felt that if there was going to be change, let somebody else make the change, you stay out of it. That's never been my way. But I was never again involved in a march.

I don't think I understood the real significance of why they were using the students. I like to refer to us as "bearable commodities" for them at that time. I came to know later the rationale behind why they used us. I have to say, in terms of my participation, I felt very much a part of what was going on. I felt that I was needed. I felt when I heard what they had to say, I responded to that spiritually. I agreed spiritually with what they were trying to do and was glad that I could be a part of it. So I think most of the children felt that this was a worthy cause. This was something that we needed to do, that we wanted to be a part of, and we had confidence in the leadership. We had confidence in Dr. King and James Bevel and the ones that spoke. They were very charismatic, and they were also very articulate. They were very specific. When you would see them, they would shake your hand. [They would say],

"Young man, young lady," [and] give you a hug: "We appreciate the fact that you are here." And we felt very much included. I did, and I think most of the students did. I think most of us probably didn't have the real sense of how valuable we were. We felt good that we could make a contribution in this small way. They needed numbers, and we helped them with the numbers.

Back at school, there was a lot of hugging and laughing and talking about what had happened, describing and joking about how someone's hair looked after they had gotten wet and who they saw running in this direction. There were a couple of students that I knew who went to jail that were out the next day. There were others that stayed in jail for four or five days. So, like the next day or two, we heard accounts from those students of what it was like. For the most part it was funny: "Yeah, they served us these peanut-butter-and-jelly sandwiches." They were fingerprinted, and they went on to tell [about how] they were carried away in a wagon and being fingerprinted and so forth. The accounts that came from the students that stayed four or five days were not quite as comical. The ladies had a lot of stories of being mistreated—not abused necessarily, but just mistreated. I think they were taken out to the Fair Park and crowded into that area. I remember several of the ladies. In fact, one lady gave the account of needing personal articles; she was there four or five days, and no one attended to her needs. She felt very deprived, disrespected. She cried when she gave this account, and this is like twenty to twenty-five years later, so I know it must have really affected her. But I think the guys were able to tough it out a little better than the girls and ladies were.

I don't remember us actually having any discussions with our teachers about what went on. I think the teachers kind of had to know and not know. I think they were proud of us but they had a business-as-usual type attitude. We did a lot of talking at lunchtime or at study periods when the teacher was not in the room. We would discuss it among ourselves in the library and just sort of compare notes on what had happened to different people.

• • •

I always left home very early. My dad worked his second job on Sunday, so he would drop us off as he went to work. Normally, I took my sister to Sunday school with my two younger brothers and me. She wouldn't let me comb her hair that morning [September 15, 1963]. I didn't want to take her anyway. So I told my mother, "She won't let me comb her hair." She said, "Okay, just go on without her." So I took my brothers, and my dad dropped us off. He was headed toward Mountain Brook. I assumed my duties as secretary. I had come through the downstairs area to pass out the attendance cards and the little envelopes where you record your money. I had done that and was heading back up the stairs, [when I] saw the girls in the bathroom sort of laughing and talking and putting on their robes. They were excited. Actually, everybody was in Sunday school class, which is probably where they should have been, but they were excited. So I walked up the steps. We had two sets of steps—well, we still do. Then [I] walked up the second set of steps and had stepped out before I stepped out into the sanctuary. We used to have the church office right there on the right.

The phone rang, and I answered the phone, and someone said, "Two minutes." Rev. [John] Cross had not made us aware—maybe he made some of the adults aware—but he had not made a general announcement to the church that we had bomb threats. I didn't know, didn't even think about what this might mean. [The caller] hung up. They said that, and then "click." I was just standing there and kind of thought about it, hung the phone up, and stepped out into the sanctuary because I had three or four more classes that I needed to give these cards to. As soon as I stepped out in the sanctuary—it wasn't two minutes, it was probably more like five seconds, the time it takes to walk from that office, maybe five or six seconds—something happened at that time. I didn't know that the church had been bombed. What I heard at first sounded like a rumble, like thunder. I remember thinking rain—it immediately came to my mind. As soon as I thought rain, all of the windows started shattering, glass came pouring in. When that happened, I heard screams all upstairs, screams. Then somebody said, "Get on the floor." We all got on the floor and were very quiet for what seems like several minutes, but it was probably only twenty or thirty seconds. Then we heard footsteps at that point; somebody had gotten up and started running. Everybody else followed. I came out of the church through the back.

I ran to the back of the church, and we went out through those doors where you normally enter on Sunday for the eleven o'clock service. [I] came down the steps, and my first thoughts immediately were to find my two younger brothers. I could see that something had happened. I think I learned in that first minute or two that I was out there that our church had been bombed. Everybody was looking for somebody. I was looking for my two younger brothers and couldn't find them. They were in the Sunday school classes downstairs. So I went back downstairs, and I remember going into the boys' bathroom first, because I looked in all of the classrooms and I couldn't find them, [so] I went in the boys' bathroom, and I didn't see them in there. Then I started in the girls' bathroom and I said, "If they went to the bathroom, they probably wouldn't be in here." But then they might, because they were little boys. They were like seven and five. So maybe they ran this way or maybe they just didn't know where to go. So I spent—this is the part I don't like talking about too much—but I spent a lot of time in the basement looking for them.

I never found them. I can tell you I spent a lot of time in that basement, but my baby brother was found on Eighth Avenue, two blocks away. He had jumped out one of those side windows when it broke and just started running. I guess [he ran] with no real sense of where he was running, just knowing that he needed to get out of there. He just ran. Someone called my mom at home to tell her that they had bombed the church. When she was heading to the church to check on us, she encountered my baby brother. She was coming, and he was coming, and that's when she found him. My dad found my oldest brother downtown. I guess a lot of kids just ran; they just scattered.

My father was headed to Mountain Brook. He worked at the Birmingham Country Club. I have a membership there now, but he was a waiter then. He heard the explosion. He said he had the radio on. My dad was a great listener of talk shows even back then. Whoever he was listening to announced within the next minute or two that the church had been bombed. He said he turned around. He never got to work; he turned around and came right back. He was also looking for us. He encountered my seven-year-old brother somewhere. By the time my dad had gotten there, they had blocked off a big portion of the area that surrounded the church. So somewhere on the boundaries and trying to get past those roadblocks, my dad encountered my brother. He took his hand and came within the boundaries looking for my other brother and myself. He found me, but my mom found my other brother at another point.

I knew there were people hurt. I had been in there looking for my brothers, but I didn't see anybody. There was a man outside saying there were people that were hurt inside. So I remember thinking that he was just trying to create a little more excitement or something. I was angry because I felt like, "Why is he saying this?" Then I got upset because I thought, "Did he see my brothers, and I didn't?" So I kept going back. At that point, I still didn't know where they were. I spent a lot of time going back to that girls' bathroom. You could actually go in [the boys' bathroom]. You could tell that there was damage, but you could actually walk around and see that, okay, here is the hand bowl and here is the toilet and whatever, and obviously no one is here. But in the case of the girls' bathroom, you couldn't see that. You didn't know what you were looking at, but you couldn't see that they were there or that they weren't there or that no one was hurt. I had been home about an hour and Mrs. [Alpha] Robertson called our house. She asked me did I see Carole. I said, "No." She asked to speak with my mom and just asked if she had seen her. She said, "No." She said, "Maybe my Carole is all right. Your Carol is at home, so maybe my Carole is all right too."

Cynthia Wesley and I were in a book social club together, the Cavalettes. There was a male social club called the Cavaliers. They adopted us or something, and we came up with the name Cavalettes. It was just something where we had parties at each other's homes. We had purchased T-shirts with our names and the club, a big C, on it. We had purchased hats and so forth. In fact, we made those purchases from John Singleton's, when it was still open, right before the church was bombed. Those items that she ordered, we took to her mother's house about two weeks after the church was bombed. Denise, I knew well. [I] didn't spend a lot of time with her because she was a lot younger than I was. I always thought she was a happy, delightful child. She was very pleasant to be around. Addie was very quiet. Addie was in my Sunday school class. I always think of them. Addie was one that didn't feel very good about herself. She was not a very attractive girl, but she was very quiet, very mannerable. In our Sunday school class, she didn't have a lot to say. We knew that the [Collins family was large], but they would come in, and we all talked and played together. I think there was probably more trouble in her than we knew at that time. I say that based on conversations I had with her oldest sister, June.

Initially I was very hurt. I was shocked. I was afraid. I was afraid because earlier that year, the Crowells' house had been bombed. That blast destroyed the foundation in front of our house. I had four brothers, and we had two sets of bunk beds. The boys that were sleeping on the top were actually thrown out of those beds. This was a bomb that went off at about three o'clock in the morning. I can't explain to you what it does to you to be awakened that time of morning. We heard this terrible, terrible noise. There was a building, a big cement building, J. M. Tull, on the street behind us. My mother said [that] the policeman said that the bomb exploded, hit the building, and bounced back, which is why we had so much damage. When the bomb exploded, it was like everything lit up. It was like daylight for what seemed like thirty seconds. It was probably about five seconds. Then it went black again, and then you heard screaming, people coming out of their homes. I could hear Mrs. [Ruth] Crowell inside my home. I could hear her screaming coming out of her home. Mr. [Toussaint] Crowell didn't wake up. He wasn't hurt, but he didn't wake up. She was trying to wake him up from the outside, hollering his name. My younger brother just developed a tremendous nervous condition [after] having been thrown out of his bed like that. So when this church explosion occurred, I think I decided it was probably just a matter of time. Both bombings had such an impact. I decided that I was probably going to be killed with one of these bombs. I was afraid. I was frightened. And it seemed there was no control. There was no way to stop what they were doing. There was no way to protect yourself.

Helplessness is what I felt. I was so withdrawn after that church bombing. I did not attend the funeral of the four girls. I remember Mrs. Robertson calling. They were asking for some of us to be flower bearers at the funerals. I told my mom, "Please don't make me go." I was [not] sure what I would see. I knew I was really hurting inside and grieving that my friends were gone. I just did not want to be—I didn't want to see them. I didn't want to be there—part of that. She kept trying to encourage me to go. Finally, the day of the funeral, she called and said, "I think I'll let her stay here." I didn't attend the funerals. I just didn't.

Back at school, the mood was very somber. We had teachers that did allow us to talk. I thought about Ralph Joseph, who was a math teacher, and Mr. [D.] Winston asked a few questions and listened to what we had to say. It was good, and it felt good to hear—very therapeutic. I remember even when [John F. Kennedy] was killed that year, Mr. Joseph was the one who made the announcement that the president had been shot. He walked around the classroom for a little bit, and then he came back up front and closed the textbook. A few students were crying, and he allowed us to talk then, just to say what was on our mind. It was difficult. That was another one of those situations where you felt that you had no control over what might happen tomorrow. Today, when things like this happen, you bring in all the therapists and psychologists, and students get a chance to talk and really get it out of their system. There was no sense of that, nor was there any sense of justice. No one was in jail, and nobody even mentioned that no one was in jail. So it was almost as if it was just a type of predestination that you couldn't do anything about. I think that may have worried me more than a lot of other things. It shook my confidence.

NOTES

BCRI OHP, vol. 35, sec. 1 (April 23, 1995). Edited by Horace Huntley and John McKerley.

1. William E. Shortridge followed Shuttlesworth into the ACMHR after the Alabama NAACP's collapse in 1956 and became the new organization's first treasurer (Andrew M. Manis, *A Fire You Can't Put Out: The Civil Rights Life of Birmingham's Reverend Fred Shuttlesworth* [Tuscaloosa: University of Alabama Press, 1999], 99).

2. It was rumored that Bull Connor rode in a tank for protection during the disturbances after the bombing of the A. G. Gaston Motel (Diane McWhorter, *Carry Me Home: Birmingham, Alabama: The Climactic Battle of the Civil Rights Revolution* [New York: Simon and Schuster, 2001], 432).

CARL GRACE

CARL GRACE was born in Fairfield, Alabama, on February 27, 1948. He described growing up in Westfield, a segregated company town owned by U.S. Steel. Grace credited his father, a steelworker and an NAACP member, with motivating him to become politically active. "My father always preached the need for voting rights and for civil rights," Grace recalled. "He wasn't a minister, but he was one that had the message in my family because he stood strong with the need for us to gain our rights." Yet despite—and in part because of—the success of black organization in Westfield, the town's residents faced the constant threat of white violence. In fact, a white security guard at U.S. Steel shot and killed one of Grace's older brothers, a U.S. Navy veteran, when he resisted arrest.

In the eighth grade, Grace moved from Westfield to Fairfield, where he attended Fairfield Industrial High School. At Fairfield Industrial, his size and strength made him a formidable competitor on the field and a leader in the rough-and-tumble world of neighborhood politics. "Back in those days, there was rivalry among blacks," Grace recalled. "Fairfield against Westfield, against Ensley, against Southside, against Collegeville, against Wenonah." While this neighborhood loyalty could bolster solidarity during demonstrations, it could also lead to violence and intimidation between groups of black people. "Even though we were marching together, we were still separated," Grace recalled. "The movement was what brought us together, but even after the march was over, there was still separatism between us."

WE SHALL OVERCOME, BUT WE WERE STILL DIVIDED

My father and mother, most of their lives were spent in the Birmingham area. My father, I'm not sure which school he went to or if he finished. I do know he did not go to school in the Birmingham area. My mother did some housework for some Caucasians years ago. But that was very limited because she had a pretty active family. She went back to Miles College and finished her high school education.

There were four boys and one girl; actually there were five, but my oldest brother I didn't know because my mother was six months pregnant with me when he was killed. A security guard at U.S. Steel killed him on his way to work. From my understanding of it, in the lot at U.S. Steel, some of the young black guys had been taking a car and joyriding and then parking it. He worked at U.S. Steel; he had done some time in the navy and had come out of the navy. He elevated his age, and they accepted him into the navy. He came out of the navy and got a job at U.S. Steel. Through the parking lot was his way to go to work every day. So from what I understand, the guard told him to halt, and he kept going, and [the guard] shot him in the back and killed him. My mother pursued it, got a detective, but back in that period of time, there weren't very many rights for black people. That's why I'm so thankful for the [1964] Civil Rights Act.

We lived in Westfield at the time. My father worked for U.S. Steel and retired in 1976. He was there approximately forty years. The first years at U.S. Steel, he worked in the plant, and the last ten or fifteen years, he worked in plant security. He checked badges at the Tin Mill gate in Westfield. I can remember every aspect of Westfield. In fact, I've got Westfield in my mind—every alley, every street, and every path in Westfield. Westfield was a town like no other town that I've ever encountered because the people were so close, and almost all of Westfield was black. U.S. Steel created it originally. We had one area where whites lived; there were about twelve houses. Blacks populated the rest of the area. All of the people with authority in Westfield were white, even though they were the minority. We had a sheriff called Mr. Vann. He was the sheriff, he was the postmaster, he was also the mayor, and he was Santa Claus at Christmastime. He visited homes with gifts. If your parents had gifts for you, they would keep it at what was considered the fire station and the post office. He would deliver them to the home at Christmastime. Westfield was very close coming up. You could leave your doors open and sleep out on the porch and leave your bicycles on the sidewalks. No problems with thievery, stealing, or killing. All of the criminal aspects of life almost were nil; it didn't exist. Westfield was a joyful place to live coming up.

There were several racial incidents from outside of Westfield coming into Westfield. I remember the Fielder twins, twin boys. The police from Fairfield came over and put them in the car, took them out to the city dump, and beat them until their heads swelled up. They were unrecognizable. The Ku Klux [Klan] came into Westfield on several occasions. My father was very active in the NAACP. They would burn crosses, and I can remember a time when one guy with a hood and a rope attempted to enter in through the bedroom while I was sleeping that night. I hollered out, and my father came with the shotgun and ran him out. He didn't fire the gun. In fact, the guy was gone before he could get into the room because when I hollered he started backing back out of the window. But we had incidents such as that because my father was the one that headed up the movement of the NAACP in Westfield during that period of time. He was very instrumental in voter registration and so forth, and the [KKK] really wanted to stop him. Anybody that spoke out, they wanted to shut them up.

We had sort of a town square there. Carlton Reese was instrumental in the civil rights movement.[1] He lived directly across the street from me. Carlton was like a part of our family; he was at our house all of the time, and we were at their house. I can remember when we were kids, they took Carlton to juvenile [detention] for looking at a white girl. They took him to juvenile and kept him there. Kept him in juvenile for approximately ten days, shaved all of his hair off and charged him with "reckless eyeballing." They created a charge—"reckless eyeballing." These type occurrences did not happen every day in Westfield as it did in other areas, because there were very few whites in the community.

In Westfield, we had Westfield No. 2 [School] and Westfield No. 1 [School]. Westfield No. 2 went from the first through the fourth [grades]. Westfield No. 1 went from the fifth through the eighth. Then, after you left Westfield No. 1, you went to Westfield High School. I went to elementary school at Westfield No. 2 and No. 1 through the eighth grade. Westfield No. 1 was a little closer than Westfield No. 2. I guess I would walk approximately half a mile. Half a mile didn't seem far at all. Kids now—half a mile, they want a ride to school. But we left in plenty of time to get to school. We always made it to school on time, and missing school was a no-no. You didn't miss school; you didn't play hooky from school. We had a truant officer; she traveled from Westfield to Fairfield. She was a big woman, a large black woman. She was very, very strict. I've got a lot of fond memories of elementary school and church. When we were all coming up, we were made—you *had* to go to church. That was a demand on all the kids. Sunday morning you had your suit on and you went to Sunday school and church. I think that's what really grounded me in my faith when the civil rights movement took place.

The summer after coming out of the eighth grade, before I could enter into high school, we moved from Westfield to Fairfield because they were tearing down all the houses. My father bought a house in Fairfield. I had practiced football at Westfield in the eighth grade, and Coach [Robert] Dickerson was expecting me to come to Westfield. I was very athletic in school. I played sports: [foot]ball, wrestling, and all types of sports were my desire. I got to Fairfield, and they had a championship team that year. In fact, we played Westfield for the championship, which was called the TB Game at that time. We played at Fair Park. They played at Rickwood and at Fair Park, but they started playing at Fair Park. We beat Westfield that year, 15–6. Both of us was undefeated that year, but Westfield had some championship teams every year after that. But yes, we left Westfield and moved to Fairfield and Fairfield [Industrial] High School.

Back in those days, there was rivalry among blacks. The kids today have gang rivals; we had city rivalries. Fairfield against Westfield, against Ensley, against Southside, against Collegeville, against Wenonah. I knew I was moving to a different city. I knew I would probably encounter some of the guys who considered themselves to be tough, and I was the toughest guy in my grade level in Westfield. So there was a guy named Donald Smith who formerly lived in Westfield. I asked him, "Donald, who is the toughest guy in the ninth grade?" He told me this guy, Eddie Godwin. I said, "I want to meet Eddie Godwin." I knew if I had to go into this place and do anything physical, I wanted to start at the top. If I could start at the top and get the top straightened out, everything underneath would fall in place. So I started with Eddie, and Eddie and I became close friends. We tussled and wrestled, but I always came out on top, so I had no problems. Eddie and I both played football at Fairfield High School. Our senior year, I was the captain of the football team and Eddie was cocaptain. So we just became real close in school, and we both were on the team in the ninth grade.

Fairfield [Industrial] High School was under Professor E. J. Oliver. He was very well known. He was very, very exceptionally strict. He didn't have any foolishness in his school. He demanded respect, and he got it. All the teachers there were very strict. Fairfield [Industrial] High School was an educational experience, but it was also an athletic experience for me. I think I got away with a lot of things as a result of my athletic ability that I wouldn't have normally gotten away with. Like sometimes, even today, something I really don't appreciate is teachers passing someone because of their basketball skills or football skills. Scholastic achievement should be demanded of kids, because very few make it in the NBA and NFL. It's good to use your athletic ability to get an education, but make sure you get that education because your athletic ability might not add up or measure up.

I believe it was my first year in high school, in 1962–63, that we marched. In 1962–63, I was a freshman. [In] 1963–64, I was a sophomore. It was something that was brewing. It was in the air. It was all over the news. It was in the community. It was in the churches. This was the message throughout the community: We've got to do something to gain respect and to get rights.

I went to Hopewell Baptist Church in Westfield. In Fairfield, I went to Mt. Pilgrim, Fairfield. My father always preached the need for voting rights and for civil rights. He wasn't a minister, but he was one that had the message in my family because he stood strong with the need for us to gain our rights. I think my father was really instrumental. He was very active in the NAACP and also in the voters' rights movement. He was getting out there and trying to get people to register to vote. In fact, he ran for city council of Fairfield. He didn't make it that year, but he was very active politically.

We were in school the day that we marched. Carlton Reese had gotten together with some others and organized the march. I was sitting in music class. We were in Miss Major's classroom, and we began to hear someone down the hall saying, "Let's go." Then all of a sudden, it sounded like horses. You could hear the footsteps coming down the hall [and voices] saying, "Let's go." It was getting closer and closer, and the closer it got, the footsteps were heavier. Someone got to our door and opened up the music class door and said, "Let's go." We all got up, and Miss Major stood in the door and tried to stop us. Oscar Porter pushed her out of the way, and we all just hit the hallway, went to the next door. We began to be the ones that opened the door [and said], "Let's go." The kids just rushed on out. Many teachers tried to stop us, and many teachers were for us going.

The biggest obstacle that we had to encounter was Professor Oliver. Everybody listened to Professor Oliver. [But] we made it through. I vaguely remember seeing him in the hallway, but what he was saying at that point in time, I don't remember. But whatever it was, it wasn't strong enough to stop us. We had that momentum, and we were going on. Everyone shelled out and went into the street, and Carlton Reese had everyone to line up. We all lined up, and he gave a speech about what we were going to do. We were going to march from Fairfield [Industrial] High School and meet a group at Five Points West. The group at Five Points West was all headed downtown to meet Rev. [Martin Luther] King, Rev. [Fred] Shuttlesworth, and other marchers. So that was the plan.

We began to march from Fairfield [Industrial] High School, went up to the west side of Miles College and over to Carline Road to Bessemer Road. When we got near Bessemer Road, we knew that if we had any problems, it was going to be between there and Five Points West because we had to contend with the Midfield, Fairfield, and Birmingham police. So Carlton at that point had everyone stop. If we had any paraphernalia, any knives, any dice, or whatever, it was time to get rid of them, because we didn't want any extra charges to be filed against anyone. Knives and dice and things began to come from everywhere. They gathered them all up as soon as we hit Bessemer Road. Marching on Bessemer Road, all of a sudden, police came from everywhere. I know the Caucasians in the area had already informed the police. Buses, paddy wagons—they loaded us up on paddy wagons and in buses; they carried us out to the Sixth Avenue Precinct. The jails were so full that they didn't have anyplace to put us. They put us on the lawn out in the yard. As we were there waiting all during the day, they brought more and more, and before you knew it, that whole yard was covered with people, wall-to-wall people. Then I was taken along with others upstairs and they put us in a cell block and began to film us. We stayed there for five days. I would think probably three-fourths of my school, if not 90 percent, participated. It was a massive march. There were hundreds of us. Everyone wanted to participate, to hear Dr. King speak.

I remember being pushed, manhandled, thrown into the bus, and thrown up the steps. The police didn't have any respect for us or anyone else that was black. You were *black*. You were just like an animal out there. You were inferior. This was their mentality during that period of time. I don't hate any—I mean, I love all people—I don't have any animosity against them, but there are certain things I can't watch on TV, like *Mississippi Burning* and some of these movies that bring back old thoughts of what happened. Now, as far as watching the actual films of what happened in the movement, yes, I enjoy watching them. I come to the [Birmingham] Civil Rights Institute to watch myself on TV sometimes. It brings back memories. Sometimes I go back to the library and get a film out or a video and watch it. Bull Connor and those guys, [George] Wallace, [John] Patterson before him, it was just like the blacks were not human.[2] I can remember my father saying "Yes, sir" to a young [white] man, younger than I, after moving back here. I told my father, "Father, don't say 'Yes, sir' to that boy. That's nothing but a boy." But it was just that mentality; it was ingrained in us from the past. I was just fortunate to see both sides. I can remember always getting on the bus and I can remember the "Colored" signs. We had to get on the back of the bus; they had a sign that would sit on the back of the seat. You knew to sit behind that sign. I didn't move the sign, but I moved from my seat a lot of times.

When I was arrested, I spent five days in jail. We still had the inner-city rivalries going on. It was calm, [and] I feel bad about the fact, but being a kid and being raised that way, I had that city mentality when someone else came in from the other city. You patted them down; if they had anything, you took it, even during jail. In jail, I sort of commanded the guys that were from Fairfield that were with me. It was quite a few of us in the cell. [If] someone else came in from Ensley or Southside, I'd tell them, "Check them out." They'd check them out, patted them down, [and] took the things. I don't feel good about that now, but I just see that as ignorance on my part and our part. But that was the mentality that we had. It was the juvenile in us at that point in time. Even though we were marching together, we were still separated. The movement was what brought us together, but even after the march was over, there was still separatism between us. We have a need to come together as a people.

In jail, there were so many [that] we were in there like sardines in a can. [There were] so many people in each cell block. In each cell block, they had what they called a dayroom where they had their picnic table where you eat at normally. They had approximately four cells with four bunks to each cell, and the doors were left open all the time. So it was just like an apartment, a four-bedroom apartment. You could travel from the cells to the dayroom and back at will. All of the guys from Fairfield claimed and possessed the bunks. Anyone else [who] came in from the other cities slept wherever they could. But it was an experience. I remember the photographers coming to the cell. All us holding our hands up singing, "We Shall Overcome." We shall overcome, but we were still divided. Most of the guys that were in there with us were our age. I think that might be the way that they did it. They did it purposely. When they decided to clean up our cell blocks, we had to go to the next cell blocks, and a lot of guys from Fairfield—our age and a year or so older—were in that cell block, and guys from other cities also were in that cell block.

I was released after five days. [Movement organizers] were asking us to stay in for five days. After five days, my mother and father picked me up at the jail and took me on back home. They were proud of me. But if I had requested to march, [my father] probably would have stood strong against it. But since it had already happened, there weren't any kind of repercussions. He was just happy that I was okay and I came out alive and I wasn't beaten like many people were beaten downtown. Dogs were not ordered against me, and I didn't have any bites or anything on me. We were just fortunate we weren't beaten, because quite a few people were beaten. In order to expel anyone, they would have to expel the whole school because school was just practically nil during that five days. I know that there were some that didn't march, but they were very few. They were in the minority. We were not expelled from school. We didn't have any repercussions in school concerning that.[3] After getting out of jail, I think my life basically took on the sports aspect of my life. I didn't get involved like Carlton or some of the other guys did. I didn't continue on. I went into the military right after high school—Vietnam and so forth.

I remember the Sixteenth Street [Church] bombing. I remember hearing [it]. I wasn't in it; I wasn't near there, but it was all over TV. It was just a sad situation. it was just unbelievable. It was like you wanted to do something. Have you ever been in the situation where you just want to do something and you know that you can't do anything? I can remember being a child, and I guess basically I just wanted some vengeance, to just be honest about it. I wanted to take vengeance. To see those kids destroyed like that.

I was in San Antonio, Texas, in the military, when Dr. King was assassinated. I was in the army. I had just left Fort Benning and jump school. I went to San Antonio to take medical training. I was a combat medic. I can remember the guys in the army. It was the same situation. We wanted to do something, but we were in the military. In the military, things are a whole lot different. I believe if I were out in the streets somewhere, I would have done something. That was really another unbelievable situation. I can remember crying because I remembered his messages. Every time Dr. King would speak, it was like I could sense an anointing on his message, and that anointing would touch me. I could feel it in my physical body. Especially the one speech about being on the mountaintop and seeing what's on the other side, that he might not get there with us, but we as a people will get there.[4] It reminds me now of Jesus Christ. He knew that he was going to die, but his death was for a reason—to free mankind. Dr. King knew that his death would be instrumental in us receiving our civil rights, and he wasn't afraid to die.

I was just thankful to be involved because it was really broadening. Everyone was committed to a common cause. We all had the same reason for being there, we all had that faith that we were going to change this situation. And in time, it changed.

NOTES

BCRI OHP, vol. 27, sec. 5 (April 9, 1997). Edited, annotated, and abridged by A. Michelle Craig and John McKerley.

1. Carlton Reese, BCRI OHP, vol. 15, sec. 3 (May 16, 1996).

2. John Patterson first gained prominence in Alabama politics after his father, Albert Patterson, was murdered in connection with his investigations into organized crime in Phenix City. After his father's murder, Patterson was appointed to take his place as attorney general (the office to which Albert Patterson was nominated at the time of his death). John Patterson used his office to attack organized crime (with the notable exception of the Klan, which supported him) and civil rights organizations, including the NAACP, which he had banned in 1956, thereby facilitating the creation of the ACMHR. In 1958, Patterson defeated George Wallace to become governor. See http://www.archives.state.al.us/govs_list/g_patter.html (accessed April 15, 2007).

3. On May 20, 1963, the Birmingham Board of Education expelled more than one thousand black students identified as youth activists. The NAACP ultimately had the decision overturned on appeal. See Glenn T. Eskew, *But for Birmingham: The Local and National Movements in the Civil Rights Struggle* (Chapel Hill: University of North Carolina Press, 1997), 308–9. On reprisals against student activists, see also Gwendolyn Gamble, BCRI OHP, vol. 12, sec. 1 (January 24, 1996); James W. Stewart, BCRI OHP, vol. 48, sec. 4 (July 15, 2003).

4. Grace is referring to King's final sermon, "I See the Promised Land," delivered on April 3, 1968, the day before his assassination, as part of his efforts to aid striking sanitation workers in Memphis, Tennessee. For the full text of the sermon, see Martin Luther King Jr., *A Testament of Hope: The Essential Writings and Speeches of Martin Luther King, Jr.*, ed. James M. Washington (New York: Harper San Francisco, 1991), 279–86.

MALCOLM HOOKS

MALCOLM HOOKS was born in Birmingham on August 25, 1948. He grew up in Riley-Travellick, a black community in the southwest part of the city. In 1963, he was a student at Wenonah Elementary. Hooks first became involved with the movement through his older brother and sister, both of whom participated in the mass demonstrations that year. "Normally I would never skip school," he recalled, "but the movement instilled in me a belief that something could be done to change the system."

Hooks's experience in the juvenile detention center after his arrest revealed the divisions that segregation and white supremacy helped to foster within the city's black community. "The overseer in the jail was a black man who called us niggers, and he was very intimidating towards us," he remembered. "It amazed me to see a black man have such opposition and hatred towards us because we were marching for freedom." Furthermore, his contact with other young black men in the detention center suggested the difficult decisions that some students faced as they attempted to reconcile their training in nonviolent direct action with the violence that surrounded them. While he remained "obedient to the movement cause," Hooks admitted that he felt the need "to protect [himself] in the face of danger."

As an adult, Hooks has worked at a variety of jobs, including serving as a manager at Sears, where he supervised both white and black employees. Looking back, he compared his struggles with the complicated legacy of racism to a person waiting for a train: "Every day he waits until finally integration allows him on the train, but once on the train, he asks, 'Where is this train going?'"

GETTING ARRESTED WAS A BADGE OF COURAGE

My mother was born in Greene County, but as an infant she moved to Birmingham. My father was born in Birmingham. I have four brothers and four sisters, and I am the middle child. My father only graduated from junior high school, but my mother finished her high school education. My father worked at the U.S. Steel factory for forty years in the ore mines and then worked in the Fairfield plant. My mother worked as a domestic worker before she became a nurse.

I grew up in the community of Riley-Travellick, located in the southwestern section of Birmingham. Riley-Travellick was composed of working families, and the community was considered a low-income neighborhood. I started first grade at Wenonah Elementary School, and after two years I attended St. Mary's Catholic School, [where I stayed] until the eighth grade. Most of my siblings attended public school except for my younger brother and me. My parents enrolled me in Catholic school because Wenonah Elementary School was extremely uncomfortable for me. Student rivalry and peer pressure made it very difficult for me to concentrate on my schoolwork, and they felt St. Mary's would be more suitable for me. St. Mary's was more structured, and great emphasis was placed on schoolwork. The teachers were more dedicated to teaching us, and the students were interested in learning. After I finished at St. Mary's, I returned to Wenonah for junior high school. The transition from St. Mary's to Wenonah was easy, because being at St. Mary's, I was able to do my work more independently without teachers having to guide me.

When I entered my junior high year in 1963, the civil rights movement in Birmingham was at its peak. The movement was visible throughout the city, and students were becoming more involved. My attendance at mass meetings had a very profound effect on me as well as some of the rest of my brothers and sisters. It was almost as if you were caught up. The feeling—it's very strange trying to explain it, because that's exactly what it was. You were caught up in a feeling. You were being directed, and we were moving almost as if we were being led to do it.

My older sister walked up to me one day after school and said she was going to participate in the student march that day. She said she was going to leave school and that my older brother was going to drive her to the Sixteenth Street Baptist Church. I decided that I wanted to attend the march with her, and the three of us went to the church for a meeting. Normally I would never skip school, but the movement instilled in me a belief that something could be done to change the system. When we arrived at the church, we listened to several speakers from the movement, and I tried to digest everything they were telling us. When I went home later that evening, I decided that I would go back the next day and participate in any way I could. The next morning, my sister came down to the school and said she was ready to go, so at the end of the period I walked out of school. That day I felt like a veteran in the struggle, and I had these strange feelings as I was being directed to different places.

The second day I went to the Sixteenth Street Baptist Church, I marched through the city, and afterwards we gathered at Kelly Ingram Park. People were singing and praying until the police came and used water hoses on the crowd. That was the first time I became fearful, when I saw dogs attacking people. I realized that water hoses hurt and that dogs do bite. I began to also realize that there was danger associated with being a part of the movement, and I was frightened by it. Later that evening, when I returned home, we were excited to tell our parents what happened that day in the park, and that's when they decided to become a part of the movement. The next day, more students began leaving from school and the principal at Wenonah started to notice. He did not say anything, and in fact he held the door open as I walked to my parents' car parked in the front. The news had gotten around to the various schools, and crowds of children left to meet at the Sixteenth Street Church.

When we arrived at the church, I was standing on the stairs waiting for the group I was assigned to line up with. As I waited, the police began using water hoses, and Rev. [Fred] Shuttlesworth, who was next to me, was hit, but luckily my father pushed me out the way. Rev. Shuttlesworth went over the railing and broke a couple of ribs and had to be hospitalized. Somehow, my father was able to see that danger was approaching, and he wanted to protect me. Once Rev. Shuttlesworth was hit, my group quickly moved into position, and I remember my brother offered me a knife. I said no, because the movement was strictly nonviolent, and I was obedient to the cause. My group continued to walk down Third Avenue North to the Holiday Inn, where we quietly took a seat in the lobby until a man from behind the desk said, "Niggers can't sit here." Five minutes later, the paddy wagons came and escorted us to [the juvenile detention center] on Tuscaloosa Avenue Southwest.

At midnight, my parents came to pick me up from jail, and I never saw a more beautiful sight than my parents waiting for me at the front. Jail was a frightening experience, because some of the guys I was in jail with were older than me, and they were not in jail for participating in demonstrations. I was in eighth grade, and these guys appeared to be teenagers, but they looked rough. There was a lot of cussing and fighting between them, and when they asked us if we participated in the demonstrations, they appeared to be curious. They began telling us what they would do if they were in the same situation, and being nonviolent was not a part of their approach. The overseer in the jail was a black man who called us niggers, and he was very intimidating towards us. It amazed me to see a black man have such opposition and hatred towards us because we were marching for freedom. I thought because we had a black man overseeing us that we would be more protected than if a white man were watching us. Because he was black, we assumed he would be sensitive to why we were there and realize that we were not there because we had done anything wrong. In fact, we were there because we were doing what was right.

When I first saw my parents, I was relieved because the supervisor had announced that no one would leave the jail that night because of the lockdown at midnight. I was able to leave, and I was the last one able to go home. I thought I would have to spend the night, so I prepared a spot on the floor for myself, and I made a pillow out of my jacket. I knew that after the lights went out that there would be a lot of fighting and arguing, so I was preparing myself for what might happen. I didn't believe that the nonviolent philosophy was going to protect me from the other juveniles I was in jail with. I was confused because I wondered how I was going to practice nonviolence in jail when I was prepared to fight. I was obedient to the movement cause, but I had to protect myself in the face of danger. Luckily, it didn't come to that.

My sister was arrested and carried to a different place, and she stayed overnight. That was another thing that weighed heavily on my mind. We were both arrested, and I didn't know where she was or what was happening to her. I knew that I just felt I was going to be all right in the situation. I didn't know what I was going to encounter while incarcerated, but I knew I was going to be okay. But I wasn't sure that she was going to be okay. I was more concerned about her than I was about myself at that time. The next evening, we discussed what happened to us the day before, and we prepared to go attend another mass meeting that night. We continued to demonstrate, but I was never arrested again because my parents didn't want us to be put in harm's way again.[1]

When I returned to school, some of the teachers allowed us to talk about our experiences, while others continued with the schoolwork for that day. My friends viewed me getting arrested as a badge of courage. If you went to jail, you were perceived as achieving something. As a child, all black children knew that you couldn't go into Woolworth's or Newberry's and eat lunch at the counter. The only night blacks were allowed at the [state] fair was on Thursday night, which was "Niggers' and Dogs' Night." On the public bus, you had to give your seat up to whites if the white section filled up. Blacks had to sit at the back of the bus and sometimes were forced to stand up because they had to give their seat to a white person. I didn't go back downtown until I was a senior in high school because the trauma of segregation was still in my mind.

I remember my first introduction to the [Ku Klux Klan]. Our house was along a busy thoroughfare, and we saw this parade on the street. We immediately realized [that] this was not an ordinary parade because of the attire, the hoods and the masks. The Ku Klux Klan was parading right there in touching distance. We ran in the house terrified. We didn't know what was about to happen. So when the movement came, we felt that whatever had to be done to change this situation was worth it. That's why it became a necessity that we take part in whatever would make this injustice go away.

By 1965, Birmingham began to desegregate, including the Alabama Theater and Holiday Inn. Something had to tell your spirit that it was okay to sit at the lunch counter now and that it was okay to sit downstairs at the movies. One day you are arrested for doing it, the next day laws say that it is okay. Habits are hard to break for black and white people. When you go outside the United States, whites have a different perception of blacks than in the United States, and it is refreshing to meet people who want to deal with you on a human level. I have traveled to Canada, London, France, and other places. In Paris, people respected you more for being a human being, not because of your race. In Canada, I felt proud of being black. In America, there is always an underlying suspicion of what people have read or their experiences with black people clouding their minds. In Canada, I was like a mystery, and people were curious.

After high school, I went to Alabama A & M University and became a teacher. I left Huntsville and started working at Sears in Birmingham during the summer break, but I eventually stayed for ten years. It was an interesting experience, because whenever I complained or had questions, I was always told that I had a white man's job and that I shouldn't complain. I stayed at Sears because the money was good, but I had to put up with a lot of nonsense. I had to work harder than everyone else because I was black, and my numbers had to be higher as well. I was one of the first black managers at Sears, and I was in charge of black and white employees. The courage I had obtained during the movement gave me the strength to deal with various people at my job. If I could face white men with fire hoses and dogs, I could definitely deal with annoying questions my white counterparts asked me. They would ask me why black men looked at white women, and I would just tell them that we looked at them as a potential customer and a good commission. My black employees expected me to be lenient towards them, and many felt that because we were both black that I couldn't tell them anything. Those are the ghosts that continue to dangle around black people after integration.

After a while, the job became too stressful, and I decided to return to teaching. I enrolled at the University of Alabama and became recertified as a teacher and then went to UAB. Afterwards, I moved to Atlanta and taught at preparatory schools and colleges before I decided to go into business for myself. It is interesting because I feel like a boy standing at the train platform waiting for the train to let him in. Every day he waits until finally integration allows him on the train, but once on the train, he asks, "Where is this train going?" The biggest question is: Where are we now, and where are we going in the future? That answer is up for us to answer for ourselves.

NOTES

BCRI OHP, vol. 37, sec. 2 (June 11, 1998). Edited, annotated, and abridged by Desiree Fisher and John McKerley.

1. For his mother's perspective on these events, see Jimmie Lucille Hooks, BCRI OHP, vol. 36, sec. 2 (May 27, 1998).

MIRIAM TAYLOR McCLENDON

MIRIAM TAYLOR McCLENDON was born in Birmingham on October 8, 1948. Although her first sense of a civil rights movement came from watching images of activists on television, she remembered reaching an uncomfortable understanding of the meaning of white supremacy while observing everyday encounters between black and white people: "I had always felt that there was something wrong between the races, and I wasn't really sure what that something was. But I didn't like the way the black people in my community would respond when a white bill collector would come around. Black men were normally very proud, aggressive men. But then, all of a sudden, they would become rather subservient in their demeanor when a white man came around, and that bothered me."

Brought to mass meetings by her mother, McClendon recalled that the youth rallies "totally engrossed" her. When she was arrested for protesting, she helped to organize her fellow students in jail, drawing on lessons learned from television: "[T]o add to our punishment, they brought us little hard biscuits, a fried piece of fatback, and some watery syrup. We looked at it and decided it was not fit for human consumption, so we threw our plates against the wall. . . . [W]e had been watching TV, so this is what you do in jail, right?"

For McClendon and many other young people who participated in the movement, these experiences served as the foundation for other, sometimes more militant, forms of activism later in life. Indeed, while McClendon believed that her experiences in the civil rights movement "taught [her] to evaluate and analyze" in the service of social change, Stokely Carmichael and Black Power ultimately produced her "great awakening": "While I enjoyed the civil rights movement and those who were preaching turning the other cheek and nonviolence as the way—I heard that and I accepted it—but I wanted to try Stokely's way. . . . He was saying, 'I'm not interested in sitting next to you at the lunch counter, or necessarily drinking at your water fountain. Let us get our own. We, as a black community, should galvanize our strength and unify to build for self.' That made sense to me."

I REALLY DIDN'T KNOW THAT I WOULD END UP IN JAIL THAT DAY

My parents were from down in the Black Belt. My father's parents and grandparents are from a town a few miles north and west of Montgomery. My mother's family was originally from an area not too far removed from my father. As a matter of fact, they grew up together. They went to the same schools and fell in love in high school. To hear him tell it, they fell in love in grammar school, and he knew when he first laid eyes on her that [she] would eventually be his wife.

I was born in Jefferson County, at Wenonah. Originally there were nine of us. The eldest died in infancy, and so there are eight remaining. My father graduated high school, went to trade school, and majored in tailoring. My mother eventually graduated high school, but she didn't do that until after she was grown and we had all come on the scene. She dropped out of high school, got married, and started raising a family. Both of them went to Powderly High School [in Jefferson County].

I started first grade at Ishkooda Elementary School. It went from the first through third grade. It was a three-room school right in the middle of the larger Ishkooda community. Ishkooda was a mining community.[1] Then I went to Powderly [Elementary] for a year. And then I transferred to Wenonah Elementary for one year. I went there for the fifth grade and found out that we couldn't return. I lived closer to Powderly Elementary, so that's where I had to go, much to my chagrin. But I went from the sixth through the eighth grades at Powderly Elementary. I went to Wenonah High in the ninth grade.

I loved school early on. I had a passion for learning, and I was an avid reader. The one thing that I remember is the fact that at some point I lost that love, that intense passion for school—not for learning but the structure. I didn't like the teaching methods. I had a peculiar way of learning, and I didn't think the instructors were able to make the material interesting enough for me. If we were assigned a reading selection, for example, I would read it and then go to class, and it really wouldn't be discussed to my satisfaction. So as a result, I ended up doing a lot of my reading outside the classroom, and I would try to talk to a classmate or my brothers and sisters about it. But of course, they hadn't read it. I think there really wasn't enough time to thoroughly digest the material and to thoroughly discuss it. I think, again, when I started taking math, I became very disillusioned because maybe I was a slow learner with the numbers, but I was turned off to math. First of all, the students scared the heck out of me [by] saying that math is hard. Then the instructor didn't make it any better. She didn't take the time to really explain it. She just whizzed through it. And back then, we didn't have tutors. So I was just kind of turned off. I stopped doing a lot of my homework and started reading other kinds of books. Now, when I was in the fifth grade, I was reading at a ninth-grade level according to the national standardized test. I was skipped a half grade in elementary school, so as a result, I ended up being one whole grade higher than I should have been. That created a new set of problems for me because when I went into the eighth grade, I should have been with the seventh grade.

I remember being very shy. I had a sister who preceded me, and I was sort of in her shadow. Cassandra was very popular. She had this beautiful singing voice and this very open personality and I was the opposite. I was a bookworm. I traveled to strange, faraway places in my book, but I wasn't very open with people at that point. People were always making the comparison between the two of us. "Are you sure you're Cassandra's sister?" I said, "Well, yes."

• • •

I started watching the movement on TV. I had watched the news with my family. Once I understood what they meant by the "civil rights movement," it made sense to me. I had always felt that there was something wrong between the races, and I wasn't really sure what that something was. But I didn't like the way the black people in my community would respond when a white bill collector would come around.[2] Black men were normally very proud, aggressive men. But then, all of a sudden, they would become rather subservient in their demeanor when a white man came around, and that bothered me, and I watched it. I don't think my peers really noticed it. They were interested, for example, in being outside and playing all the little games that kids normally play. I played some, too—don't get me wrong. But I preferred the company of books to the company of the kids.

My mother went to a mass meeting, and I wanted to go, and she took me. Sitting in the audience and listening to Dr. [Martin Luther] King touched on that mysterious something inside me. I knew that they were addressing the race question, and it had never really been addressed [for me] before. I thought, "Okay, finally! Let me kind of investigate this and see where this will lead." Back then, they separated the mass meetings. They had one for the adults, and they had one around the corner for the youth. I started going to the youth meeting and just became totally engrossed.

The meeting was a lot of singing and rallying. They discussed the critical issues, the same issues that were being discussed in the larger mass meeting with the adults, but they tailored it to fit the temperament of the student. Again, I just became totally absorbed and fell absolutely in love with Rev. James Bevel. I remember Carlton Reese was there playing away at the piano, leading us through song. You had people who were there on a weekly basis, who were kind of on the front line, the foot soldiers.

There were a number of us who already were involved in the movement, again, through the mass meetings. We knew they were coming to our school because they told us. They said, "We want you to walk out and go with us downtown because we're trying to make a statement. We want to send a message." I heard them, and it really didn't sink in to me what they were actually saying until I saw some of the guys walking up and down the hallways calling the students to come out. I looked out there and I saw them, and I said, "Oh, okay. Now is the time." There were a number of us who just got up, walked out of class, and we walked [about seven miles] from Wenonah High School to downtown Birmingham to Kelly Ingram Park.

We walked, and we sang and chanted. In retrospect, [when] I stop and think about it [now], I say, "Wow, that's a long way." But back then, we were young. I was thirteen or fourteen years old, and I walked long distances anyway. I would walk from Ishkooda to Cairo Church of Christ to revival meetings. We only made that long walk that one time. Again, we were trying to make that statement, so we walked from Wenonah to downtown Birmingham. That was the same day that I got arrested. There were in excess of one hundred of us from Wenonah. When I say that, I really hadn't given any thought to [the reality of the demonstration] prior to that. I'm very serious. I had not asked my parents' permission. I really did not know that I would end up in jail that day. I thought I would walk downtown and march, the same kinds of things that I had done many times in the past, and then go home.

When we got to Kelly Ingram Park, we were split up in different groups, and each group had an assigned area. My group's assigned area was the Atlantic Mills Thrift Store. And my parents, of course, shopped there. We had this big family, and you know how difficult it was to feed and clothe everybody in those days. So I was familiar with the store. The specific reason that we were picketing at Atlantic Mills was because they had no black sales clerks, no black managers. We couldn't drink at the [water] fountains. We couldn't use the bathrooms other than the one designated for "Colored." That didn't make sense to me, because if not the majority, a large portion of their clientele was black. I thought it only made sense that we should be employed there if we were going to spend our dollars there. So we went there to picket the store.

The store manager came out. We had our little signs, and we had formed our little circle, and we started marching and singing. He came out and demanded that we stop, but of course we kept going. He stepped almost directly in front of me, and in order to avoid colliding with him, I said [to myself], "Let me stop and see what he has to say." So he proceeded to tell us that if we did not leave the premises immediately, he would call the police and have us arrested. I'm standing there. There was no leader of that group. I didn't make myself leader or anything; he just happened to stop in front of me. I had to decide then and there for myself whether or not to walk away or to continue marching, so I just stepped around him and continued marching and singing, and everybody else did the same thing. He immediately called the police. There were between twenty and twenty-five of us, and all were arrested.

The police car seemed to materialize almost immediately, but I imagine maybe three to five minutes passed. They apparently were nearby because of the climate. They knew things were happening. They shot down there in about two or three paddy wagons, and we were loaded into them and driven to Sixth Avenue Jail on the south side. They took our fingerprints. They took our photographs and background information. Again, it still had not sunk into me that I wasn't going to go home. After the processing, they put us back in either a paddy wagon or bus—I'm not exactly sure which. But we were transported. I think it was a bus, because we were with kids from other schools. We were taken to the county jail. I think we stayed about three or four days at the county. I'm not very clear. But then we were transported to the [state] fairgrounds, Fair Park Arena, where we remained several more days.

The most vivid memory that I have [of] being incarcerated is the sweatbox. That kind of overshadows everything else. The sweatbox was a small room, closet size, and you had to step down into it—just a few inches, not far. They had water at the bottom of it. It was like a big steel coffin because the sides were metal and the door was metal. This was the place where they took you for punishment.

I was punished because I wasn't a good girl. The first time I was taken to the sweatbox was because one of my cellmates was ill and complaining of headache and stomachache and was just really balled up and in pain. I and a couple of girls in our cell block called for the warden. At first she ignored us. We took some tin forks or cups and banged them up against the jail cell and made a lot of racket. She came in and wanted to know why we were calling for her. We explained that the girl was sick, and we wanted to know if we could get some type of medical attention for her. She laughed and walked away. Bear in mind that we were young and not used to this type of treatment, and here is this girl who [was] obviously ill. We were frightened, so we started banging again. We said, "Wait a minute, did you not hear us? She's sick." Then she came and took all of us except the sick girl to the sweatbox. This is in the county jail. I don't know how long we were there, maybe an hour or less.

I thought only three or four could fit in the sweatbox comfortably. The first time we were put in there, there was no one else in there, just the three or four of us. We just kind of stood around, laughed and told jokes, and they finally came and let us out. We said, "Hey, now, that wasn't so bad. If that's all the punishment we're going to get, we'll just keep on banging." And when we got back, they still hadn't done anything for the girl, so we watched her all night, in pain. That following morning, to add to our punishment, they brought us little hard biscuits, a fried piece of fatback, and some watery syrup. We looked at it and decided it was not fit for human consumption, so we threw our plates against the wall. Now, again, we had been watching TV, so this is what you do in jail, right? We're acting out what we had seen when an inmate wants to show displeasure. The girl was still sick. We started banging against the bars again. This time, when they came and got us and took us to the sweatbox, they said, "Okay, now you've done it. You're going to the sweatbox." We had it the day before, so we really didn't think that much about it. But when they took us the second time, it was very different. When they opened the door, it was already jam-packed with girls, and the heat from the bodies just kind of hit us in the face. I just stood there, and they said, "Come on, go on in." I didn't move because I was about to turn around and say, "It's already full. It can't hold any more." And then they pushed us in there. I was the last one to go in because I just stood there. They finally pushed me in, and I could feel the bodies being pressed back. The warden and one of her assistants had to push the door. They had to use their body weight to close the door. It was just that packed. The girls were crying and moaning. There was absolutely no air.

After coming out of the sweatbox, it was probably the next day that we were transferred to the fairgrounds. That evening, the newspaper was coming to do a story on the kids in jail, so they had to kind of put on the dog. It was a fun day. They gave the girls fried chicken, banana pudding, mashed potatoes, and gravy. Now, we were absolutely famished. Remember, we had thrown our breakfast against the wall and had no food in the interim. And when we questioned it, they brought us the same thing we had for breakfast: a strip of fatback; the cold, hard biscuit; and the watery syrup. We just threw a fit, but to no avail. So we just had to sit there and watch the girls eat and enjoy their feast. Interestingly enough, I couldn't get a single person to share.

My father came to pick me up from the fairgrounds. When I got home, I started talking to my mom, and I said, "Weren't you worried about us?" She said, "No, because when you didn't come home, we knew you were in jail." That surprised me, because I didn't know that my parents knew me well enough to know that if [movement leaders] came to my school, I would be one of the first to get up and go. But of course, parents always do. She continued to go to the mass meetings, and they were explaining the process to them and explaining to them that they didn't want them to come and bail us right out. They [wanted] us to stay in jail for a few days. They wanted us to just fill up the jails and even once they were full to keep coming, and that's pretty much what happened.

When we returned to school, there were no negative repercussions.[3] It was as though it never happened. Although I didn't realize it, that sweatbox experience really traumatized me because I didn't talk about it. I talked about it maybe a little bit to my parents and my family that first day that I got out, but after that, I just never discussed it again and didn't realize that it was a sore spot for me until many, many years later, when I was talking to someone, and I mentioned the sweatbox, and they wanted to know what the sweatbox was. I started explaining it and just broke down and started crying, and I [thought], "Where did that come from?" Once that happened, I realized that there was a little problem area for me, and I wrote about one aspect of my experience. It was just enough to kind of get it out because it was cathartic for me. I have actually started a book.

I continued to demonstrate but was never arrested again. I continued to picket and demonstrate. I wore out many pairs of shoes. I was driven. And even after I graduated high school, there wasn't much activism going on at my high school. We went to jail, those of us who walked to downtown Birmingham, and then we came back to school, and it was pretty much business as usual.

The real activism didn't start until I attended Miles College. I wanted to go away to college, but I was only sixteen and my parents wouldn't have it. I had to go to Miles College so that I could remain under their watchful eye. My freshman year, Stokely Carmichael came to Miles College to speak. That, I think, was my great awakening. Stokely spoke to me. He touched a chord in me that had never been touched before because he was verbalizing many of the ideas and concepts that I felt but had not given expression to. So while I enjoyed the civil rights movement and those who were preaching turning the other cheek and nonviolence as the way—I heard that and I accepted it—but I wanted to try Stokely's way. He was very forceful, and he was talking about Black Power. He was saying, "I'm not interested in sitting next to you at the lunch counter or necessarily drinking at your water fountain. Let us get our own. We, as a black community, should galvanize our strength and unify to build for self." That made sense to me.

On campus, I started working with other like-minded individuals, and we had a little underground newspaper. We would go out into the community and try to register people to vote. We continued doing many of the same kinds of things that were being done through the SCLC, but we also tried to raise people's level of consciousness. And we were very quick to call people Uncle Toms if they didn't do what we wanted them to do. So in this underground newspaper, we had what we called a Tom of the Week Award. Those professors, for example, who we felt were impeding the progressive thinking, we honored them with that award, and we put it in the paper. They didn't know who was publishing the paper, so we could be very, very forthright and write exactly what we thought and felt.

My years in the movement taught me to evaluate and to analyze. They sowed the seeds or laid the groundwork for everything that came after. It allowed me to give expression to my thoughts and it provided an outlet for me to put those expressions into some type of practice. When I was out marching, picketing, demonstrating, going door-to-door, registering people to vote, that was something that I could actually do. That was something concrete, and I felt that I was making a difference, and that was important to me. I don't know what direction my life would have taken had I not been involved in the movement. I can't even imagine it, because I'm so much of a doer. It's so important for me to attack injustice wherever I see it that I guess I would have had to be a different kind of person to not have been involved in the movement.

NOTES

BCRI OHP, vol. 11, sec. 4 (November 8, 1995). Edited, annotated, and abridged by A. Michelle Craig, Horace Huntley, and John McKerley.

1. On Ishkooda, see also David P. Earle, BCRI OHP, vol. 13, sec. 2 (March 6, 1995); Jimmie Lucille Spencer Hooks, BCRI OHP, vol. 36, sec. 2 (May 27, 1998); Horace Huntley and David Montgomery, eds., *Black Workers' Struggle for Equality in Birmingham* (Urbana: University of Illinois Press, 2004), 151–52.

2. On bill collectors, see also Jimmie Lucille Spencer Hooks, BCRI OHP, vol. 36, sec. 2 (May 27, 1998).

3. Some student activists were targeted for reprisal by the Board of Education. See Glenn T. Eskew, *But for Birmingham: The Local and National Movements in the Civil Rights Struggle* (Chapel Hill: University of North Carolina Press, 1997), 308–9.

SHIRLEY SMITH MILLER

SHIRLEY SMITH MILLER was born in Birmingham on January 9, 1949. She became involved in the movement through her parents, a miner and domestic worker. Miller was one of the first black students to desegregate West End High School, a process during which she felt tremendous isolation: "Being the only black student was an experience that you had to get used to. You got used to the fact that people were going to ignore you."

WE WERE JUST OUT THERE

My mother was from Calhoun, Alabama, in Lowndes County. My father was from Planters, Alabama. I had two brothers. I didn't have any sisters. I grew up in the western section of [Birmingham], which at the time, when we were growing up, was between Titusville and Mason City. It was called Montevallo Park. It's right off Martin Luther King Drive. Actually, the old house is still there on Nassau Avenue.

Now, my father had very little schooling. As a matter of fact, my mother taught my father how to sign his name for checks and stuff. My mother finished high school. She worked outside of the home when my younger brother was in the ninth grade. It was domestic work. My father started out working for the ore mines. Once they closed the mines [in the early 1960s], then they transferred [workers] to the steel mills.

When [the demonstrations] first started, I was in the eighth grade. We were completing the eighth grade. I think when we were first asked to leave school it was in April, I think around Easter of '63. My mother was always involved in the church. My church was an active church, and my pastor has always been active in the civil rights movement: New Pilgrim Baptist Church with Rev. N. H. Smith Jr.[1] So we were always active anyway. My mother always went to the movement meetings. I attended meetings with her. At the meetings, there was a lot of praying, a lot of singing, and a lot of preaching. You always left with a euphoric feeling, like you could do anything, go anywhere, and beat any odds when you went. It was like everybody was [in] one accord. As a child, I don't know if I listened to everything they were saying, but I know a lot of it sunk in. I was thirteen years old. I was old enough to know some of what was going on, but not old enough to know all of it. I did listen, and it had a profound effect.

The day that we all left school, I don't remember how the day got started. I guess it started like any other day. They had already told us in the mass meeting the night before. We would always go to the mass meeting the night before and then go to the demonstrations. My mother had written a note [to the principal]; she was trying to do it right. It was saying that we were leaving, and he just let us go. The next day, I don't think we went at all.

The first time, not a whole lot of students left school. When we left school, we came home, and then the man across the street, Mr. [Fred] Davis, took us downtown. When we arrived, we saw a bunch of other kids, grown people, police, Bull Connor. I remember the first day that we actually demonstrated, we just went downtown. We didn't go to the church or anything. After we went to the movement that night, they told us how to always go. I think we went to Immaculata [Our Lady of Fatima Catholic School in Titusville]. It was a church. The youth met there with Rev. James Bevel. He met with us to tell us how and what to do when you got in the marches. [He told us] how to react nonviolently. They would always take up a collection of anybody handling any type of weapons. I never will forget that, because we had all kinds of knives and this and that. We didn't have any guns among the students, but we had all kinds of things that could be used [as weapons]. They would always take that up before you went out. They told you how to stand, how to brace yourself for licks, and how not to say anything.

The first time I remember demonstrating, we didn't have sense enough to know really what we were doing. We were just out there. We were out of school, and we were just out there with a group of people. We had never really seen that many of our people together doing anything like that, so it was just exciting to us. I don't know if I thought about anything, but I was there, and I wanted to be there. I didn't encounter the police dogs directly. We were always in the back, and we got some water on us, but I never felt the full blast. But to be there to see—Have you ever seen a fire hose put on somebody? Everybody was just splashing up against the wall and on the ground and everything. We got wet, but we did not get the full blow of that. I never will forget.

The hoses and the dogs were frightening. When they brought the dogs in, we ran. That was frightening. When I see that statue [in Kelly Ingram Park] now, I think about that. The dogs were growling, and everybody was scared of them dogs. We ran back. We would run back to the end of the park, and then we went back to the church. After that, we all gathered up. We would always have our little meeting place. Sometimes we would go back to the church; sometimes we would go back to the car. We would go home. Then [we would] go to the mass meetings and then come back the next day. Definitely when the dogs came, we would fall back. We definitely fell back. Like I said, with the water hose, we never got the brunt of that because we were not right up front. When you talk about people, I'm talking about wall-to-wall people.

We stopped and went back to school. We didn't stay out of school. If I'm not mistaken, we were out that Thursday and Friday, and that Sunday was Easter. When we returned, the majority of the students in the classes knew where we [had been]. Some of the kids were like, "Where are you going? We can't go. My mama said that we couldn't go." A lot of people didn't have the permission of their parents to do it. Some just went, and their parents didn't know it. You have to realize that a lot of parents were really afraid for us. I never will forget my aunts from out of town calling my mama [and] asking if we were in the marches. She said, "Yeah, they were right there." So it was a kind of place where some people wanted to go, and some people didn't. It wasn't like everybody wanted to go there. And the principal, I think, wanted to go along with it, but the fact that they were working for the [Board of Education] and all, they just didn't. I don't remember any teacher making any comments, really. Some of them, you could tell by what they said that they were for it, but they just really couldn't [show it]. But they suggested to me that they wished that they had been there.

When I finished the tenth grade, some friends and I decided that we would be our part of integrating the schools. We [thought we] would [all] go to Ramsay High School to integrate it. [But] by me living on the other side of Montevallo Road, I ended up going to [West End High School] by myself, and my other friends, about three or four of them, went to Ramsey. I almost didn't go because of that. I didn't want to go there by myself. Then I said, "No,

I'm going to go anyway." So at the end of the tenth grade, when we went to the eleventh grade, they went to Ramsay, and I went to West End. That was our plan: we were going to integrate it.

When I went in '65 [to West End High School], there was one other black young lady there [Carrie Delores Hamilton Lock].[2] She finished with me in high school. We finished West End together. I had no idea when I got there who would be there or how many other blacks would be there at all. When I first went, it was Delores and I in the twelfth grade, and there was one other young lady who was in the ninth grade. That was it. There were three black girls in a school of probably [fifteen hundred] people.[3]

My mother took me the first day [for registration]. They were nice, but they were not overly nice. Like when you go to the doctor or when you go to sell them something, they treated you with respect but not anything other than that. There were some incidents. Delores came the year before I did, so she ended up having a lot more traumatic things than I did. At that time, West End High School had a vacant lot across the street. When she first came, she said the Ku Klux Klan stayed over there and were hollering, "Nigger, go home. Nigger, go home." When I came, I never really saw any of those people, but there was that same attitude with some of the students and the teachers. [They] dared not say that, but some of them, you felt that they felt that way: "Nigger, go home," and nigger this and that. You just [ignored] it.

[Delores and I] had one class that we took together. I can't remember now which one it was. Being the only black student was an experience that you had to get used to. You got used to the fact that people were going to ignore you. Some people acted like they didn't want to sit by you. I just got used to the fact that when I was in school, that until Delores and I went to lunch or something or I saw Vera [Marcus, a sophomore], I really wasn't going to have any communication with anybody. We simply accepted that as being [the norm].

I had been in the band at Ullman [High School], and I wanted to get back in the band [at West End]. They were saying that they had a long waiting list, and they really didn't need anybody in the band. So I just said forget that. We were in a few clubs, believe it or not. The Spanish Club, Careers Club—those were some of the clubs we were in. They did their cheerleaders and that kind of thing a little differently from everywhere else. At the schools I was used to, if you wanted to be in it, you just got in it. They used to always elect officers for things. I remember one of us, I think it was Vera, that ran for office for something. Of course, she didn't win. We did some things just for the heck of it. We auditioned for the choir. Of course we never got chosen. They said we were good, and I knew that I could sing because I have always sang. But for whatever reasons, we never got in the choir.

Then there were these little kids would say ugly things. I remember one time I really got into a competition with this boy because he called me a nigger, [so] I kicked him into a locker and kept going. We didn't get in any trouble. I didn't get sent home or nothing like that. I remember one time I had an asthma attack. I remember the teacher's name was Baughan, Mr. [G. C.] Baughan. He was teaching chemistry. He told my mother, "Maybe she's having an asthma attack which is caused by stress and trauma. Maybe all of her experiences here have caused that." Which it didn't. I've had asthma all the time. What he was trying to say and suggest to her was that maybe the strain was causing me to have the asthma attack. He said, "Now, if this keeps happening, maybe you need to think." He was trying to tell her [to make me] go back to the other school and all. But that [wasn't] the problem.

After we left school [in the afternoon], we never really did come back [for extracurricular activities]. They didn't want us there, and we obviously didn't want to be there. We kept up our social life [in our communities]. In fact, we didn't even have a prom at West End High School. We had a banquet, and we just chose not to go. I participated with Ullman's prom, and I believe Delores participated with her ex–high school's prom.

Our graduation was fine. It was uneventful, because I had all my folk there and Delores had all her folk there. We had our graduation in the auditorium at the school. Nothing happened there. My math teacher was another teacher that sticks out in my mind. I can't remember her name; I just remember her face. She wasn't really indifferent, but the first time I ever got an F in any subject was from her. It was not fair and equal. Now, the books were different. The books I had at Ullman High School compared to the books I had at West End High School were like night and day. Some of the labs and all that they had there were up-to-date. The classes, some of them had air-conditioning in them, even at that time. There were a lot of differences. The testing system was different. They did their testing similar to what they do in college. We weren't really used to that, so we had to get used to that. I know I was getting As and Bs at Ullman, and when I first got to West End, I had to get adjusted. That was the first F I got. I remember that. The next semester I got a B. We had to get used to the kind of testing system that they had.

The principal was Mr. [Steven] Ham. He was never ugly acting, but he never was encouraging that much either. I remember one time, my mother had to come up there to talk to him about something. Maybe it was when I got that F. I was really upset about that because I had never got that low of a grade before. I was determined to show her and them that I am not stupid and I can do the work. That's why I worked very hard the next semester and got a B and got out of that class. Most of the teachers never really said anything ugly to you. They just kind of ignored you a lot of time when you had your hand up. They would call on just about everybody before they called upon you. Of course, you had to go and explain a little more than everybody else had to go and explain.

There were never any teachers around when we got into a confrontation. Most of the time the confrontations were with students, in the hall or in the lunchroom. They tried to say little things. If you were walking down the hall, everybody would get on the other side of the hall. That kind of thing. I never got into a situation where somebody tried to beat me up or anything like that. Delores used to be really, really angry about some of the stuff they did. Some of it I took in stride because she was more traumatized, especially with the adults acting the way they were. She was afraid to go to the bathroom. Some of the bathrooms I didn't go in. I just said, "Look, I'm here. I'm going to be here. So y'all might as well get used to it." That was the kind of attitude that I took.

NOTES

BCRI OHP, vol. 37, sec. 1 (June 10, 1998). Edited, annotated, and abridged by A. Michelle Craig and John McKerley.

1. See Paul Littlejohn, BCRI OHP, vol. 18, sec. 3 (June 24, 1996).

2. Carrie Hamilton Lock, BCRI OHP, vol. 10, sec. 5 (October 18, 1995).

3. In 1967, there were at least twenty black students at West End, including eight boys. Almost all (and all but one of the boys), however, were freshmen. (*Resumé*, 1967, Southern History Collection, Birmingham Public Library)

WASHINGTON BOOKER III

WASHINGTON BOOKER III was born in Marengo County, Alabama, on January 20, 1949. After moving from Demopolis as a child, Booker lived on Seventh Avenue North and later in Loveman's Village, a housing project. According to Booker, he and his friends had become politicized by their daily experiences of segregation long before the organization of mass protest in 1963. In the movement, they saw an outlet for the self-respect and self-assertion that white supremacy had denied to their elders (especially black men) and that they were determined to seize. Rather than simply being participants in a protest strategy designed by others, Booker and his friends turned the marches and meetings into vehicles for their own forms of dissent, community, and camaraderie. Still, Booker described his participation in the movement as a transformative experience. "I think the movement was the beginning of consciousness," he observed. He joined the U.S. Marines in 1967 and later saw combat in Vietnam. While in the military, his contact with black nationalists from other parts of the country further radicalized him. He also interpreted his relationship with the Vietnamese through the lens of his run-ins with the Birmingham Police Department. "The Viet Cong were painted as the bogeymen, and we were the good guys from the West come in to save the poor ignorant savages from the bogeymen," he recalled. "Of course, the savages really didn't want to be saved; they looked at us like we were barbarians coming in from the West. In our relationship with the police, the police were much the same way." After returning to Birmingham in the early 1970s, Booker joined other veterans in founding the Alabama Black Liberation Front, an affiliate of the Black Panther Party.

WE WERE THERE FOR ACTION

I came to Birmingham when I was four. I have one sister; she's two years older than me, and I was born in 1949. My father finished high school and joined the navy. He is a well-read man. He loves books, and he loves to read and listens to tapes and anything that can give him information. He has a high school diploma, but he is fairly well-read, which makes him educated beyond those years. My mother went to Alabama State [College] on a choir scholarship and was there for two years.

My father worked in and retired from the plant in Demopolis. They pressed plywood. It was a plywood factory. At an earlier age, he worked about ten years delivering for a store in downtown Demopolis. It was the top-of-the-line store in Demopolis. He delivered packages for them.

My mother was an orthodontist assistant. She worked for Dr. Farmer on the south side [of Birmingham], starting in the late '50s. Before then, she worked over the mountain. She caught the bus and went to the white folks' house. Eventually, she got on doing [domestic] work, and she liked it. She left there in the mid-'60s, walked out when they asked her to do the windows. She didn't do windows, so she left. [She] had a quarter, and I think the bus cost fifteen cents, but she walked out. She had such a reputation for doing good work that she was hired by Dr. [Richard J.] Westbrook, who was in the City Federal Building for fifty years. She worked for him for twenty-five years.

I went to Ullman High School but did not graduate. I got a GED. I was asked to leave. I was just so far above the rest of the students, they felt like I shouldn't finish. They felt I was so grown that I should just go on out in the world. After I left Ullman, I did the all-American thing: I joined the Marine Corps. It was 1967, September 7, when I went into the Marine Corps and on to Vietnam.

I was in an infantry unit, First Battalion, Third Marines, Bravo Company. I like to say that we ran the welcome center between North and South Vietnam. Our area of operation was along the border between North and South Vietnam. We ran patrols, search-and-destroy patrols. We looked for enemy units moving in and through the area and closed in and destroyed. I'm a combat veteran.

• • •

When we first came to Birmingham, I lived on Seventh Avenue North, two doors up from Poole's Funeral Home. We stayed in a two-story tenement house. We had one room. My mother and my sister slept in the big bed, and I slept in the roll-away bed. There was a common kitchen, and the people had rooms in the two-story house. On Seventh Avenue, we had a tub that we poured boiled water into and put cold water in the tub to take a bath. There was no such thing as hot water in the house. The bathroom was a room a little bigger than a closet. It had a commode that sat right in the middle of the floor, and there was no light in it. There was one sink in the house, and it was of course on the other side of the wall from the bathroom, all the way to the back of the house. And there was a coal stove in the house. My mom would get up in the morning and make the fire in the stove and get back in the bed until the room got warm.

I was about a block and a half from Kelly Ingram Park. On the corner of Fifteenth Street and Seventh Avenue, there was Poole's Funeral Home. Their father was starting to get old at that time, and they were grown men, and they were running the funeral home. Aubrey Bushelon, who now runs Bushelon Funeral Home, was working for the Poole family. If you go farther west on Seventh Avenue, there was the Ballard House that was owned by Ma Perkins. She also owned the Zanzibar Hotel, where the Birmingham Black Barons lived. This was right next door to my house. I would sometime go to the store for members of the ball team. They would give me balls, old bats, little bitty bats, and that kind of thing. Sometimes they would put me on the bus and take me out to Rickwood Field, and I would sit in the dugout. I didn't know then that I was with a part of history, the old Negro League. There were black businesses on both corners on the south side of Seventh Avenue, but on the north side of Seventh Avenue, Vincent's Grocery Store was on one corner, which was an Italian business, and Fagin's Grocery Store was on the other corner, which was another Italian business. And right across Sixteenth Street on the northeast corner, there was a coal yard. We stayed [on Seventh Avenue] until 1959.

In 1959, we moved to Loveman's Village, where we had hot and cold running water, [a] bathtub, and thermostat. We moved up in the world. When we moved to Loveman's Village, one of the biggest arguments my sister and I ever had was over who was going to be the first to take a bath in the bathtub. There was a heater, a gas heater, with a thermostat that came on whenever it got cold. There was no light that would come in. If you closed all the doors and turned off all the lights, you couldn't see light coming in from the outside around the windows and through the closets. You could go in the closets in the old house on Seventh Avenue and close your door and you could see light coming in from the outside because it wasn't insulated. Loveman's Village was brick. It was warm, and it was well lit, and we had moved up in the world. I think we moved in maybe July, August, or something like that. School hadn't started, so we were on vacation. We were all wonderful until we went to school. Then the other kids informed us that we lived in the projects.

[The] Birmingham Police Department was an occupying force in our community. It was the source of the ultimate terror. People would threaten their children by telling them, "The police gonna get you." In Vietnam, we were like the policemen trying to run the bogeymen out the country. The Viet Cong were painted as the bogeymen, and we were the good guys from the West come in to save the poor ignorant savages from the bogeymen. Of course, the savages really didn't want to be saved; they looked at us like we were barbarians coming in from the West. In our relationship with the [Birmingham] police, the police were much the same way. There was no communication other than "Come here, Nigger," a lick upside the head, or to shoot. There was no human communications. There was no talking—none of that. They terrorized the community. It was a rare weekend passed that one or two folk maybe didn't get killed by the police.[1] This is what they do to you: they'd call you and make you stick your head in the [police car] window, right. Then they would roll the window up [on your neck], all the while calling you "Boy" and "Nigger." Then [they would] hit you on your head. You were lucky if that was all you got away with. They'd beat people to death. People were terrified of the police.

There was all kind of organizations [in the black community]. Almost everybody went to church. [Even] what you would call the baddest kids at the school, they went to church. It was really, really an exception to find a family in the black community that didn't go to church. But anyway, the church had ushers, matrons, youth programs, that kind of thing. There was the Boy Scouts. We had a Boy Scout troop in Loveman's Village. We had the [YMCA]. I was lucky enough to go to a Y camp. They had slots for poor kids. I could get in one of those slots, and I'd get a chance to go out to Camp Fletcher and [play] with the kids whose parents had paid to send them out there. But anyway, it was a good experience, and I'm thankful for it. There were singing groups. As a matter of fact, my mother sang with the Gospel Harmonettes, which was a gospel group. Churches would be packed on Sunday night because one of those groups would be coming to town, or one of the small auditoriums or the Masonic Temple and other places where they would have concerts [would be packed]. Then there were social and savings clubs. Later on, after Honeybowl was built and Starbowl was built, everybody bowled. That was the thing in Birmingham. If you were anybody in Birmingham, you went to the bowling alley. And people formed bowling clubs, and lot of black folks still bowl today.

We had a club. Our club was called the Coachmen. All of us would just kind of get together. [We] figured everybody else had a club, so we had a club of our own. We had parties, and we went to other people's parties. We all wore the same T-shirts or something. We didn't sell dope and do drive-bys. We weren't really that tough. There were gangs, though they weren't called gangs. There was always a group of fellows who hung together that carried pocketknives and were always looking to jump on somebody. They would go to another side of town or go to a party for the express purpose of getting into a fight and cutting somebody. Yeah, there were folk out there like that. They were in the minority. We would sponsor bus trips to Atlanta to go over to the big park and spend the day over there and go to the dance hall.

• • •

I remember the first day that I went [to a demonstration in Birmingham]. The march was starting from St. Joseph Church. It was all the way down on Sixth Avenue. We were standing across the street, facing north. The steps came out of the church, and the church faced south. The people were coming out of the church, and the police was meeting them in the streets. Some people behind us threw some bottles and some bricks. The police saw where it came from and rushed into the crowd. When they rushed into the crowd, I just fell. I fell in front of one of the police officers, and he fell over me, and the brother got away. He ran and got away. And so when I went home that day, I felt like I had really, really done something, that I had aided and abetted a fellow revolutionary. That was the first day. We didn't go to jail when the call came to fill the jails up with the children. We did not go at first because we had run-ins with the police on a daily basis. We knew them to be torturers and murderers, and the idea of voluntarily submitting yourself to be taken away by them took us a while to get used to. [We] finally decided we would go, and we all got arrested and went to jail.

I felt like black folk were standing up. I grew up with Stepin Fetchit [a Hollywood producer's image of black manhood], I grew up with Tarzan movies, I grew up with *Amos 'n' Andy*, [another caricature of black people] where the only black folk who were really on TV then were buffoons or lackeys or cowards. The movement represented courage. It was black people standing up saying, "I'm a human being. I have a right to be treated like a human being," even more so than [about] the jobs. As a child, I may not have understood the demands to be a clerk at Newberry's. I understood access to public facilities because I went down to Newberry's, and I would have to walk by and look at the white people sitting at the counter eating a banana split. I swore to God I was going to get me one. More than anything else, I wanted a banana split behind that counter. They looked so good, but you couldn't go back there. You had to go over to the other side, go down into the basement, and stand up. You could get a hot dog, maybe a hamburger, I don't know. You couldn't get all the things you could get upstairs at the lunch counter. I felt we wanted to go there. As a child, I wanted to go there because I saw the white kids go there. But even more than that, it was the thought that black people were standing up [and] that they were showing courage. I felt as though I had never seen a black man talk or speak with defiance or self-assurance to a white man. Not in real life. If a white man walked up—he could be twenty years old, [and] it could be black folks sitting around who were sixty years old—you couldn't miss the skinning-and-a-grinning because that's what they had to do to survive.

I attended the mass meetings. I went to the churches and sat inside. They would ask you [to] give your pocketknife up voluntarily. They made speeches. For the most part, we would go in and kind of circulate around, seeing who we could see. We knew what we were going to do, and we just really weren't into the speeches. We all wanted to see Martin Luther King. Once we saw him, [and we thought], "That was cool. Now who else you see? Do you see anybody over there that looked good? Where they from? They outside?" It was that kind of thing. Not to say we were not serious—we were very serious about what we had to do—but we were just prepared to do it when it came time. We really did not need to be pumped. We were ready to go. In 1963, I was fourteen years old.

We were there for action. The day I went to jail, we knew it was going to be a good day. The group was about fifty or sixty of us that left school. We came down the railroad track, and after we got off the railroad track, [we] came down First Avenue and turned left onto Sixteenth Street. As we got up to the top of that little rise, we could see all the way up Sixteenth Street down to about Eighth Avenue. We could see just a whole bunch of folk coming, and we figured that they were coming from North Birmingham or coming from Carver [High School] or something like that. So we started running. Something just went through the crowd. We were coming for business. We [were] coming to face the police, to face the dogs, to do whatever we had to do.

Those were magic times. When we came over the hill, we saw the kids coming from Carver. Then, as we got down to Sixth Avenue, we all just kind of got on both sides and went down on Sixth Avenue to the church. I think when we crossed Fifth Avenue, everything was blocked off from there. And we kind of made our way down, and the police was rolling their eyes, looking at us, because people were coming. As we got there, and these kids got there, we looked down Sixth Avenue, and there were kids coming in a big group like ours. It may have been maybe twenty-five, it may have been twenty. When you are fourteen years old, twenty people could be a hundred people.

We had snuck out of school. I heard people say that the leadership didn't want to use the children and that it was some of the field-workers' idea. But as soon as the idea got around among the kids, it was over. We liked it, and we moved on it.[2] Other folk had already gone to jail, and we knew what to expect. We knew how it went. We knew what was going on, all right. But this was the day that we were going. My mother dropped me off. I went in the school, through the school, and out to the courtyard. Other folk were already out in the courtyard. It was understood that we were going today: "We going? You going? We going, too."

So as we started leaving the school, other folk got with us, and others caught up with us. We saw folk on their way to school that turned around and joined in as we walked downtown. We didn't start singing until we got up near the church. We sang outside in the streets before we went in the church so we can come back out and be arrested. We just sang and taunted the police. Our favorite thing was "I Ain't Gonna Let Nobody Turn Me Around," and our favorite verse was "Ain't gonna let Bull Connor." It gave us a good feeling to be able to stand there and tell Mr. Eugene "Bull" Connor, "We ain't gonna let you." It made us feel powerful. But anyway, then we go inside, they make the speeches, they pass the basket and ask everybody to put their pocketknife in the basket and if you got any weapons. They told us what to do, how to protect ourselves if you were pushed or shoved. They went through all that. We had heard all of this before because we had seen other folks go. We had seen some of the first group of folks, when it was small, when the adults were going, and we had seen other kids go. We knew the routine. Like I said, we already knew, and though we were sitting there, and they were making the speeches, we may have been talking among ourselves—halfway listening and halfway talking—because we had already decided on the plan. The plan was laid. We knew what we were going to do. They were in charge, [and] we knew they had to make their speeches and go through their changes.

So we moved out. We came out of the church. We turned left, and we started up Sixth Avenue. We started east on Sixth Avenue, and the people at the front were met by policemen who said, "Y'all got to go. If you don't, we gonna arrest you." And then they started herding us, and the people came in from both sides. They started herding us towards the buses and loading us on the buses because they had the buses parked there. It had become an assembly line.

When they first loaded us up, they took us over to the city [jail]. But at the city jail, it was just like a madhouse. You couldn't see the police for the kids and the demonstrators. We were outside in the big courtyard. All the cells were already full, and it must have been a processing center at that point. We were just outside, and rumors were spreading about where we would eventually go after they figured out what the heck to do with all these little nappy-head children.

We were there for about four or five hours. We talked to the police face-to-face because the guards didn't have guns, and they were just completely surrounded. It was like folk on all sides, and they seemed a little troubled about it. I guess they had never seen anything like this. Anyway, they kept us there for about four or five hours, and then they loaded us back on the buses and took us to Juvenile Court.

At Juvenile Court, they split the boys and the girls up. I remember it was starting to get late in the evening, and we had been going all day. We were kind of settling down, and this sister got up and started singing the Lord's Prayer. We sung out there for a while. We sang movement songs; we sang church songs. The people in the building came to the windows, opened the windows, and were looking out. It was just really, really an emotional thing that happened. We left there that night about eight.

They loaded all the boys, and they took us to Jefferson County Jail, which was just about full. They put us in the cells up on the eighth floor. We were just in the hallway in the cell block. The front of the cell block is a big iron door. You go through that door—it could be either to the right or to the left—but what you immediately come in is the dayroom. There were two or three long tables where the guys sat during the day and played cards. I don't think they had TVs at that time, but that's where you ate your meals and played cards and generally sat around and did things during the day. If you go on back from there, then there are cells. I think in this block they had four-man cells, which means they had two bunks up here and two bunks up there and a commode in the middle. There may have been three, four, [or] maybe five cells on the back. Normally, what happened was you would put the prisoners inside the cells and close the doors to the individual cells.

We slept on the floors in the cells, on the floors in the halls, on the tables and on the floors in the dayroom. They were just packed in there. We had literally filled up all the jails in the county. One thing I remember, when my mother finally came and got me after five or six days [was that] they were coming in with new boilers, new pots and new pans and stuff like that. It must have been a logistical nightmare to have to feed all of these people and take care of them. You have to remember, at this point, all the news media from all over the world was in here, and everything [officials] were doing was being closely scrutinized. Needless to say, it hassled them to no end. We were credited with breaking the back of Birmingham.

You know what my sister would say? "See, I knew he would go down there, 'cause he just so bad." My mother was afraid and proud because she knew that they would kill me. When we were little, they used to say, "I'd rather kill you myself than let the white folks kill you." That was a real thing, and so she was proud. But she was also afraid. She had told me not to go down there.

I think the movement was the beginning of consciousness, the beginning of the awareness of self. I know the obvious things you would think would be the integration and access to public facilities. All those things were obvious benefits. But I think the most important benefit was the self-esteem that it gave black people: the feeling that we can do something.

· · ·

When I returned from Vietnam, home was different, but I was different, too. I was a combat veteran. I had been in combat, I had fought for this country, and I made the same mistakes that black men had made since the Civil War. There were riots after World War I because the black troops went to France, and they sat with the mademoiselles, and they thought they were free. When they came back here, there were riots in eastern cities and cities in the Midwest. Partly it was the attitude that they came back with, expecting that they could now be real Americans, and they could enjoy all of the privileges that other Americans enjoyed. Of course, that wasn't the case. After World War II, it was the same way. I don't think it was as bad after Korea, for some reason. I guess it bears examining, but it just didn't have the same kind of effect. Because of the civil rights movement, the peace movement, and the nationalist movement that was afoot in the black community, we got education in [Vietnam]. We started to interact with people from up north and up east who knew about folks like Malcolm X. In Alabama, there was a "cotton curtain." News didn't come in, and news didn't get out. We were shocked to find out some of the things that had gone on in some of the other parts of the country that we never heard about.

Like what was happening with the Nation of Islam. We knew there was a small group of Black Muslims here. We had heard tales about what they were doing in places like Chicago and New York, but it wasn't [in the newspaper or on television]. Those kinds of things just weren't reported down here. So we were behind in terms of that movement. We led the charge in the civil rights movement, but the Black and Proud movement—the Black revolution, the Black identity, Black independence movement, if you will—we came late to that. Most of us got those kind of ideas from our interactions with our cousins from up north and some of these other places. So we came back quite militant. Plus the riots happened while I was in 'Nam, and we didn't find out about them. A lot of things were going on in this country too. I was in 'Nam in '68 and '69. There were things happening here that we didn't find out about until much later.

I came home from 'Nam in May of '69, and I got out of the Marine Corps in '70. When I got back to Birmingham, I had a new attitude and new knowledge. James Brown had made [the song "Say It Loud, I'm Black and I'm Proud"], plus we thought things had changed while we were in 'Nam. We made two mistakes. Two things we thought had changed hadn't changed. One, we thought that America had become a fair and a more just place and that black people now shared equally in the American dream. Two, we became conscious and close while we were in 'Nam. We developed a camaraderie, a sense of brotherhood that we thought was even stronger back here.

Police brutality was rampant here. There were people coming from the service. The "old wine," the old racist segregationist[s] who were on the police department, was saying, "You back here now. I don't care where you been, who you think you is. You back in Birmingham." So that kind of thing was going on. The community was a little bit more militant. There was militancy in the community, and we returning Vietnam veterans brought back militance to the community. At the same time, the police were becoming more repressive and oppressive. That's what we ran into.

I hooked up with some fellows when I got back here. Three of them were Vietnam veterans. Mombozi was a middle-class college student that hooked up with us. [Wayland] "Doc" Bryant had come from Carolina and had been fooling around with the movement for years. We started an affiliate of the [Black] Panther Party. It was called the Alabama Black Liberation Front. We adhered to the principles and ideology and teachings of the party, and we sold the Black Panther newspaper. Among other things, we fought police brutality by doing everything from investigating and documenting cases of police brutality when we went out into the community right on their heels. We had two offices. We had one in Roosevelt City, and we had another over in Titusville, in a place they called Newmongo, a Little Korea. People would call. Let's say the police was going to somebody's house in Collegeville. [The police had] kicked the door in and roughed their mama up and their sister and just kind of beat up everybody, which [the police] would do. We would get a call. We would shoot over there [and] talk to everybody who was a witness. We'd get their story; we'd get it all down. There was a young man, a young council member, who had decided that he was going to fight things, so we hooked up with him. We decided that we would go up there and meet with him. Doc would take him the information, and he would get up in the council meeting and boom, boom, boom, he would blast them. He had the acceptability and the credibility in the community that we had been denied. They ran a media campaign against us. They told the community that we were a threat to the community, that we were militants, and that we were danger-ous, blah, blah, blah, blah, blah. But the information we gave him, he was able to use to bring attention to the situation. This was [future Birmingham mayor] Richard Arrington.[3]

We started a breakfast for kids program. We went to the merchants in the neighborhood and said, "You make your money off of these people, but their kids go to school hungry in the morning." Of course, we got this from the [Black Panther Party]. We said, "You're going to donate and give us grits and eggs and food." And they said we were extorting. "Hell," we said, "no, we're just putting something back." We were making sure they were putting something back. So we started running breakfast for kids programs, we held political education classes, and we would teach the kids songs. They said we were "indoctrinating" the kids with our ideology, which is why the federal government eventually co-opted the program nationally. The federal gov-ernment now provides breakfast for children at school for those who can't afford it. But the concept came from the Panther Party.

Encounters with the police happened all the time. One of the first ones I can remember is when we followed the example of the party and got copies of the city codes. When [the police] came into our community, we would get in the car and get right behind them. And if they stopped anybody, we'd get out and observe. We would say, "The man has rights. [You] have to read him his rights." Of course, they would get angry. In the beginning, they didn't know how to deal with it. I think a lot of it had to do with just that they were really stunned because here were some black men in Birmingham, Alabama, walking up to the police, saying, "Look, you can't do that to this man. This man has a constitutional right to defend himself against you if you violate his rights." Of course, they didn't want to hear none of that. We had one confrontation up on Sixth Avenue where a brother was selling the papers and they called the police on him. He called it in, and we called some other folk. It ended up that we were all up there on Sixth Avenue armed, with the police. It was defused. It all just fizzled out. We left; they left. Nobody was arrested. The brother had the right to sell the newspaper. But [the police thought] that black people didn't know their rights [and] that they could just buffalo this brother. These officers, they approached and told him, "Get on. You can't stand out here and sell that." He called us. They called reinforcements, and we all ended up on Sixth Avenue. There were cases where they stopped, we stopped, and there were words back and forth. I just think that they were not ready for armed black men. They had never had to deal with this kind of situation before, and it kind of threw them off. Of course, today, they have tactics and deal with it lickety-split.

There was a shootout in Tarrant City. A woman was going to be evicted, and she had no place to go. We were idealist[s]. We could not understand how you could just take a black person's home. The lady was in her sixties. She had been living there and was renting from one of these slumlords. Somebody called us and said, "Look, they're going to put this lady out in the street, and she got nowhere to go. She got no family." So we went out to the house. I was not in the house when the sheriff finally came, but a gunfight broke out, and obviously [the police] brought enough folk. They had fifty to sixty deputies. Ronnie [Williams] was shot in the neck. Doc might have been shot too. Ronnie was shot, and [Harold Robertson] was shot. Mombozi didn't get shot, but I think maybe two or three of the fellows got shot. Then one of the brothers named Robert Jakes, from North Birmingham, they broke him and he testified against everybody else and said it was a conspiracy. I think Doc ended up with five years. Ronnie ended up with five years. Ronnie never served his. He left and went to Oregon. The governor of Oregon refused to extradite him back to Alabama because he said that the judicial system was unfair to blacks and that he couldn't get a fair trial. He lived there until he died four or five years ago. Doc, of course, went and did three years.[4]

I remember one night—when I think about this, it sends chills—one night we were going to ambush the police simply because some idiot came to headquarters and started saying, "Y'all always talk about what y'all gonna do, but y'all ain't gonna do nothing. Y'all scared of the white folks. Y'all ain't gonna do nothing." Doc wasn't there, but Ronnie was there. It kind of worked us all into a frenzy. We loaded up our arms and set up an ambush. It just so happens we made this guy go with us, and he broke before we could spring the ambush. It would have been a terrible thing, just a senseless act of murder with no real political purpose. It would have been hard to defend in hindsight. Hindsight is twenty-twenty. It would have been hard to defend. It didn't happen because he jumped up and threw his rifle down and took off. So when he ran, we all got up and said, "We ain't gonna do this." I look back at that, and I think that's the closest [to murder we came], and it was stupid.

I see Birmingham now in hindsight as a center for change. Birmingham has produced a lot of leaders, great thinkers. People have left here and gone to other parts of the country. This has been a movement town, and it is a movement town. And I think the reason it became a movement town is because at one point, it was the most racist place on the face of the earth. Tough times make tough people. Growing up in a tough town like Birmingham was what made the people. Black folk who came out of here were tough people, and I think that toughness has pushed this city forward. Their toughness has caused this city to continue to grow and build and move in spite of what anybody may say or what may happen. And I think it's because of the toughness of the town. And to my way of thinking, [it] is one of the world's great cities today, and it has a bright future. Strangely enough, because of those tough times, tough people are now able to build. We are not inside, not by a long shot. We ain't where we ought to be, but we ain't where we were, either. Hopefully, we will get there, wherever that is. I think that self-determination, the right to decide your own destiny as a people, is something. [It] is a right that belongs to every group of people, race, and ethnic group on the earth. I think we as black folk have to realize that it is right and just for us to want to determine our own destiny.

NOTES

BCRI OHP, vol. 1, sec. 2 (January 5, 1995). Edited, annotated, and abridged by Horace Huntley and John McKerley. This interview has been extensively reorganized for clarity.

1. Booker's numbers are an exaggeration, though police brutality against the black community was an ongoing problem. According to one study, the police killed "ten black men, the majority teenagers or young adults," between January 1966 and March 1977 (Robin D. G. Kelley, *Race Rebels: Culture, Politics, and the Black Working Class* [New York: Free Press, 1996], 91).

2. On student groups' leadership of the Birmingham protests, see also Miriam McClendon, BCRI OHP, vol. 11, sec. 4 (November 8, 1995); Gwendolyn Gamble,

BCRI OHP, vol. 12, sec. 1 (January 24, 1996); Annetta Streeter Gary, BCRI OHP, vol. 36, sec. 4 (June 4, 1998).

3. On Arrington, see also Jimmie Lucille Spencer Hooks, BCRI OHP, vol. 36, sec. 2 (May 27, 1998).

4. On September 15, 1970, officers were serving an eviction notice on Bernice Turner at 222 Jefferson Boulevard in Tarrant. Jefferson County sheriff Mel Bailey later told the *Birmingham News* that the police had been tipped off that the Panthers had planned "to trap deputies" at the house. Bryant, Williams, and Robertson were wounded in the gun battle, and police arrested two other Panthers, Robert Jakes and Brenda Joyce Griffin. According to the paper, "All five [were] charged with assault with intent to murder and resisting a court order" (*Birmingham News*, September 15, 1970; *New York Times*, September 20, 1970). Since the 1970s, historians and activists have documented numerous cases in which the Federal Bureau of Investigation worked with local law enforcement to entrap members of radical organizations such as the Black Panther Party during this period. See Robin D. G. Kelley and Earl Lewis, eds., *To Make Our World Anew: A History of African Americans* (Oxford: Oxford University Press, 2000), 546–47; Taylor Branch, *Pillar of Fire: America in the King Years, 1963–65* (New York: Simon and Schuster, 1998), 243.

CARRIE DELORES HAMILTON LOCK

CARRIE DELORES HAMILTON LOCK was born in Birmingham on May 17, 1949. Both of her parents were from Birmingham. Lock grew up in the small black community of Rising, located near Rickwood Park. She was first exposed to the civil rights movement through her parents. In contrast to the young people who stressed the impact of seeing black men humiliated by the threat of white violence, Lock emphasized her memories of a cadre of black men, including her father, who conducted active (and sometimes armed) resistance to white supremacy in Rising. "None of these men were afraid of whites," she recalled. "They were not afraid. They were protectors of the community. If something happened, they would take care of it." After terrorists bombed the home of attorney Arthur Shores, she remembered that her father and other men in the community "would sit on the porch at night, . . . with shotguns and rifles, and they would sit on the porch all night just to make sure that white people didn't harm us." Lock's activism culminated in her participation in the desegregation of West End High School. "That was 1964–65 school year," she recalled. "Twenty-two signed up the Sunday before. One showed up. Me."

INSIDE THE SCHOOL, IT WAS CHAOS

I have an older sister, Cheryl. I'm the second in line. [Then there is] my brother, William; my brother, Bernard; and my sister, Nancy.

My mother and father both went to Parker High School. My father was a minister. He was minister at First Baptist Church in Ensley. He also worked and retired from the U.S. Postal Service. He was a mail handler here in Birmingham and retired after twenty-something years. My mother did work outside of the home. She worked as a nurse, and she was involved in our child rearing. But I would have to say that my father was an early Mr. Mom. He took care of the kids. He did the cooking, he did the washing, and he did the ironing.

I started first grade at Brighton Elementary School, and I went there for the first and the second grade. I can remember my first-grade teacher was Mrs. Austin. I have all fond memories of my childhood. I went to Princeton Elementary School. It was all-black at the time. Princeton remains a premier elementary school. During the time that I went to school, it was a very good school, and the community was always involved. We had a principal, Ms. Lucille Boyd. Our teachers were all involved with the kids. I had no idea that we were poor because back then everything was based on integrity instead of money. So my parents had plenty of integrity, [and] I thought we were rich.

The foremost thing that I remember about Rising is that it was four blocks east and west and four blocks north and south. That was our world. We had four blocks by four blocks, and we were a very closely knit community. All of the parents knew each other. All the time my mother and father worked, they would leave very early and come back very late. The neighbors were in charge of us. If anything happened, rest assured, the neighbors were going to tell. During the '50s and the '60s, [our] neighbors worked as teachers, nurses, nurse's aides, domestics. [They were] proud domestics, but [the] people that I knew as porter men were [also] proud people. They worked to send their children to school. I just remember a dignified lifestyle during that time.

I went to Parker High School in the ninth grade. My grandmother and grandfather lived in the Smithfield area, and at my grandmother's house, I had my own room. I had all the privileges that an only child has. My grandfather was a minister, and he always wore a black suit, a white shirt, and a black tie. He would take me to school and have me sit in the back. He would get out and come around to the side; it was like I had a chauffeur. So of course, all the kids thought we were rich. Of course, we were not. But everybody thought that my grandfather was my chauffeur. I felt like a princess. My older sister is less than two years older than I, so she was at Parker. But she lived with my mother and father, and I lived with our grandparents. When I would get mad at my parents, I would go to my [grandparents], just like kids are today.

As children, we were very aware of whites. We were very aware of the two worlds that we lived in—the black world, the white world. My parents always had *Ebony* magazine around and *Jet* magazine, and we understood. We knew about Emmett Till, the young boy that had been killed and his body mutilated.[1] We knew about lynchings. We were very aware of how black people disappeared, never to be heard of again, how black men would be shot in the back walking the streets, and the police would say they were shot in self-defense because these people were robbing or killing. We were very aware of the terrible things that were happening in the black community. Every day, there was something to let black people know that they were not safe. [Whites] would intimidate our parents and tell them, "If you go to these meetings, you're not going to have a job." The jobs that they had, they couldn't make a living for their children anyway, so it didn't matter. They would sit on the porch at night, my father and other men, with shotguns and rifles, and they would sit on the front porch all night just to make sure that white people didn't harm us. They would go to other communities and band together and watch over the houses to make sure that people were not bombed in their sleep. There was somebody in every block. After I went to West End [High School], they sat up all night across the street from our house, in the back of our house, on the side of our house.

But as children, we were not afraid. I never saw the police in our community. We lived in a very quiet community, a family community. As a matter of fact, when I was in the eighth grade, I never knew anybody that was divorced. None of my friends' parents were divorced. I didn't know what that meant. We might have been poor people, but we were a proud people with dignity. I remember that if there were ever any conflicts in the community that they would come to the men, my dad, other men. If young boys got in trouble, their parents threatened to tell my dad, other fathers. They would be in big trouble. At that time, all men disciplined all the children. Just recently, my mother and I were talking. I said, "When you are young, you don't question anything." There were people that I called aunt so-and-so or cousin so-and-so, and you never really knew if they were blood relatives or not. It didn't matter, but you didn't question it.

My parents were active in the movement. They would go to the mass meetings at Sixteenth Street Baptist Church. My father was a minister, [and] my grandfather was a minister, and at that time all ministers were vocal characters in the movement. They kept the community abreast of what would be going on and what should be going on.[2] My father had a very personal stake in the movement. My father was very outspoken. He was not afraid of white people. He always said what was on his mind, and it often got him in trouble. For example, when we were very small children—maybe I was six or seven—we were on the way to the hospital to pick my mother up, and the police stopped my father. [The police] got really smart. They said something [like], "Get out of the car, Boy." And of course, we were on the back seat, and my dad said, "Who are you calling 'Boy'?" And the cops said, "You're going to be in trouble." My dad said, "If you put your gun on top of the car and fight me fair, I'll show you who a boy is." And they took him to jail. I can remember that it was cold, that it was very damp, raining, and the police left us standing on the sidewalk. My mother had just gotten out of the hospital. We had never made it home. They left us there—children, small children, and my mother [was] not dressed. She didn't have a coat. She was coming from the hospital. They took my father to jail, but he was not afraid. Whenever people got in trouble in the community, [it was] my father, along with some of the other men, that everybody came to when somebody was in trouble. None of these men were afraid of whites. They were not afraid. They were protectors of the community. If something happened, they would take care of it.

The mass meetings were very intense. Even as a child, you knew that there was something special in the air. At the meetings, it was like church, but it was different from church. I can remember on the stage, Dr. [Martin Luther] King, Mrs. [Coretta Scott] King, Fred Shuttlesworth, Jesse Jackson, and Julian Bond. Julian Bond and Jesse Jackson were young boys. They didn't look much older than we were, but they were there. And Rev. [Abraham L.] Woods and another older gentleman [Ben Owens], they called him Sunshine. He's dead now. Sunshine was always close to my parents, and he kept us all informed of what was going on. We would sit in [the meeting] as though it was church, and they would tell us what to do. The strategists were the men. They would say, "We're going to walk down this street. When the police come, then we'll come from the other street, and when the other police come, we'll come." They were very smart. As a child, I loved the meetings because I always thought that black people were smarter than the cops because they were always surprised. And I can remember that they would always send somebody to infiltrate the meeting and how Dr. King would stand on the podium and call them out. It was as though he knew who the Judas was. [The informant was] a black person that would be sent in. We called them the Uncle Toms. I can't label all people that. There were some people there [who] for whatever reason, the white man would demand that they report back, that they would bring back information. And for whatever reason, they had to do it. Some were known, and some were unknown. I just remember that Dr. King would speak to them as "Judas." Then there were whites that would stand in the back of the church and take notes.[3] I can remember Bull Connor [when I was] a child, and the police that they would be outside of the church. They were very visible. They always wore sunglasses. You could see the malice on their faces. You knew that they meant you harm. But they were very bold about infiltrating the church. They didn't have any respect, but we prevailed. Some of us went because it was fun until the four children were killed. When you're very young, you don't know why, but you're caught up in the emotions. My parents talked to us. They knew that something would come, eventually come. I'm not saying that they had the foresight to see what eventually did happen, but I knew they wanted something better for their children.

During demonstrations, I remember just being in the crowds and running. To say that I was bitten by a dog—no. To say that I was knocked down by the water hoses—no. But we were in the crowds when the dogs were turned loose. We were in the crowds when the water was turned on, but there were so many people. I can remember when they would pick demonstrators up, and we were still very young. I can remember when all of the city jails were full, and then they started putting people in the Bessemer jails. And when the Bessemer jails were full, they started putting people in the Fair Park, every conceivable facility. Blacks had come to realize that going to jail was no big deal. There was nothing criminal about it, so I knew older teenagers who would go to jail and be released and go back the same night to get arrested again. I was never arrested there. Later on, I had my share.

· · ·

I thought [going to Parker High School was] the greatest thing that has ever happened to me. It was so big, it was so huge, and I was such an adult. I just thought this was the greatest thing in the world. Most of the people there knew my parents. The teachers knew my dad and my mom, so we couldn't get away with anything, because people would call your parents then. You didn't dare get in trouble because that would just be the end of it. I felt very special there. I worked for the principal, so I had my own principal's pass. My teachers were very good. I was freshman representative to the Student Council, so I got a chance to go to assembly on a weekly basis and stand on the stage. That was very important.

Dr. King asked all the children, all the students, to integrate the schools, and there were twenty-two [students who] signed up for West End. There were other numbers signed up to the other schools, but specifically I remember twenty-two signed up for West End. That was 1964–65 school year. Twenty-two signed up the Sunday before. One showed up. Me. My father drove us—my mother, my father, and myself. When we arrived, I can remember the Klan marching down the sidewalk in their hoods, in their robes, and I believe this was the first time that I had seen the Klan. There were mobs there. It was a mob scene, but I will always remember the robes and not being afraid. The closer we got to the school, I felt privileged, and I felt honored. I was not afraid. Maybe I should have been afraid, but I was not afraid because I had my father there. I can remember getting to the school door, and we had to say, "Excuse me, excuse me." And they didn't want to let us through, and they would say, "Nigger, go home. Nigger! Nigger! Go home, Nigger!" And the more they said that, the prouder I got, and the more I held my shoulders back and I smiled. But there were a lot of angry whites there. My father and my mother talked to me, and they said that the West End area was a poor area and that's where poor white trash lived and that we were better than that. Those people were acting that way because they didn't know any better.

My mother and father prepared me for what would happen, but they had no idea as to what really happened. I remember the principal being very old and very nervous. He was probably thinking that no blacks would come, that we wouldn't dare come. And then I showed up. Inside the school, it was chaos. What happened was just awful. If there were twenty to twenty-five kids in one class, they would all sit in the front row, two and three to one seat. They would leave four rows, and I would sit on the last row. There would be four empty rows between us. I could not go to the restroom when the other students went to the restroom. I had a special time to go to the restroom—a special designated time, whether I had to or not. And one particular day, when I was in the tenth grade, I had to go at the time when the other kids were in there. I remember that this was the first time that I had new books. I had brand-new books for the first time, and one of the students knocked my books over in a sink full of water. Heaven and hell couldn't help her right then. I didn't care. I beat her from A to Z, and I didn't care. There were many girls in there, but I would have taken care of all of them. It was the first time in my life that I had brand-new books. My father had probably taken his whole two weeks' salary to pay for my books. I was so proud. They were wrapped in newspaper. I had trimmed the newspaper and bound the books. I was so careful not to get any scratches on them. No dirt. They were protected because they were new books.

I'm sure that the white girl wished that she hadn't started that. I told her to pick them up, and she knocked them on the floor again. I said, "Pick them up." And she said something about she didn't listen to a nigger—something about a nigger. After that I don't remember, except that when I finished with her, you couldn't really tell what she was made of. But we were both sent to the principal's office, and the principal expelled me, and I called my dad. My father came to get me. When I got home, we called the Sixteenth Street Baptist Church, and my dad called Washington [D.C.], and he talked to [deputy U.S. attorney general Nicholas] Katzenbach. They sent somebody there. There were three white men that came that night. They came to my home. They wanted to know what happened, and I told them. They wanted to be very sure that I hadn't initiated the fight.

I cannot remember if I went back the next day, but this was a very critical point, because whites didn't know how they were going to handle the situation in the schools. There were no rules. They really didn't know how to handle it. I was the only black child there, and it seemed like two thousand of them. The principal was very angry. The attorney general had sent people—I don't know who the white men were—to the school to talk to him. It would have been very easy to suspend me, get rid of me, and never see me again, but my father said, "No." He asked me, "Can you handle it?" My father would always ask me, "Can you handle it?" But he knew that I could. I knew that he expected me to, and I knew that somebody had to do it.

My brothers and sisters were supportive. Whatever had to be done is exactly what we did. My brothers were younger, and perhaps they did not understand as much, but my sister did. My sister was fearful for me. My sister was very protective of me. They were always fearful that something might happen to me. If the other kids were let out of school at 3:00, then my dad had to pick me up at 2:30. I was never allowed to go out of the door when [white students] were going out of the door. For the entire three years that we were there, they said they couldn't protect me.

There were a total of three black students when I graduated. There were two of us graduating [in 1967]. I believe Vera Marcus was in the tenth grade at that time. [Her sister], Patricia Marcus, had gone to West End in 1963 and graduated. There were no black males involved in the school at all.[4]

I grew up fast. I matured probably faster than the kids around me. It made me very strong. It made me very bitter, but it made me very proud, and I knew that I had been set aside. I knew that for whatever reason, whatever would come in my life, that I would be able to handle it, that if I had gone through that, that I could handle anything.

After high school, I went to Tuskegee Institute. I graduated [from high school] on Sunday afternoon, and the next Sunday afternoon, I was leaving for college. That had nothing to do with West End. At Princeton Elementary School, in fifth grade, we knew where we were going to college. Our teachers had told us where we were going to college. We knew all about Tuskegee. I knew in fifth grade where I was going to go to [college]. By the time we were in seventh grade, I think our teachers had probably already filled out our applications for college in our minds. Mrs. Catherine Smith, Catherine Eileen Smith, had gone to Tuskegee, and she would say, "Class, these are the songs that you will sing at Tuskegee, and these are the things that you will do at Tuskegee." And of course, "This is what you'll have to wear at Tuskegee." Everybody went to Tuskegee. We were programmed. I never applied anywhere else. [At Tuskegee], it was wonderful to be around black people, to be around people going to college. It was a new day. It was a proud day. It was just wonderful. I spent two years at Tuskegee. From Tuskegee, I got married, and I moved to Atlanta, Georgia. Then I lived three years in Germany, and from Germany I came back to Chicago. I finished [at] Northeastern Illinois University. I have a master's degree in public administration and business from the University of Texas, San Antonio.

As a result of my experiences at West End, I sure learned how to survive. You sure don't know that *no* is in the vocabulary. You sure don't know that *can't* is in the dictionary. You don't know that you can't do things. You certainly are not intimidated by people, because you faced Satan himself every day. My life was better because people died before I had to go through those doors. I'm saddened when I see West End High School now. I'm saddened by the way the children act today, that they don't take their education seriously. I'm saddened when they don't want to go to college. I'm saddened when they go to college and it's not important to them. They must know that everything came at somebody's sacrifice. That's what I want them to know. Somebody bled, somebody cried, and somebody died for you.

NOTES

BCRI OHP, vol. 10, sec. 5 (October 18, 1995). Edited, annotated, and abridged by Horace Huntley and John McKerley.

1. In 1955, two white men in rural Mississippi murdered Emmett Till, a fourteen-year-old black youth from Chicago, for allegedly whistling at the wife of one of the men. The images of Till's mutilated body in *Jet* magazine and other publications helped to bring worldwide attention to white supremacist violence in the rural South.

2. On Birmingham's black ministers and the movement, see Glenn T. Eskew, *But for Birmingham: The Local and National Movements in the Civil Rights Struggle* (Chapel Hill: University of North Carolina Press, 1997), 229.

3. See Gwendolyn Gamble, BCRI OHP, vol. 12, sec. 1 (January 24, 1996).

4. In 1967, there were at least twenty black students at West End, including eight boys. Almost all (and all but one of the boys), however, were freshmen. (*Resumé*, 1967, Southern History Collection, Birmingham Public Library)

AUDREY FAYE HENDRICKS

AUDREY FAYE HENDRICKS, born in Birmingham on May 22, 1953, was one of the youngest students arrested during the Children's Crusade. Like many children, she became a part of the movement through her parents. During her time in detention, she recalled the police attempting to use the children as informants: "They would ask silly questions about our mass meetings. They wanted to know whether we talked about any communist plots, or did we plan to overthrow the government or something silly like that. I told them we talked about nonviolence and discrimination at our meetings, not communism."

As an adult, Hendricks came to see the period as a time of considerable change that had a mixed legacy for the city's black men and women. After living in Dallas for several years, she decided to return to Birmingham; her Texas friends and coworkers thought she "must have been insane to want to return to what they felt must be an awful place for a black person." While she feared that history "would show that they were probably right," she still found that "the personal fears of my friends and coworkers were the fears that spelled home for me." Hendricks died on March 1, 2009.

AT EIGHT YEARS OLD, I DECIDED . . . THAT I WOULD GO TO JAIL

My mother is a Birmingham native, and my father is from Boligee, Alabama, which is in Greene County, Alabama. I was born in Birmingham. I have one other sibling. I am the oldest of two girls. My mother finished Booker T. Washington Business College. My father unfortunately did not finish elementary school. My father was a laborer and worked for Jim Dandy,[1] and my mother [worked] as a secretary for Alexander and Company, a black insurance company. We lived in a community known as Titusville. It is on the southwest side of Sixth Avenue and Center Street. Our community was well mixed financially. We had the well-to-do and the laborers, but as far as racially, our community was 100 percent black. From my perspective, it was a nice neighborhood. We had a recreational park, Memorial Park, which was not too far away, in walking distance. Cops were seldom seen in the neighborhood unless there was a break-in. The cops were never there just to harass us.

I attended school at Center Street Elementary for four years. Later, I went to Our Lady of Fatima private school. From the fifth through the eighth grade, I attended the Immaculata High School at Our Lady of Fatima on Fourteenth Street South. I and a few other black students were enrolled into Ramsay High School in 1971. The administrators at Ramsay were not prepared for the immediate desegregation at all.[2] When we, the black students, arrived, the white students had already begun their classes for the year. We black students sat in the auditorium for about the whole first week there. The administrators did not know what to do with us. All the black students became very close. It was a pretty difficult time for us, so we all bonded together. There was some hatred between black and white children at Ramsey, whites hating blacks and vice versa. There was some name-calling and a couple of fights, but not a whole lot. Every year it got better and better between the races. Besides the togetherness that was shared by us black students, one of the things I remember most about Ramsay is the difference in cultural experiences. It was just the smallest differences that could be noticed between blacks and whites. For instance, blacks are kind of cold-natured when compared to whites. All of the white students would be complaining that it was too hot when we had the windows down in the classrooms during early fall, and all of us black students would be complaining that it was too cold when the windows were up. We blacks would come to school all bundled up with sweaters.

After graduating from Ramsey, I left Birmingham and moved to Dallas, Texas, to attend Bishop College. As far as I know, I was the only person from Birmingham there at that time. People had their usual misconceptions about Birmingham in Dallas. They thought we all lived in shotgun houses and had unpaved dirt roads. For four years, I lived in Dallas and worked at the Dallas Department of Mental Health and Retardation. There I worked in a residential setting with children who have emotional problems. After my four years in Dallas, home began to beckon me. I soon decided that it was just time to return to Birmingham. Upon announcing to my friends and coworkers, they thought that I must have been insane to want to return to what they felt must be an awful place for a black person. History would show that they were probably right. But as a child, I had grown up around the civil rights struggle; the personal fears of my friends and coworkers were the fears that spelled home for me.

• • •

At eight years old, I was attending mass meetings at Sixteenth Street Baptist Church. I was there because my mother and father were so involved. Whenever there was a meeting, we three were there. I don't ever recall missing a meeting. The meetings were very organized and very emotional. If there were a plan to march, we would always be reminded to be nonviolent. Before marching, people would leave their weapons on the table—knives and that sort of thing. The movement had a great impact on the community. There were so many people attending the Sixteenth Street mass meeting that we soon outgrew Sixteenth Street and had to have two different mass meetings on the same day. One would be for the youth, and the other one would be for the adults, but the meetings would talk about the same issues. The difference was primarily to do with location. You didn't really have to be a youth to go to the youth mass meeting and vice versa. The split meetings were for space and convenience. I don't ever remember seeing a [policeman] at any of the meetings. If there was one, he would have to have been white, and I didn't see any white people.[3]

At eight years old, I decided one day that I would go to jail over a protest march. My family and friends were proud of me for my decision. My fourth-grade teacher, Mrs. Wills, cried when my parents told her that I was going to jail and that she should not be expecting me at school for a while. She did not cry because I was going to jail, I suppose; I think she cried because I was so young [and was] making such a conscious effort to help in the struggle. She was overwhelmed, I guess.

Me and a couple of other children followed through with the plan and marched. I was too young to know why I would be arrested, but I knew that I would be. I didn't know anything about having a permit, but I saw nothing wrong with marching and telling the world that it was something going on that I did not like. On my march, we did get arrested. I never saw a water hose, but I did see the police dogs, even though they were about a half block away from where we were apprehended. I spent two weeks in juvenile detention. There the rooms were like dorm rooms, with bunk beds. We were basically just sitting around all day in the recreation room, kidding around or something. We didn't have our school lessons or anything, so we missed our lessons. We were just there. The only thing that happened to me while I was there was the constant questioning done by plainclothes white officers. They would ask silly questions about our mass meeting. They wanted to know whether we talked about any communist plots, or did we plan to overthrow the government, or something silly like that. I told them we talked about nonviolence and discrimination in our meetings, not communism. That was about all that really took place there. For me, there was no harassment or anything. From my perspective, we were just there.

The worst thing that ever happened during the movement also occurred the year that I had gotten arrested. It was September of 1963 that the city of Birmingham, jokingly known as "Bombingham," witnessed its worst bombing of all, the bombing of the Sixteenth Street Baptist Church. I remember the sadness of those times, and I remember one of the four little girls, Denise McNair. She attended Center Street School while I was there. In fact, her mother was a teacher at Center Street. They say that she was so distraught from the news that they had to hold her up. After the Sixteenth Street bombing, I was not particularly involved anymore after that, but there were some great accomplishments that I had gotten to be involved in.

I think the biggest accomplishments that came out of the movement in the beginning were better jobs for the adults. My mother in particular was able to leave Alexander and Company and work for the federal government, which she would not have been able to do prior to the demonstrations. People began to do things that they could not do before. People began going into restaurants that at one period of time they could not do anything but look inside. For me, the movement allowed me to go to Ramsey High School, which was not available for me before. There was just an abundance of things that had not been available before. I think the movement helped the relationships between blacks and whites as well in some respects.

NOTES

BCRI OHP, vol. 6, sec. 4 (June 1, 1995). Edited, annotated, and abridged by Nakeshia Jackson-Leverette and John McKerley.

1. The Western Grain Company was a Birmingham-based firm that produced the Jim Dandy brand of dog food (History of Savannah Foods and Industries, http://www.referenceforbusiness.com/history2/65/Savannah-Foods-Industries -Inc.html [accessed April 24, 2007]).

2. Richard Walker had desegregated Ramsay in 1963 (Diane McWhorter, *Carry Me Home: Birmingham, Alabama: The Climactic Battle of the Civil Rights Revolution* [New York: Simon and Schuster, 2001], 506).

3. The police also paid black informants to report on the meetings. See James Roberson, BCRI OHP, vol. 18, sec. 2 (June 25, 1996).

Birmingham, Alabama, has meant many things to many people. For most African Americans, the city has been synonymous with segregation, hatred, fear, terror, white supremacy, bombings, castration, and police brutality. Segregation was law as well as custom, a combination that created a debilitating attitude of white superiority and African American inferiority that many accepted as being normal in this abnormal setting.

Birmingham residents of African descent can relate to such negative depictions of the city, but there has always been another Birmingham that few outsiders knew. We loved and defended that Birmingham against verbal assaults from friends and relatives in other parts of the country.

That love obviously did not lie in the same things that white Birmingham stood for and perpetuated and profited from. Rather, we took pride in the black people who made a difference in their children's lives. That Birmingham was a black mother of four who "with only God's help" put two children through college and two through vocational school on a salary of three dollars per week. The mother could neither read nor write, but she was determined that her children would not be deprived of a formal education. She said, "I didn't want my children working in no white folks' kitchen." That Birmingham was where a couple raised eleven children in a five-room house and demonstrated that even under the most adverse conditions, they could succeed. Pride in Birmingham would come when an iron ore miner, the father of six children, went to Europe to defend this country and returned to help his wife prepare those children for the rigors of a segregated life. White Birmingham knew little and cared less about this black Birmingham. My son, who claimed to hate Birmingham and tried to get as far away as possible when he attended college, called from school in Upstate New York and admitted that he had defended this place that he thought he hated so much.

Home for most people is a place to be loved and respected. Many natives of Birmingham feel no different.

This belief is not universal. Many black people have been threatened by, been uncomplimentary regarding, abandoned, and denied any connection to Birmingham or to the South. Plenty have been embarrassed because of the inhumane treatment accorded to the region's African Americans. Other black people have expressed confusion and bewilderment about the "weak" responses African Americans mustered in the face of white supremacy. When I was in the military, one man told us that he was from Cleveland, Ohio. When we learned that he was from Meridian, Mississippi, he cried. Another GI told people that he was from "PA," hoping that they would assume he meant Pennsylvania. In reality, it was Pineapple, Alabama.

African Americans' love/hate relationship with the South has engendered a long tradition of struggle. In Birmingham during the 1930s, Harriet Flood and Helen Long challenged the terror tactics that were commonplace. In the 1940s, the interracial International Union of Mine, Mill, and Smelter Workers defied the attempts of the city, the state, and TCI to subjugate black workers. In the 1950s, when Alabama outlawed the NAACP, the ACMHR took up the cause, laying the groundwork for the struggles of the following decade by questioning the lack of blacks on the police force and in the civil service, encouraging blacks to begin to defy segregation on city buses and in schools, and launching challenges to discriminatory practices at stores and lunch counters.

In this light, then, it is not surprising that Birmingham's African American community took on the adversarial white supremacist status quo in 1963. Rev. Fred Shuttlesworth and the city's other ministers forged a movement that challenged racism in all walks of life. The last months of 1962 and the first months of 1963 were pivotal in changing the legal status of African Americans in this city. Attorney David Vann led the effort to change the form of government, removing the notorious Bull Connor, who symbolized the worst of white supremacy in the city, from the halls of power. And beginning on April 1, 1963, daily demonstrations turned up the heat on the racist status quo until the Children's Crusade pushed the segregationist regime out of the kitchen.

Between 1961 and 1965, Birmingham changed forever. After the revolution, African Americans rode at the front of the bus, sat at desegregated lunch counters, attended the Alabama Theater, and went to school at Graymont and Ramsay. Some of the city's African Americans believed that we had arrived and that the movement was over. However, much work remained. When black people moved to West End, whites moved out. Though legal discrimination was vanquished, the public school system became increasingly black. Churches remained almost completely segregated.

Yes, we should celebrate the civil rights victories. The foot soldiers made tremendous sacrifices for the good of the city. The Birmingham Civil Rights Institute is a memorial to the struggle and to those who struggled. However, the problem of the color line remains unsolved, and we still face problems related to race, class, religion, gender, and economic disparities. They remind us of the distance yet to be traveled.

Horace Huntley, Director
Oral History Project
Birmingham Civil Rights Institute

HORACE HUNTLEY is an assistant professor of history at the University of Alabama, Birmingham, the director of the Oral History Project at the Birmingham Civil Rights Institute, and the coeditor of *Black Workers' Struggle for Equality in Birmingham*.

JOHN W. McKERLEY is a faculty research associate and assistant editor with the Freedmen and Southern Society Project at the University of Maryland, College Park.

The University of Illinois Press
is a founding member of the
Association of American University Presses.

Composed in 10.5/13 Adobe Minion Pro
with Memphis and Avenir display
by Jim Proefrock
at the University of Illinois Press
Designed by Dennis Roberts
Manufactured by Cushing-Malloy, Inc.

University of Illinois Press
1325 South Oak Street
Champaign, IL 61820-6903
www.press.uillinois.edu